W9-ASF-804

America, Russia, and the Cold War 1945-1971

AMERICA IN CRISIS

A series of books on American Diplomatic History
EDITOR: *Robert A. Divine*

America, Russia, and the Cold War

1945-1971

Second Edition

WALTER LAFEBER
Cornell University

John Wiley and Sons, Inc., New York • London • Sydney • Toronto

Library of Congress Cataloging in Publication Data

LaFeber, Walter.
    America, Russia, and the cold war, 1945–1971.
    (America in crisis)

    Bibliography: p.
    1. U. S.—Foreign relations—Russia. 2. Russia
—Foreign relations—U. S. I. Title. II. Series.
E183.8.R9L26   327.47'073   70–38955

ISBN 0–471–51137–4
ISBN 0–471–51138–2 (pbk.)

Printed in the United States of America.

10 9 8 7 6 5 4 3 2 1

For Sandra

Foreword

"THE UNITED STATES always wins the war and loses the peace," runs a persistent popular complaint. Neither part of the statement is accurate. The United States barely escaped the War of 1812 with its territory intact, and in Korea in the 1950's the nation was forced to settle for a stalemate on the battlefield. At Paris in 1782, and again in 1898, American negotiators drove hard bargains to win notable diplomatic victories. Yet the myth persists, along with the equally erroneous American belief that we are a peaceful people. Our history is studded with conflict and violence. From the Revolution to the Cold War, Americans have been willing to fight for their interests, their beliefs, and their ambitions. The United States has gone to war for many objectives —for independence in 1775, for honor and trade in 1812, for territory in 1846, for humanity and empire in 1898, for neutral rights in 1917, and for national security in 1941. Since 1945 the nation has been engaged in a deadly struggle to contain communism and defend the democratic way of life.

The purpose of the series is to examine in detail eight critical periods relating to American involvement in foreign war from the Revolution through the Cold War. Each author has set out to recount anew the breakdown of diplomacy that led to war and the subsequent quest for peace. The emphasis is on foreign policy, and no effort is made to chronicle the military participation of the United States in these wars. Instead the authors focus on the day-by-day conduct of diplomacy to explain why the nation went to war and to show how peace was restored. Each volume is a synthesis combining the research of other historians with new insights to provide a fresh interpretation of a critical period in American diplomatic history. It is hoped that this series will help dispel the illusion of national innocence and give Americans a better appreciation of their country's role in war and peace.

ROBERT A. DIVINE

Preface

C HAPTER x has been completely rewritten and Chapter XI has been added covering the years from 1967–1971. Clarifications of the text and corrections have been made on twenty other pages. Because I was determined to keep the price of the new edition as low as possible, I reluctantly decided not to rewrite the first two chapters dealing with the initial causes of the Cold War. Highly significant work has been published on that problem since 1967; moreover, some critics of the first edition correctly observed that my linking of the American economic policy of 1942 to 1945 to the policy makers' anti-Communist rhetoric of post-1947 was not as strong as it might have been. The recent volumes of Lloyd Gardner, Thomas Patterson, Gabriel Kolko, and David Green, among others, superbly analyze these links. I especially wanted to incorporate the important work of Richard Freeland, who has shown in detail how the initial anti-Communist pronouncements unloosed on Americans through publicity surrounding the Truman Doctrine and Marshall Plan, were chiefly desperate attempts to force a reluctant public to support foreign policies actually based on the economic requirements of the American political economy. These requirements were the pivotal assumptions of the Administration's Cold War policies, but because the requirements were complex, sometimes abstract and, therefore, lacking the political prowess and simplicity of straight anti-Communism, the public heard primarily the negative, anti-Communist rhetoric. Americans finally and enthusiastically supported policies that they never fully understood for reasons other than those that mainly shaped these policies. The results included McCarthyism, Vietnam, and subsequent disillusionment. These results are examined in detail in this edition.

I am grateful to many friends who assisted with this edition. Myron Rush of Cornell, Lloyd Gardner of Rutgers, and Robert Divine of Texas gave the revision the same helpful reading that they gave the first manuscript five years ago. Helpful discussions, information, and criticism were provided by Thomas McCormick, University of Wisconsin; Joel Silbey, Richard Polenberg, David Mozingo, Michael Kammen, Mack Walker, Arthur Rovine, and Benjamin Batson, all of Cornell; Samuel McSeveney of Brooklyn College; Gaddis Smith, Yale; David Millar, Hamilton College; Charles Chatfield and Richard Ortquist, Wittenberg University; Raymond O'Connor, the University of Miami in Coral Gables, Florida; the late William L. Neumann, Goucher College; Thomas A. Bailey and Barton Bernstein, Stanford University; Norman Graebner, University of Virginia; Kenneth H. W. Hillborn, University of Western Ontario; and a memorable (for me, at least) 1970 seminar of Cornell undergraduates, which resulted in many useful lessons, including the stimulating insights that these students provided into the development of the multinational corporation. I am deeply indebted to friends at Wiley, particularly to Carl Beers, Editor, Carolyn Jenkins, Editorial Assistant, and Dennis Hudson, Production Manager. I also thank Mrs. Sylvie Turner and John Stewart of the John F. Kennedy Library; John E. Wickman and Edwin A. Thompson of the Dwight D. Eisenhower Library; Miss Ruth Lengelsen of the Mt. Carmel, Illinois Public Library; and—as always—the superb Cornell Library Staff headed by David Kaser and Giles Shepherd. Research for this revision was made possible by the funds of the Colonel Return Jonathan Meigs First (1740–1823) Fund, which was created with funds left by Dorothy Mix Meigs and Fielding Pope Meigs, Jr. of Rosemont Pennsylvania. Finally, and most important, I sincerely thank the teachers, students, and general readers who have found this book useful. I hope that those who read the book, although they might not always agree with it, will be stimulated to rethink the importance of history as well as the nature of American and Russian foreign policies.

WALTER LaFEBER

September, 1971

Preface to First Edition

STUDYING THE COLD WAR teaches many lessons. One of them is that although the 1945 to 1966 era might be well described in 850 words or, certainly, 850,000, it is very difficult to analyze those years in 85,000 words. This is especially true, first, when an author attempts (as I have done) to delineate a general thesis that domestic policy influences foreign policy; second, when he tries to give something of the picture of both sides—Russian and American; and third, when in such a short space he attempts to deal with problems in Europe and the newly emerging world in chronological sequence, not in terms of geographical units. This book is not Europe-oriented, and I hope that one of its contributions is to point out where and why American foreign policy began to pivot away from Europe and to focus on the newly emerging areas. With respect to the sequential development, I have had to skip around more when handling these problems chronologically, but then that is how it happened, together in both time and space, not just in space.

In writing this book I have accumulated many obligations. My thanks are given in the acknowledgments at the end of the book.

April, 1967

Contents

MAPS

(Maps by John V. Morris)

Contents

America, Russia, and the Cold War 1945-1971

CHAPTER I

Open Doors, Iron Curtains (1945)

IT WAS OCTOBER 1945 and war had never ended. The new issue of Russia's leading doctrinal journal, *Bol'shevik*, warned its readers that Marxists must not lapse into pacifism, since the "imperialist struggle," which ignited World War II, continued to rage. The Soviet Union, *Bol'shevik* proclaimed, would never retreat from wars waged "for the liberation of the people from landowning, capitalist slavery." In Washington, meanwhile, President Harry S. Truman delivered a speech larded with references to America's monopoly of atomic power. In one sentence the President attacked Russia's tightening hold in Eastern Europe: it is one of the "fundamentals" of American policy, Truman announced, that "We shall refuse to recognize any government imposed upon any nation by the force of any foreign power." A week later, M. Vjacheslav Molotov, People's Commissar for Foreign Affairs, answered Truman. Peace cannot be reconciled with an armament race "preached abroad by certain especially zealous partisans of the imperialist policy," Molotov admonished. "In this connection we should mention the discovery of atomic energy and the atomic bomb." [1]

As the *Bol'shevik* editorial illustrated, the triumphant wartime alliance had already split on ideological, economic, and political issues. The Truman and Molotov speeches explained the immediate causes of the split: the dropping of an iron curtain by the Soviets around Eastern Europe, and the determination of the

---

[1] *Bol'shevik* (August, 1945), especially pp. 48–59; Harry S. Truman, "Restatement of Foreign Policy of the United States," *Department of State Bulletin*, XIII (October 28, 1945), 653–656; Vjacheslav Molotov, *U.S.S.R. Foreign Policy* (Shanghai, 1946), pp. 7–8.

world's sole atomic power to penetrate that curtain. At the Potsdam Conference, a month before Japan surrendered, Churchill blurted out to Stalin that "an iron fence" surrounded parts of Eastern Europe. "All fairy-tales!" Stalin blandly replied. Months earlier, however, American officials had arrived at Churchill's conclusion. On April 12, 1945, Harry S. Truman, Vice-President of the United States, former Missouri politician and Senator, and a man who was to become known as one not reluctant to make decisions, suddenly became President of the United States. Truman's knowledge of foreign policy issues was pitifully weak, partly because his predecessor, Franklin D. Roosevelt, had seldom invited his opinion on international problems. Truman evidently learned quickly about Soviet moves in Eastern Europe; in any case, he made a rapid policy decision. Eleven days after becoming President, Truman invited Molotov to the White House and proceeded to give the Russian a stern lecture against trying to lower an iron fence around Poland. An astonished Molotov retorted, "I have never been talked to like that in my life." "Carry out your agreements," Truman replied, "and you won't get talked to like that." [2]

The roots of Truman's complaint went back at least to the nineteenth century. Since becoming a major world power in the 1890s, the United States had viewed anything in the world resembling Stalin's iron fence as incompatible with American objectives. An open, free world had no such divisions. Russia had historically been a chief offender in this regard. American officials had faced problems similar to Truman's, not only with the signing of the Nazi-Soviet Pact of 1939 or after the Bolshevik Revolution threatened to spread over Eastern Europe in 1917-1920, but during the first major clash of American and Russian interests in the 1890s. At the end of that decade the United States, having expanded westward across a continent and a great ocean, and Russia, sweeping eastward through Siberia, confronted one another on the plains of China and Manchuria.

It was a presentiment of events half a century later. Their policy differences sprang from the American determination to

---

[2] Harry S. Truman, *Memoirs. Volume One: Year of Decisions* (Garden City, N. Y., 1955), p. 82.

keep China politically sovereign and whole for purposes of exploitation by the burgeoning United States industrial complex, while the Russians, who could not economically compete on such terms, tried to assure themselves political leverage and markets by creating exclusive spheres of influence. The Czar, like the Soviets in 1945, also attempted to create buffer states between Russian soil and the ambitions of Great Britain, the United States, and especially Japan. After several years of cold war, Japan broke the Czar's power in the Far East in the Russo-Japanese war of 1904-1905.

The Japanese then set off on their own career of empire. This climaxed in a conflict caused in large measure by the Japanese determination to spread their own type of fence around China while the United States insisted on an open-door policy. In Europe, Great Britain further isolated Germany by joining the Franco-Russian alliance. When this realignment of power led to World War I, the United States faced the terrible choice that would continually haunt its officials in the twentieth century. Colonel Edward House, President Woodrow Wilson's closest advisor, defined the alternatives in August 1914: "If the Allies win, it means largely the domination of Russia on the Continent of Europe; and if Germany wins, it means the unspeakable tyranny of militarism for generations to come." [3]

The danger posed to American interests by Russia's possible domination of Europe immeasurably worsened in 1917 when the immense potential of Russian national power was abetted by an ideology supposedly driven by historical law and dedicated to world revolution. The Allies first tried to topple the Lenin government with force. Intervention between 1918 and 1920 by British, Japanese, and American armies, however, somberly demonstrated the futility of this kind of preventive war; the Russian people reacted against the foreign armies with a renewed and stronger allegiance to the Bolshevik government. Meanwhile, Woodrow Wilson's fear that Bolshevism would thrive in war-ravaged Europe became real in 1919 when Communist governments came to power for short periods in Hun-

---

[3] Quoted in Arthur S. Link, *Wilson: The Struggle for Neutrality, 1914–1915* (Princeton, 1960), p. 48.

gary and a part of Germany and threatened other European nations. At the Versailles Peace Conference in 1919, the victorious Allies, aware that armed intervention had not brought the Russian Communists to their knees, tried another approach. With the shadow of Lenin and Trotsky overhanging every discussion, the Western powers, as young, embittered Walter Lippmann phrased it, created a *cordon sanitaire* across Central and Eastern Europe to isolate Russia. Lippmann argued instead for a "sanitary Europe," warning that the use of such states as Poland, Rumania, Czechoslavakia, and Jugoslavia to separate the Russian peoples from the West could never develop into a long-range solution.[4]

Wilson coupled this reconstruction of Central Europe with a declaration of August 10, 1920, which indicated that the United States hoped to mellow or, preferably, break up the Bolshevik regime with a policy of nonrecognition. Other Western nations, however, refused to follow this lead. The British opened formal trade relations with Russia in March 1921. A major Soviet breakthrough followed a year later when the two outcasts, Germany and Russia, reached agreement on several important issues in the Rapallo Pact. This and the Nazi-Soviet Treaty of 1939 proved that regardless of any ideological division, Germany and Russia could readily compromise and join hands when they thought it was in their common interest. In February 1924, the British recognized the Soviet government *de jure* and set off a chain reaction of recognition by nearly all major powers except the United States.

Americans by no means ignored the Soviets. A United States Relief mission distributed over sixty million dollars worth of aid to the Russians in the early 1920s. American businessmen, encouraged by Secretary of Commerce Herbert Hoover, surged into the Russian market. Between 1925 and 1930, trade between the two nations grew to nearly $100 million, or twice the prewar figure; this was rather remarkable, given the failure of the State Department to recognize that the Soviets officially existed. The trade declined rapidly in 1931 and 1932, and urged on by demands of American businessmen for formal political

---

[4] Walter Lippmann, *New Republic* (March 22, 1919), supplement.

relations, Franklin D. Roosevelt finally extended recognition in November 1933. (Perhaps Roosevelt worried about how Americans would receive the news; he had the Soviet delegation arrive in Washington at the same time that Prohibition was being lifted.)

The Russians welcomed recognition. They cared less about increased trade, however, than about cooperating with the United States to stop Japanese aggression in the Far East. Roosevelt refused to respond to this Russian appeal, and the State Department assured the Japanese that opening relations with the Soviets contained no hidden meaning for Japanese policies in Asia.[5] The New Deal maintained this policy of non-cooperation throughout the decade, receiving strong support from many American liberals, even former Communists, who in the post-1936 period became bitterly disillusioned with Communism after Stalin began his bloody purges and signed the Nazi-Soviet Pact. After the war, these liberals would not forget their earlier disenchantment with the "God Who Failed."

Hitler's invasion of Russia in June 1941 forced a four-year partnership upon the Soviets and Americans. Despite the wartime cooperation and the goodwill generated by $9½ billion of lend-lease materials sent to Russia, conflicts erupted over war strategies and plans for the postwar peace. In 1942 and 1943, Churchill and Roosevelt indicated readiness to open a second front in Western Europe. Their backs to the wall, the Soviets seized upon these indications as ironclad pledges. When the Allies invaded North Africa and Italy, thus stalling the second front invasion until mid-1944, Stalin became increasingly suspicious and resentful. Nor did the Russian dictator care for the Anglo-American refusal to assure him that after the conflict the Soviet borders would essentially be those recognized by the Nazi-Soviet treaty, that is, that the Baltic states and parts of Poland, Finland, and Rumania would be absorbed by Russia. The United States instead asked Stalin to wait until the end of the war to settle those territorial problems. As the conflict came

[5] Stanley K. Hornbeck to Secretary of State Cordell Hull, Oct. 28, 1933, and Hornbeck to William Phillips, October 31, 1933, 711.61/333, Archives of the Department of State, Washington, D. C.

to a close, American policy-makers realized that these issues would have to be discussed in the context of a new world balance of power, since the Allies had destroyed Germany and Japan, two nations which historically had blocked Russian expansion in Europe and Asia.

The Cold War consequently developed on a foundation of a half century of Russian-American distrust and apprehension. These early years, especially the shock of depression and disillusionment in the 1930s, forged four major assumptions upon which the United States built its initial post-World War II foreign policy.

①Washington officials first assumed that foreign policy grew directly from domestic policy; American actions abroad did not respond primarily to the pressures of other nations, but to political, social, and economic forces at home. Policy-makers could consider the economic the most important of these forces, a not unreasonable conclusion given the national crisis endured in the 1930s. ②The ghosts of Depression Past and Depression Future led officials to a second assumption: the post-1929 quagmire had been prolonged and partly caused by high tariff walls and regional trading blocks which had dammed up the natural flow of foreign trade. Such economic dislocation had inexorably led to political conflicts which, in turn, had ignited World War II. Free flow of exports and imports was essential. ③Third, the United States, quadrupling its production while other major industrial nations suffered severe war-time damage and forced liquidation, wielded the requisite economic power to establish this desired economic community. The use of this type of power, moreover, would allow the United States and the world to deemphasize military power and return to peace-time conditions. ④Finally, Washington policy-makers determined to use this gigantic economic power. Unlike the 1930s, the United States would not sit on the side-lines; indeed, it could not afford to do so.

One week after Japan surrendered, Secretary of State James F. Byrnes elaborated upon these four assumptions. "Our international policies and our domestic policies are inseparable," he began. "Our foreign relations inevitably affect employment in the United States. Prosperity and depression in the United

States just as inevitably affect our relations with the other nations of the world." Byrnes expressed his "firm conviction that a durable peace cannot be built on an economic foundation of exclusive blocs . . . and economic warfare . . . . [A liberal trading system] imposes special responsibilities upon those who occupy a dominant position in world trade. Such is the position of the United States." In announcing the American intention to re-order the world, he uttered a warning as well as a policy assumption: "In many countries throughout the world our political and economic creed is in conflict with ideologies which reject both of these principles. To the extent that we are able to manage our domestic affairs successfully, we shall win converts to our creed in every land." [6] John Winthrop had not expressed it more clearly at Massachusetts Bay. Only now the City Upon a Hill had been industrialized and internationalized.

American officials hoped that this process would primarily occur through the United Nations, the World Bank (the International Bank of Reconstruction and Development), and the International Monetary Fund. The World Bank had a treasury of $7.6 billion (and the authority to lend twice that amount), which would guarantee private loans given to build facilities in war-torn Europe and the underdeveloped areas. The International Monetary Fund possessed a fund of $7.3 billion to stabilize currencies so that multilateral trade could be conducted without sudden currency depreciation or wide fluctuations in exchange rates, two ailments which had almost destroyed the international economic community in the 1930s. The United States hoped that such international agencies would minimize exclusive and explosive nationalisms and maximize economic and political interchange. Of course, there was one other implication of this policy: American economic power necessarily made the United States the dominant force in these organizations. In March 1946, Secretary of the Treasury Fred Vinson became the first chairman of the Board of Governors of both groups.

---

[6] *Documents on American Foreign Relations, VIII (1945–1946)*, edited by Raymond Dennett and Robert K. Turner (Princeton, 1948), pp. 601–602; the best historical treatment of this developing view is in Lloyd C. Gardner, *Economic Aspects of New Deal Diplomacy* (Madison, Wisconsin, 1964).

At home, the Truman Administration moved rapidly to implement this multilateral approach. Congress renewed the Reciprocal Trade Agreements Act of 1934, a powerful lever in lowering tariff walls at home and abroad. Conversely, the Export-Import Bank, since 1934 the central American agency in extending *bilateral* overseas credits for the purchase of American exports, received notice that its $3.5 billion authorization would terminate in mid-1946. At that point, Congress wanted the Bank's functions picked up by the new United Nations organization, the World Bank, and the International Monetary Fund. Rapid demobilization of American armed forces also fitted into the pattern. Pressured by the public demand to "bring the boys back home," determined to use peaceful economic pressures instead of military force to reorder the world, and disturbed by the long string of wartime unbalanced budgets, the President reduced a 3.5 million-man army in Europe to 500,000 men in less than ten months. If American interests demanded the quick use of military force, the Administration could exploit its monopoly of the atomic bomb. That was the not-so-hidden stick back of America's economic carrot.

Bernard Baruch caught the essence of the American tactics: if the United States can "stop subsidization of labor and sweated competition in the export markets," the elder statesman exulted in March 1945, and prevent the rebuilding of war machines in the world, "oh boy, oh boy, what long-time prosperity we will have." [7] Amidst such excitement, however, one question plagued American officials: would all the former Allies play the game according to American rules? Within a year after the German surrender, France and Great Britain gave most of the appropriate pledges.

France cooperated despite the fierce independence of Charles de Gaulle, President of the French Provisional Government, and despite nearly two centuries of conflict between French and American political interests in both the New and Old Worlds. French dependence upon American aid demanded that de Gaulle swallow his pride and travel to Washington in August 1945 to ask for a one billion-dollar loan. After nine months of hard

---

[7] Bernard Baruch to E. Coblentz, March 23, 1945, Papers of Bernard Baruch, Princeton University Library, Princeton, New Jersey.

negotiations, the United States granted the money, receiving, in return, French promises to curtail governmental manipulation and subsidies, which had given French producers and exporters advantages in the international market. This agreement perfectly fitted Byrnes' dream of the postwar world, but it missed the roots of Franco-American conflicts. French and American officials continually clashed over occupation policies in Germany, and de Gaulle insisted on reestablishing the French colonial empire in Southeast Asia despite strong pressure from Washington to keep the area independent and open to the capital of all nations. ("I told him," Baruch recalled of a conversation with de Gaulle, "what the Mormons had done for Utah which was practically wilderness when they reached there."[8])

The British proved even more compliant, since, unlike the French, they fell into line politically as well as economically. Long-suffering England had little choice. Two wars had destroyed the shipping and export industries, which had traditionally paid for the importation of over half of England's food staples and nearly all of its raw materials except coal. Despite nationalization of some key industries by the newly elected Labour Government of Clement Attlee, and despite the importation of 300,000 Italian and German prisoners of war to serve as laborers, Britain faced a trade deficit of nearly $1.5 billion in 1946. The United States responded in December 1945 by signing a loan agreement for about $3.8 billion to be paid back with an annual interest which would approximate 1.6 percent. (The British had hoped to obtain a larger loan interest-free.) In return, the United States exacted stiff concessions. The weary British dismantled much of their Imperial Preference system, promised that the pound sterling and the Imperial trade would move throughout the world with a minimum of restrictions, and received severe warnings from Washington about further nationalization of industry. Assistant Secretary of State William Clayton, who negotiated the agreement, confided to Baruch, "We loaded the British loan negotiations with all the conditions that the traffic would bear." [9]

---

[8] "Memorandum for James F. Byrnes," August 27, 1945, Baruch Papers.
[9] "Memorandum for Mr. Baruch" from William Clayton, April 26, 1946, Baruch Papers.

Triumphant economically, the State Department began to move against British political policies in Europe. In October 1944, Churchill had shown some doubt about American plans for an open, multilateral world when he traveled to Moscow and worked out with Stalin a deal which gave Russia control of Rumania, Bulgaria, and Hungary and assured Great Britain a free hand in Greece. The two men agreed to split control of Yugoslavia between them. The United States immediately disavowed these negotiations, but Russian armies in Eastern Europe and ruthless British suppression of a revolt in Greece (in which Stalin did not raise a hand) made the American disavowal academic. United States opposition, however, never wavered. A State Department memorandum of late June 1945 informed Truman that although spheres of interest did in fact exist in both Eastern Europe and the Western Hemisphere, "Basic United States policy has been to oppose spheres of influence in Europe. . . . American policy must be attuned to events in Europe as a whole. . . ."[10]

This memorandum exposed a central problem in American diplomacy, for while Washington firmly set itself against spheres of interest in Europe, it moved to strengthen its own sphere of interest in the Western Hemisphere. Unlike its policies elsewhere, however, the State Department did not attempt to achieve this through economic tactics. The economic relationship with Latin America and Canada could be assumed; none had to be developed. During the war most Latin American nations linked themselves closely with the North American economy by feeding cheap raw materials to war industries. After the war, and despite American promises to the contrary at the Mexico City Conference in February 1945, Latin American economic needs were neglected in Washington while American money and goods flowed to Europe.

Economically, the United States failed to meet its first postwar test with the problems of an underdeveloped area. An inauspicious revival of Roosevelt's "Good Neighbor" approach, this failure also heralded the crisis to come in the post-1954 era when

---

[10] Department of State, *Papers Relating to the Foreign Relations of the United States: The Conference of Berlin (Potsdam)* (Washington, 1960), I, 262–264.

the newly-emerging nations forced their way toward the top of the State Department's list of priorities. In 1945-1946, the problem was different: how could the United States reconcile its general multilateral, open-door-to-all approach elsewhere with its traditional policy of maintaining Latin America as its own sphere of influence? The answer lay in Article 51 of the United Nations Charter. This provided for collective self-defense through special regional organizations to be created outside of the United Nations, but under the principles of the Charter. Latin American officials had pushed for this provision in the hope of regaining the preferential position in American policy that they had enjoyed during the 1930s. Washington policy-makers had other reasons. These were best explained by Arthur Vandenberg, Republican Senator from Michigan, architect of the bipartisan approach to postwar foreign policy, and former "isolationist" turned "internationalist."

How far Vandenberg had turned is debatable. He fervently believed in the internationalization of the Atlantic Charter freedoms framed by Roosevelt and Churchill in 1941, particularly the freedom of "all peoples to choose the form of government under which they will live." These principles, Vandenberg grandiloquently proclaimed in 1945, "sail with our fleets. They fly with our eagles. They sleep with our martyred dead." And they must be had by all, especially those in Eastern Europe. His growing fear of the Soviet Union weakened his hope that the United Nations, encumbered by the Russian veto in the Security Council, could effectively enforce these freedoms. The Western Hemisphere, however, could be protected. Teaming up with Assistant Secretary of State Nelson Rockefeller, Vandenberg formulated Article 51. "We would," Vandenberg candidly explained, no longer "have to depend exclusively on the Security Council" in American affairs.[11] The Senator wanted the best of both worlds: exclusive American power in the New and the right to exert American power in the Old.

This view was not a radical departure from pre-1941 policies. United States objectives in Latin America remained the traditional goals of the Monroe Doctrine: order, exclusion of extra-

---

[11] Arthur H. Vandenberg, Jr. (ed.), *The Private Papers of Senator Vandenberg* (Boston, 1952), pp. 134, 187.

hemispheric influences, and equal economic opportunity for United States citizens. These terms, however, became increasingly interchanged with the phrase "anti-communism." Article 51 provided a weapon which might ward off "communism" in the short run. For the long run, a comprehensive economic and social reform program was needed, and given Latin American dependence upon the United States, the program's success would depend upon help from Washington. The United States was not interested in such a program and would not be for more than a decade. Europe came first. In the meantime, Vandenberg and other American officials were content to preserve American freedom of action in the hemisphere through Article 51.

With considerably more brutality and less regard for the formalities of the United Nations Charter, Joseph Stalin also constructed his postwar policy upon the necessity of maintaining freedom of action in spheres he considered vital for Soviet economic and strategic requirements. Within a year after Hitler's demise, American open-world diplomacy crashed against Stalin's iron curtain, and only Vandenberg's vehicle of Article 51 remained to cart away the pieces.

Regardless of the threat, whether economic or atomic, Stalin had reasons for not lifting the curtain. For strategic and psychological purposes, he divided Germany and then maintained buffer states between Germany and the Soviet Union. The Soviet peoples and leaders alike viewed almost everything in their lives through the memories of the horrors that struck from 1941 to 1945.[12] The Germans "will recover, and very quickly," Stalin observed at a banquet in April 1945. "Give them twelve to fifteen years and they'll be on their feet again. And that is why the unity of the Slavs is important."[13]

Such predictions were confirmed in Stalin's mind by his own peculiar interpretation of Marxist-Leninist doctrine. All Soviet rulers have cloaked their policies, no matter how divergent, with this doctrine, and, in the post-1945 years, have used it not only

---

[12] Ralph K. White, "Images in the Context of International Conflict," in *International Behaviour*, edited by Herbert C. Kelman (New York, 1965), p. 271.

[13] Milovan Djilas, *Conversations with Stalin* (New York, 1961), p. 114.

to rally the Soviet people against foreign threats, but to rationalize the power of their regime and silence internal dissent. To
outside observers, doctrine can consequently act as a weather
vane; once officials have decided upon a policy, they justify it
with appropriate doctrine, and the doctrinal changes then indi-
cate policy changes.

Stalin's use of this doctrine in 1945 differed little from the
dogmas used during the bitterest East-West confrontation between 1937 and 1941. Perhaps this similarity resulted in part
from the remarkably stable membership of the Politburo (the
policy-making body of the Central Committee of the Communist
Party), whose membership in 1945 was almost exactly that of
1939. The similarity could also be ascribed to Stalin's belief that
his warnings in the 1920s and 1930s regarding capitalist encirclement of the Soviet Union had proved accurate. The war-time
alliance with the West apparently did not dent Stalin's outlook.
His views of Western democracy, the danger of capitalist encirclement, the inevitability of war, the nature and sources of
imperialism, and the impossibility of disarmament evidently
changed very little between 1939 and 1945.

Soviet journals muted these beliefs during the German onslaught of 1941-1942, for Stalin was shrewd enough to ask the
Russians to sacrifice themselves for "Holy Russia," not for the
Communist party. The old dogmas began to reappear with the
Red Army victories of 1943 and arguments among the Allies regarding the second front and postwar boundaries. By 1944 and
early 1945 Soviet articles, for the first time since 1941, explored,
with appropriate Marxist terminology, the importance of unemployment in the United States. In April 1945, Eugene Tarle, a
leading Soviet academic figure, told a Moscow audience that
Anglo-American contributions to the Great Patriotic War had
consisted of little more than goodwill.[14]

With his doctrinal house more orderly, Stalin consolidated his
personal power by raising his close associate, Lavrenti Beria,

---

[14] John S. Curtiss and Alex Inkeles, "Marxism in the U.S.S.R.—The Recent
Revival," *Political Science Quarterly*, LXI (September, 1946), 349–364;
Frederick C. Barghoorn, "Great Russian Messianism in Postwar Soviet
Ideology," in Ernest J. Simmons, editor, *Continuity and Change in Russian
and Soviet Thought* (Cambridge, Massachusetts, 1955), p. 541.

chief of the Secret Police, to the rank of Marshall of the Red Army, and promoting himself to Generalissimo. Red Army officers, who controlled the only power capable of challenging Stalin's control, slowly disappeared from public view.[15] In August 1945, rumors circulated that Stalin would shortly announce a new Five-Year Plan. Such a plan would cut two ways for the Soviet dictator, since its required regimentation would maximize his own power, while compelling the Russians to resurrect rapidly their war-torn economy.

These same objectives were accomplished by the Red Army's occupation and consequent communization of Eastern Europe. Doctrinal demands and neurotic personal ambition partly explained Stalin's policies in this area. But the overriding requirement dictating this policy was the Soviets' need for security and economic reconstruction. Here Stalin's dilemma became strikingly evident. If he wished quick economic reconstruction, he would need American funds, since the United States possessed the only sufficient capital supply in the world. To obtain those funds, however, Stalin would have to loosen his control of Eastern Europe, allow American political and economic power to flow into the area, and consequently surrender what he considered to be the first essential of Soviet security. Through absolute control of Eastern Europe, Stalin might obtain both security and, through forced drafts upon those European economies, the economic resources needed for Soviet reconstruction. Russia had lost one quarter of her capital equipment, 1700 towns, 70,000 villages, nearly 100,000 collective farms and more than twenty million dead during World War II. In 1945 Soviet steel production sunk to only one eighth the amount of American production. Control of Poland, Rumania, Hungary, Bulgaria, and East Germany (as well as the Baltic States which Stalin had absorbed in 1940, and Manchuria in the Far East) enabled the Soviets to drain vast quantities of goods and laborers to refurbish their economy. Stalin imposed a communist system over most of these areas, not because the historical inevitability of Marxism had come to pass, but because, in the Russians' view, both their security and eco-

---

[15] Raymond L. Garthoff, *Soviet Military Policy, A Historical Analysis* (New York, 1966), pp. 42–44.

nomic requirements could be found in such a system, and the success of the Red Army presented a unique opportunity to act. As Stalin remarked in the spring of 1945, "Whoever occupies a territory also imposes on it his own social system."

For American policy-makers dedicated to creating a Western-democratic world built on the Atlantic Charter Freedoms, Stalin's moves posed the terrible problem of how to open the Soviet empire without alienating the Soviets. Given their assumptions of how the postwar world must work, Washington officials had little choice but to attempt to stop the descent of the curtain around Stalin's domains. Otherwise the world would be divided, as in the late 1930s, into separate and hostile blocs. In these dilemmas lay the roots of the Cold War.

The first test came in Poland. During the darkest days of 1941 and 1942 when the German armies drove toward Moscow, Stalin insisted to Western officials that after the war Soviet security required the annexation of large areas of Polish soil. Consequently, when the Russians formally agreed in early 1942 to the Atlantic Charter's provision that "all peoples" have the right "to choose the form of government under which they will live," Stalin added a significant reservation: "Considering that the practical application of these principles will necessarily adapt itself to the circumstances, needs, and historic peculiarities of particular countries, the Soviet Government can state that a consistent application of these principles will secure the most energetic support on the part of the government and peoples of the Soviet Union." [16] The first half of the reservation clearly indicated that the Soviets had no intention of allowing the history of 1919-1939 to repeat itself; if they could gather the requisite power, Eastern Europe and particularly Poland, across which German armies had invaded Russia twice in less than twenty-five years, would come under *de facto* Soviet control. American diplomats attempted to soften this policy at the Moscow Conference in October 1943 and again at Yalta in February 1945, but the Russians refused to yield.

---

[16] Martin Herz, *Beginnings of the Cold War* (Bloomington, Indiana, 1966), pp. vii–viii and, for the following account in which I have drawn heavily from Herz's analysis, see pp. 50, 69, 176, and particularly Chapter IV of his book.

When, therefore, the discussions at Yalta reached the substantial question of the composition of the Polish government, the Soviets announced that the basis of that government would be the Communist-controlled Lublin group. This move threatened largely to exclude from power the Polish government-in-exile which had lived in London during the war; that regime had angered Stalin by demanding that Poland regain its pre-1939 boundaries. Churchill and Roosevelt finally acquiesced in Stalin's two demands that Russia receive large areas of eastern Poland, and that the Polish government be reorganized on the basis of the present provisional government which was dominated by the Lublin group. The British and American leaders, however, did not believe that this agreement gave the Soviets a veto power over the future course of Poland, although the Russians proceeded to interpret the understanding in precisely those terms. Churchill and Roosevelt also thought they had scored by getting Stalin's signature on the "Declaration of Liberated Europe," a document that soon became a highly contentious issue in Soviet-American relations. In the "Declaration," the three powers agreed to destroy all Nazism and Fascism, to follow through on the Atlantic Charter principle of allowing the liberated peoples to create their own democratic institutions, and to hold "free elections" at the "earliest possible" time. The important debates centered upon the crucial phrases that would explain how these laudable objectives were to be reached, and here the Soviets got their way. Instead of accepting an American suggestion to insert a phrase that would establish machinery to carry out these principles, Molotov succeeded in including a simple promise that, if problems arose, the three powers would "take measures for the carrying out of mutual consultation." In such "consultation," unanimous agreement would have to be reached for further action; that is, the Soviets could veto any new Western moves in Poland and Eastern Europe.

Critics have attacked these agreements on the grounds that American officials surrendered Eastern Europe to Russia at Yalta, and that the Russians broke their word. The critics cannot easily have it both ways and actually cannot argue either way with any consistency. Churchill and Roosevelt did not surrender Poland; given the presence of the Red Army in Poland, the nation was

not theirs to surrender. The two Western leaders were playing for the highest stakes with weak hands. They hoped to keep the game going and maintain some form of Russian cooperation until their hands could be strengthened with postwar American economic power. On the other side, the Russians argued that they did not break these agreements, at least not until they believed they were forced to do so in the post-1946 years. They held "mutual consultations" (although this did not mean that such consultations necessarily would lead to different policies), and they allowed "free elections" (although the Russians were extremely careful to insure that "free" in this case was compatible with their view of Soviet security requirements).

The Soviet approach to East European governments varied. In Rumania, which had been an ally of Hitler and whose troops had actually invaded Russia, the Soviets first attempted to rule through a government in which the Communists were a minority. Two weeks after Yalta, however, Stalin issued a brutal ultimatum demanding that the Communist party obtain power within two hours to restore "order" or else Russia would "not be responsible for the continuance of Rumania as an independent state." On the other hand, the Soviets held elections which allowed a non-Communist government to gain power in Hungary, suffered an overwhelming defeat in elections in the Russian-controlled zones of Austria, supervised elections in Bulgaria, which satisfied British if not American officials, and agreed to acquiesce in the coming to power of an independent, non-Communist government in Finland (a nation against which the Russians had fought a bloody war in 1939-1940) if that government would follow a foreign policy friendly to Russia. Historical events, particularly the two German invasions, led Stalin to place Poland in the same category as Rumania, not Finland.

Soviet concern over Western attitudes toward Eastern Europe grew in March 1945 when, at the same time that Americans demanded a voice at Warsaw, reports reached Stalin that United States officials were considering the negotiations of a secret surrender of German forces in Italy. These reports contained enough truth so that Roosevelt was unable to relieve Stalin's fears that the Americans were cooperating with German efforts to move Nazi armies from Italy to the Soviet front. In 1944-1945, moreover, the United States had effectively excluded Russian representation from the key commission which controlled the Italian occupation. The Soviets later used this precedent to exclude Americans from a similar commission in Rumania. Another bitter Soviet-American dispute erupted over voting procedures in the new United Nations organization.

These arguments sharpened the feelings over the crucial Polish question. In a letter of April 24 (the day after the Molotov-Truman confrontation noted at the beginning of this chapter), Stalin answered Anglo-American complaints about Russian actions in Poland by observing that "Poland borders on the Soviet Union, which cannot be said about Great Britain or the U.S.A. . . . I do not know," he continued, "whether a genuinely representative Government has been established in Greece, or whether the Belgium Government is a genuinely democratic one. The Soviet Union was not consulted when those Governments were being formed, nor did it claim the right to interfere in those matters, because it realizes how important Belgium and Greece are to the security of Great Britain." The Soviet dictator concluded: "I cannot understand why in discussing Poland no attempt is made to consider the interests of the Soviet Union in terms of security as well." Stalin held fast to his views on the Provisional Government and on territorial boundaries that gave Russia a huge section of Poland. He recompensed the Poles by moving their boundary to the Oder-Niesse rivers, well inside eastern Germany.

By the time the Potsdam Conference met in July 1945, the United States recognized the Soviet-controlled Polish government, but throughout the summer and autumn attempted to weaken Soviet control by using relief materials and equipment badly needed by the Poles to force Poland to accept, as the State Department said, "a policy of equal opportunity for us in trade, investments and access to sources of information." [17] This policy failed before it could ever get under way, and the failure left an enduring mark on postwar American policy. Vandenberg had drawn the appropriate conclusion as early as the Yalta Conference. The Polish settlement there "was *awful*," he had written;

---

[17] Department of State, *Potsdam*, I, 715, 784–785.

if anything ruined the new United Nations, it would "be the ghost of Poland."[18] Stalin had drawn his own conclusions.

A greater test began in Germany. At Yalta, the Big Three agreed to govern Germany temporarily after the war by dividing it into four sections: Russia would control the northeastern provinces between the Oder-Neisse and Elbe rivers, Britain the northwest, and the United States the southern areas. France later received control of two Rhineland states in the American sector. Each area was to be governed individually by the military commanders of each power. Together, the commanders formed the Allied Control Council which, by unanimous decision, would lay down rules for reuniting Germany. The rub lay in the requirement of unanimity, since the powers were badly split on policy objectives.

In the early months of the Cold War, the United States and Great Britain hoped to keep Germany politically whole and, after destroying her war-making potential, restore industry to a self-supporting level; the Allies would thus not have to expend their own resources to keep Germany alive. The Soviets, supported in large part by the French, preferred a politically-divided, economically-weakened Germany. Stalin's tactics included demands for huge reparations to be taken out of the German industrial complex. He liked the figure of $20 billion with $10 billion going to Russia. At Yalta, Roosevelt agreed that the $20 billion figure might be the starting point for negotiations, but during the summer of 1945, American and Russian delegates meeting in Moscow failed to reach agreement on this crucial question.[19] The collapse of these talks forced the issue to be worked out at Potsdam where it became part of a deal: the West essentially surrendered the disputed Oder-Neisse area by allowing Poland to "administer" those lands, and the Anglo-Americans took a long step toward their goal of making Germany self-sufficient by winning Russian assent to a proposal which gave the Soviets 25 percent (instead of a fixed figure) of German capital equipment from the Western zones. Fifteen percent of this, however, was to be ex-

[18] Vandenberg to Baruch, February 15, 1945, Baruch Papers.
[19] "Summary of Procedure of Allied Commission on Reparations," Vol. 19-A, Papers of Richard A. Scandrett, Cornell University Library, Ithaca, New York.

changed for agricultural products from the Soviet sector. In their own zone, the Soviets received *carte blanche*, and now that their opportunities in the Western areas had been sharply cut, they accelerated their divestment of industrial machinery and laborers from eastern Germany.

By the end of 1945, chances for a united, open, and self-sufficient Germany had largely disappeared. The French adamantly opposed any central administration. In the Soviet zone Stalin destroyed the Prussian landlord class, nationalized industry, and forced political parties to accept Communist control. In the American zone, General Lucius Clay, head of the American Military Government in Germany, pushed for the raising of German industrial production until the State Department on December 12, 1945 allowed the ceiling placed on that economy at the Potsdam Conference to become a minimum instead of a maximum level. Clay's arguments received strong support from important American industrialists. Alfred P. Sloan, President of General Motors, reminded Bernard Baruch (who wanted to keep Germany under tight control) of General Motors' accomplishments in prewar Germany ("it was frequently passed on to us by the German Economic Ministry that we had contributed much to the expansion of industry in Germany") and urged loose controls over all but war industries so that Germany would once again become attractive to American investors.[20] Throughout Germany, the Allied Control Council lost power, and American, French, British, and Russian commanders assumed supreme authority in their zones.

Little else was possible, for as Stalin had remarked, each occupying power imposed its own system on its area. The division of Germany was set. Poland and Eastern Europe were sinking behind a Soviet iron curtain. The question now became: how would the world's most powerful nation respond to these frustrations of its dream for the postwar world?

---

[20] Sloan to Baruch, November 30, 1945, Baruch Papers.

CHAPTER II

The Declaration of Cold War (1945-1946)

AMERICAN OFFICIALS RESPONDED to the crisis in Germany and Eastern Europe by devising three tactics which, they believed, would draw back the enveloping curtain. First, throughout the summer of 1945, the Truman Administration hoped that the American possession of atomic bombs would, in the words of Secretary of War Henry Stimson, result in "less barbarous relations with the Russians." Stimson believed that world peace was unobtainable until "Russia's secret police state" opened itself to the fresh winds from the West. More to the point, James F. Byrnes, soon to be Secretary of State, informed scientists Leo Szilard and Harold Urey in June 1945 that the bomb "would make Russia more manageable in Europe."[1] Eastern Europe remained sealed off, however, even after Hiroshima and Nagasaki endured the terrible birth agonies of a new era in world history.

Stimson now advised changing tactics. In a memorandum of September 11 to President Truman, the retiring Secretary of War prophesied "that it would not be possible to use our possession of the atomic bomb as a direct lever to produce the change" desired inside Eastern Europe and Russia. If Soviet-American negotiations continue with "this weapon rather ostentatiously on our hip, their suspicions and their distrust of our purposes and motives will increase." Stimson urged direct, bilateral discussions with the Soviets to formulate control of atomic

---

[1] Louis Morton, "The Decision to Use the Atomic Bomb," *Foreign Affairs Quarterly*, XXXV (Jan. 1957), 334–353; Leo Szilard, "Personal History," *University of Chicago Roundtable*, September 27, 1949, pp. 14–15; Gar Alperovitz, *Atomic Diplomacy* (New York, 1965).

energy and write a general peace settlement.[2] Few top-level, bilateral Soviet-American talks took place, but discussions did occur in the Council of Foreign Ministers. A stalemate soon resulted at the first meeting of the Council in London in September 1945, when Molotov insisted that the Allies recognize the Rumanian and other Russian-supported governments in Eastern Europe before the actual writing of the peace treaties.

Having failed to budge the Russians in face-to-face negotiations, even when backed by atomic bombs, the State Department next tried to buckle Stalin's iron fence with economic pressure. An Office of Strategic Services report of September 1944 had indirectly warned against such tactics, observing that by demanding great internal sacrifices, the Russians "could carry through this reconstruction with its domestic resources, without foreign loans or reparations."[3] The State Department either did not read or believe such reports. When Stalin asked for a six billion dollar loan in January 1945, the State Department refused to discuss the matter unless, as Ambassador to Russia W. Averell Harriman remarked, Stalin became more receptive to American demands in Europe. After the German surrender in May, President Truman, following Congressional legislative authority, abruptly cut off Lend-Lease aid. Three months later, the Soviet dictator asked for a one billion-dollar loan. Somehow, the United States government lost this request, but it was discovered after the failure of the Foreign Ministers Conference in December. On March 1, 1946 the State Department offered to discuss the loan if the Soviets would pledge "non-discrimination in international commerce" by accepting membership in the World Bank and the International Monetary Fund.[4] Such membership required the Russians to open their records and territory to international agencies, which were necessarily dominated by American capital and personnel. On March 13, 1946, the Soviets officially announced a Five-Year Plan in order to rebuild heavy industry and to ensure "the technical and economic independence of the Soviet

---

[2] Henry S. Stimson, *On Active Service in Peace and War* (New York, 1947), pp. 638–650.

[3] Enclosed in "Memorandum" for Baruch from Samuel Lubell, March 1945, Baruch Papers.

[4] *The New York Times*, April 21, 1946, p. 17.

Union," as the official Russian announcement phrased it. Two days later, Stalin bluntly refused the American offer.

These failures also infected non-European problems. The triumphant war-time coalition collapsed, as it had triumphed, on a worldwide scale. The extent of the breakdown precluded hopes for a permanent settlement almost anywhere on the globe. More important, it made American officials ponder the awful possibility that Stalin's ambitions included not only strategic positions in Eastern Europe, but the imposition of Communist regimes upon Asia and the Middle East.

Stating the Soviet dictator's alternatives in this way no doubt badly distorts his true policies. Attempting to foster a Communist revolution in China during the 1920s, Stalin had suffered disastrously in 1927 when Chiang Kai-shek turned and purged the Communist influences inside the revolution. Thereafter Stalin became extremely careful in supporting revolutionary movements which he could not directly control. Stalin's thrusts after 1944 were rooted more in the Soviets' desire to secure certain specific strategic bases, raw materials, and above all, to break up what Stalin considered to be the growing Western encirclement of Russia. The distinction was important; in view of the general breakdown in Europe, however, American officials saw little reason to worry about such distinctions in formulating Asian policies. The Soviets had to be stopped, whatever their motives.

They were first confronted in Korea. After thirty-five years of occupation, Japanese armies were, according to Soviet-American agreement, disarmed north of the 38th parallel by Russian troops and south of that line by American soldiers. Lengthy Russian-American conferences failed to unify the nation. Neither side wanted to chance the possibility that a unified Korea might move into the opposite camp. The Russians rapidly consolidated Communist power in the north, but American authorities encountered great difficulty in establishing order in the impoverished and nearly politically illiterate south where fifty-four different parties sought power. In 1948 the United States attempted to break the deadlock by proposing unification through nationwide elections under United Nations supervision, but the Russians refused to cooperate. American officials nevertheless held the election in the south, and Syngman Rhee, a strongly anti-Soviet conservative who had spent many years in the United States, won the presidency. In September, the Soviets retaliated by establishing a "People's Republic" in the north, and then scored a propaganda victory by withdrawing their occupation armies amidst great diplomatic fanfare. An American army and a divided Korea nevertheless remained.

In Japan, no similar problem over unification occurred. General Douglas MacArthur controlled the occupation not only to the exclusion of Russian authority, but sometimes by overlooking the wishes of the government in Washington. When an occupation agreement was signed by Allied officials on January 30, 1946, the Russians were nowhere in sight; even Australia was allowed to send occupation forces only as long as it promised not to interfere with American authority. MacArthur then purged from public life many who had been associated with Japanese militarism and drafted a constitution which established a figurehead Emperor, a two-house Diet, a bill of rights, and a clause in which Japan renounced war for all time. Elections in April 1946 and the following April brought a semblance of representative government. More important, the elections isolated the Japanese Communists and allowed MacArthur to say that Japan had overwhelmingly repudiated Communism. To the General, as to Washington officials, this was central. In a conversation with Secretary of Navy James Forrestal in July 1946, MacArthur viewed Japan "as the western [sic] outpost of our defenses," blasted "left-wing writers in the American press," and then compared America in its crusade against Communism to the agony of Christ at Gethsemane, for "Christ, even though crucified, nevertheless prevailed."[5]

In using such vivid but characteristic phrases, MacArthur particularly had the American position in China in mind. Unlike the situation in Japan, the Russians prominently entered the Chinese scene before the Japanese surrendered. At Yalta, Roosevelt, pressured by urgent military and political advice (including MacArthur's) secured Stalin's promises to enter the Pacific War and recognize Chiang Kai-shek as the leader of China. In return,

---

[5] James F. Forrestal, *Forrestal Diaries*, Walter Millis (ed.) (New York, 1951), pp. 177–178.

the Soviets received substantial concessions: the lease of Port Arthur as a Soviet naval base, internationalization of the port of Darien, joint Sino-Soviet operation of the Chinese-Eastern and South Manchurian railroads, possession of southern Sakhalin and the Kurile Islands, and a plebiscite to be held in Outer Mongolia (which in October 1945 voted to become independent of China by the amazing score of 483,291 to 0). Chiang and Stalin agreed to these terms in a Treaty of Friendship and Alliance on August 14, 1945. The State Department and such periodicals as Henry Luce's *Time-Life* publications, which kept close watch over American interests in Asia, cheered the treaty.

By the spring of 1945, the United States was keeping very close watch on Soviet activities in and around China. Washington feared Russian Communists much more than the Chinese variety. On April 23, George Kennan, Chargé of the American Embassy in Moscow, warned Washington that Stalin's apparent friendliness toward Chiang was deceptive because the Soviets believed that Chiang could unify China "only on conditions which are acceptable to the Chinese Communist Party." Russian policy, Kennan argued, would continue as it had been "in the recent past: a fluid resilient policy directed at the achievement of maximum power with minimum responsibility" in areas on the Soviet border. Kennan then made a clear delineation of Soviet motives: they were "dictated by the strategic necessity of protecting in depth the industrial core of the U.S.S.R."[6]

The State Department listened to Kennan. On December 5, 1945, General of the Army George Marshall set off on his famous mission to reconcile Nationalists with Communists in order, in the General's words, to avert "the tragic consequences of a divided China and of a probable Russian reassumption of power in Manchuria, the combined effect of this resulting in the defeat or loss of the major purpose of our war in the Pacific."[7] Few American officials dissented from Kennan's and Marshall's analyses of the Russian danger. In addition, these policy-makers

---

[6] Department of State, *U.S. Relations With China* (Washington, 1949), pp. 96–97.

[7] Tang Tsou, *America's Failure in China, 1941–1950* (Chicago, 1963), pp. 355–356.

wanted a strong and friendly China which could fill the power vacuum in the Far East left by a defeated Japan. Whether a China which would be both strong and friendly could be created was a question which the West had avoided facing for a hundred years.

By the end of February 1946, Marshall succeeded in working out a tentative settlement, including a cease-fire between Nationalist and Communist forces. This was the closest the United States or the Chinese themselves would come to a peaceful settlement of the civil war. By mid-April, the arrangement had collapsed. Marshall later placed much blame on Chiang for this disaster, although he noted that towards the end of the negotiations the Communists also were unwilling "to make a fair compromise." A discouraged Marshall urged that the Kuomintang, Chiang's chief channel of power, be forced to enter a coalition with all "liberals," whether Communist or non-Communist, under the leadership of Chiang.[8]

Believing that he could defeat the Communists militarily and that the United States had no alternative but to provide him with all the resources he might require, Chiang refused Marshall's suggestions in the spring of 1946. The Chinese leader sadly miscalculated. Although outnumbered five to one, the Communist armies of Mao Tse-tung had increased their power dramatically since the late 1930s; by late 1945 they controlled at least 225,000 square miles and more than 105 million Chinese. Communist power rested on this well-drilled army, and also on the peasants, comprising four fifths of the population, who despised the landlords upon whom Chiang depended for much of his strength. As the war intensified in 1946, the Communists also profited from a tremendous inflationary spiral which nearly wiped out the middle class and forced Chiang's officials to keep up with the rising prices with increased corruption. Finally, as the State Department had feared, Communist armies obtained a treasure when in March and April 1946, the Soviet occupation troops in Manchuria suddenly withdrew, leaving behind vast stores of Japanese arms and equipment. Chiang now launched a military offensive into Manchuria. Successful at first, the Nationalists overstretched

---

[8] *U.S. Relations With China*, pp. 686–689.

their supply lines. By autumn, Mao's troops began successful counterattacks.

With the Russians taking great pains to emphasize their formal recognition of Chiang as the leader of China, American officials were hard put to place the growing disaster in China within the standard Cold War context. John Carter Vincent, chief of the Far Eastern Desk in the State Department, precisely explained the growing dilemma: "We are not going to wash our hands of the problem, [but] we are going to keep out of involvement in civil warfare."[9] It became impossible to do both at once. By the spring of 1947 Chiang was losing power rapidly. Truman tried to help, or at least put a new face on American policy, by replacing Vincent and sending a new mission led by General Albert Wedemeyer. The President's policy assumption, however, remained the same: Chiang was not worth the commitment of American troops or of large amounts of American materiel.

This policy assumption could rest in large part on the apparent Russian retreat in Korea, Japan, and, by mid-1946, China. The diplomatic situation in Asia changed qualitatively, in the eyes of State Department officials, between the time of Kennan's and Marshall's warnings of 1945 and the Russian withdrawal from Manchuria in 1946. Such a view followed logically from the American inclination to view international events in the context of the developing Russian-American confrontation. On the other hand, this same context forced United States officials to give top priority to European affairs. Given the more blatant and direct Soviet policies in Eastern and Central Europe, and moved by the historic ties to a Western Europe whose immediate industrial and power potential was much greater than that of China, Washington policy-makers could do little else. As China dropped down the list of American diplomatic priorities in 1946, these two elements—Washington's determination to blunt and roll back all Soviet threats, and an equal determination to keep Western Europe within the American camp—fused and exploded into a dramatic Russian-American crisis in the Middle East.

---

[9] John Carter Vincent, "Our Far Eastern Policies," in Vincent, *et al.*, *America's Future in the Pacific* (New Brunswick, New Jersey, 1947), pp. 6–10.

For nearly a century, the Middle East had formed the lifeline of the British and French empires. More recently, it had become the source for Europe of one of the most critical natural resources, oil, and American interests had moved into a dominating position in controlling that resource. The Soviets struck at two junctures on this lifeline, Iran and Turkey. Their first thrust came in Iran when Stalin violated a 1942 Occupation Treaty signed with Great Britain in which both parties had promised to pull their forces out of Iran six months after the end of hostilities. The American and British troops withdrew; the Russians, however, not only refused to evacuate their troops, but demanded oil concessions approximating those obtained by Anglo-American companies, (and promised by F.D.R. to Stalin in 1943), and then supported a revolt of the Azerbaijanian population in northern Iran. In February and March of 1946 Soviet tanks and equipment rumbled toward the Iranian border. With the crisis at a peak, Byrnes sent a stiff note to Moscow on March 6 demanding immediate withdrawal of Russian forces. On March 24, Iran and Russia announced that the Red Army would shortly be withdrawn, bilateral negotiations would begin between the Iranian government and the Azerbaijanians, and a joint Iranian-Soviet oil company would be formed subject to ratification of the Persian Parliament (the Majlis). The Red Army left by May 6 and the Iranian army quelled the northern revolt merely by marching into the area. Most important, the oil company, which had been the primary reason for Stalin's moves in Iran, was rejected by the Majlis in early 1947. The Soviets had suffered a major diplomatic defeat.

Russian interest in Turkey was more complex. It had developed from historic Russian-Turkish antipathy, Soviet determination to gain joint control of the strategic Dardanelles (the key link between the Black Sea and the Mediterranean), and Stalin's inherited Georgian trait of hating everything Turkish except Turkish tobacco. In March 1945 the Soviets revived an ancient Russian demand for partnership with the Turks in the control of the Straits. Quiet diplomatic probing by both the Russians and the United States followed until August 1946 when Stalin sent a note to Turkey, which Under-Secretary of State Dean Acheson interpreted as a Soviet attempt to dominate Turkey, threaten Greece, and intimidate the remainder of the Middle East. Acheson advised a showdown with the Russians. Truman agreed: "We might as well find out whether the Russians were bent on world conquest now as in five or ten years."[10] The Soviets soon learned from Washington that Turkey would continue to be "primarily responsible" for the Straits.[11] The State Department then ordered reinforcement for an American naval unit (including Marines) which had been sailing in the Mediterranean since early spring. The *Franklin D. Roosevelt*, the most powerful American carrier, moved into the area. By the autumn of 1946, Soviet pressure on Turkey had considerably eased.

Stalin no doubt believed that, because of its war-time sacrifices and geographical location, Russia had as much right to Iranian oil and control of the Straits as any other power. Thwarted in these areas, in February 1946 Stalin brought charges in the Security Council against the British repression of the Greek rebellion and British and Dutch attempts to suppress revolution in Indonesia. The bitterest outburst occurred three months later at the Paris Foreign Ministers Conference. British Foreign Minister Ernest Bevin angrily announced that although "nineteenth century imperialism in England is dead," he was "driven to the suspicion sometimes that our place has been taken by others." Molotov immediately brought Soviet views into focus:

Nineteenth century imperialism may be dead in England, but there are new twentieth century tendencies. When Mr. Churchill calls for a new war and makes militant speeches on two continents, he represents the worst of 20th century imperialism . . . . Britain has troops in Greece, Palestine, Iraq, Indo-China and elsewhere. Russia has no troops outside of security zones and their lines of communication. This is different. We have troops only where provided by treaties. Thus we are in Poland, for example, as our Allies are in Belgium, France and Holland. I also recall that Egypt is a member of UNO. She demands that British troops be withdrawn. Britain declines . . . . What shall we say of UNO when one member imposes its authority upon another? How long can such things go on?[12]

[10] *Forrestal Diaries*, p. 192.

[11] *Documents on American Foreign Relations*, Dennett and Turner (eds), VIII, 865.

[12] *Private Papers of Senator Vandenberg*, pp. 277–278.

Bevin made no effective reply and the meeting hastily adjourned.

In February and March 1946, Stalin and Churchill issued the appropriate declarations of Cold War. In an election speech of February 9, Stalin announced that Marxist-Leninist dogma remained valid, for "the unevenness of development of the capitalist countries" could lead to "violent disturbance" and the consequent splitting of the "capitalist world into two hostile camps and war between them." The Soviets must prepare themselves for a replay of the 1930s by increasing industrialization, the collectivization of agriculture, the development of basic industry at the expense of consumer goods and, in all, the enormous sacrifices demanded in "three more Five-Year Plans, I should think, if not more."[13] There would be no peace, externally or internally. These words made a profound impact on Washington. Justice William Douglas, one of the reigning American liberals, told Forrestal that Stalin's speech meant "The Declaration of World War III."[14]

Winston Churchill delivered the Western reply at Fulton, Missouri on March 5. After a significant introduction by President Truman, who asked Churchill to speak his mind, the former Prime Minister launched into an exaltation of American power with the plea that Americans recognize that "God has willed" the United States, not "some Communist or neo-Fascist state" the possession of atomic bombs. To take proper advantage of the "breathing space" provided by these weapons, Churchill asked for "a fraternal association of the English-speaking peoples" operating under the principles of the United Nations, but not inside that organization, to reorder the world. This unilateral effort must be undertaken because "From Stettin in the Baltic to Trieste in the Adriatic, an iron curtain has descended across the Continent," allowing "police governments" to rule Eastern Europe. The Soviets, Churchill emphasized, did not want war: "What

---

[13] J. V. Stalin, *Speech Delivered by J. V. Stalin at a Meeting of Voters of the Stalin Electoral Area of Moscow, February 9, 1946* (Washington, Embassy of the U.S.S.R., March, 1946).

[14] *Forrestal Diaries*, pp. 134–135.

they desire is the fruits of war and the indefinite expansion of their power and doctrines."[15]

The "iron curtain" phrase made the speech famous, but as Churchill himself observed, the "crux" of the message lay in the proposal that the Anglo-Americans, outside the United Nations and with the support of atomic weaponry (the title of the address was "The Sinews of Peace"), create "a unity in Europe from which no nation should be permanently outcast." The Soviets accepted this as a direct threat to their power in Eastern Europe. Within a week Stalin attacked Churchill and his "friends" in America who, like Hitler, held a "racial theory": that those who speak the English language "should rule over the remaining nations of the world." This, Stalin warned, is "a set-up for war, a call to war with the Soviet Union." The Russian dictator reminded Churchill that twice in recent history Germany had attacked Russia through Eastern European countries which "had governments inimical to the Soviet Union." Anyway, Stalin added, contrary to Churchill's belief, Communism in "Europe" is "normal," "the law of historical development."[16] Western officials observed that Stalin did not limit this conception of Communism's power to the area east of the Elbe.

Within a three-week period after the Churchill speech, Stalin launched a series of policies which, in retrospect, marks March 1946 as a milestone in the Cold War. No doubt these policies had been evolving for months and years. The timing and the concentration of the moves, however, have significance, for during that month the Soviets rejected the terms of a $1 billion American loan after having worked for such a loan over the previous fifteen months, refused to become a member of the World Bank and the International Monetary Fund, formally announced the start of a new five-year plan, built up and then stepped back from a confrontation with the West in Iran, timed the evacuation of Manchuria so that the Chinese Communists would benefit from materiel left behind by the Red Army, and made a crucial change in Russian economic policy toward East

---

[15] Text in *The New York Times*, March 6, 1946, p. 4.
[16] Interview in *Pravda*, reprinted in *The New York Times*, March 14, 1946, p. 4.

Germany. The Kremlin also initiated an intense ideological effort to eliminate Western influences, purify and propagate Stalinist dogma, and deify Stalin himself. The name of Andrei Zhdanov soon became synonomous with this campaign. One close observer described this supposed "intellectual" of the Politburo as "short, with a brownish clipped mustache, high forehead, pointed nose, and sickly red face," who "had some knowledge of everything," but did not know a single field thoroughly, "a typical intellectual who became acquainted with and picked up knowledge of other fields through Marxist literature."[17] Zhdanov prophesied that Marxism-Leninism had a messianic destiny, "the right to teach others a new general human morality."[18]

By the early summer of 1946, these ideological developments became embodied into policy toward that touchstone of the Cold War, Germany. Reparations were the central issue. In late 1945, Byrnes had attempted to meet Russian fears of a remilitarized Germany by proposing that the Big Four powers sign a treaty unifying Germany and guaranteeing German demilitarization. In late April 1946, Molotov rejected this because of a key Russian policy change on reparations. Sometime during the spring, the Soviets stopped removing machinery from eastern Germany and determined instead to produce goods in their zone, where labor and resources were more readily available, and then ship the products to Russia. While Molotov was rejecting Brynes' overture, General Lucius Clay was informing Russian commanders in Germany on May 3, 1946 that no more reparations would be moved from the Western zones. Molotov's and Clay's moves were decisive moments in the Cold War, for they terminated any hope of useful negotiations on Germany.

Byrnes analyzed this growing rigidity in a highly-publicized speech at Stuttgart, Germany, on September 6. The Secretary of State announced that Germany must develop exports in order to be "self-sustaining," refused to recognize the Oder-Neisse boundary for eastern Germany, specified that Germans should be given primary responsibility for running their own affairs

---

[17] Djilas, *Conversations With Stalin*, pp. 149–150.
[18] Barghoorn, "Great Russian Messianism," in Simmons (ed.), *Continuity and Change in Russian and Soviet Thought*, pp. 545–546.

DIVIDED GERMANY IN A DIVIDED EUROPE, 1946

Moscow

RUSSIA

SWEDEN

POLAND

DENMARK

Oder R.

Neisse R.

Elbe R.

Berlin

EAST
GERMANY

CZECHOSLOVAKIA

HUNGARY

YUGOSLAVIA

ALBANIA

Hamburg

WEST
GERMANY

Frankfort

Danube R.

AUSTRIA

ITALY

NETHERLANDS

Bonn

Rhine R.

SWITZERLAND

BELGIUM

LUXEM.

GREAT
BRITAIN

English Channel

Paris

FRANCE

SPAIN

Berlin

EAST
GERMANY

Elbe R.

Hamburg

WEST
GERMANY

Frankfort

Railroads   Highways   Air routes

33

(this was particularly frightening to the Russians and the French), and emphasized that American presence in Central Europe would not be withdrawn. This was the first time a high American official had publicly said such things. The speech, however, was historical, not prophetic; it simply summarized events of the previous eighteen months.

A second occurrence in the summer of 1946 intensified the Cold War. Since Hiroshima, the terrible specter of atomic energy had overhung every diplomatic exchange. In December 1945, the Big Three Foreign Ministers attempted to deal with this horror by establishing an Atomic Energy Commission tied to the Security Council of the United Nations. On March 16, 1946, the United States released its own plan for the control of atomic energy, the so-called Acheson-Lilienthal proposal. This report suggested a series of stages through which the world could pass to international control of atomic weapons; throughout this transition period the United States, possessing the only atomic bombs, would remain in a favored position while other nations agreed to be inspected by international agencies. A month later Bernard Baruch was named by the President to be the first American delegate to the United Nations Commission. American policy soon began to assume new forms. Deeply suspicious by nature, Baruch distrusted the Acheson-Lilienthal Report, partly because he had not sat on the committee, and partly because it said nothing about the Russian veto on the Security Council.

Baruch determined to eliminate any Russian power to veto inspections or sanctions. The Acheson-Lilienthal Report, on the other hand, said nothing about the veto; it planned to obtain Russian agreement to general principles and then discuss the veto problem. Top American military officials supported Baruch. Admiral Chester Nimitz, Chief of Naval Operations, and Admiral William D. Leahy, Truman's chief military adviser, urged, in Nimitz's words, that little be done on atomic energy until a "satisfactory peace" could be established.[19] Baruch became increasingly bitter about Acheson (whom he mistakenly accused of recording their telephone conversations), and those "One

---

[19] Nimitz to Baruch, June 11, 1946, and Leahy to Baruch, June 11, 1946, Navy Department, Atomic Energy, Baruch Papers.

Worlders" like Joseph Alsop and Walter Lippmann, "whom I can't understand any more"; all of these men criticized Baruch's insistence on immediately removing the veto power.[20] But he finally triumphed by convincing Truman that the United States must be tough with the Russians earlier rather than later. After recalling the dismantling of the American Navy in the 1920's and Stimson's troubles in Manchuria in 1931, the President agreed: "we should not under any circumstances throw away our gun until we are sure the rest of the world can't arm against us."[21] Military and political advisers bolstered this view by avowing that Russia could not build A-bombs for at least five to fifteen years. Only a few scientists warned that the period might be considerably shorter.

In a dramatic speech at the United Nations on June 14, Baruch presented his plan: atomic energy would be controlled through international management of the necessary raw materials and inspection by international agencies; no vetoes of these controls and inspections would be allowed; majority vote would rule. In the realm of peaceful uses of atomic energy, an Atomic Development Authority, again free of the veto, would establish atomic plants not according to need (as in underdeveloped areas or in large stretches of Russia), but according to strategic and geographical criteria; this criteria would allow more plants in Europe and the United States. Furthermore, by controlling a majority within the Authority, the United States could also control the development of the industrial uses of nuclear energy *within* the Soviet Union. The Soviets countered by demanding destruction of all atomic weapons, the cessation of their production, agreement of all powers not to use these weapons, and then a discussion of controls. Negotiations stalled until October when the Russians agreed to international inspection and eliminating the veto on day-to-day inspections, although not eliminating it on punishment of violations. Baruch retorted that either the Rus-

---

[20] Acheson file, Atomic Energy, Baruch Papers, especially telephone conversation between Baruch and Acheson, November 26, 1946.

[21] "BMB [Bernard M. Baruch] Memorandum of Meeting on June 7, 1946 with the President and J. F. Byrnes," Truman File, Atomic Energy, Baruch Papers.

sians must accept the entire American plan or there would be no plan. There was no plan. Instead, Congress established a United States Atomic Energy Commission under the Atomic Energy Act of 1946. Under strong military pressure, the act prohibited any exchange of information on the use of atomic energy with any nation until Congress should decide by joint resolution that "effective" international controls were in force.

A year after Japan's surrender, the Pandora Box of atomic energy remained open, Byrnes' speech illustrated the deadlock over Germany, and Russian-American discussions on loans and credit agreements had collapsed. American plans to use multilateral, international agencies to weaken the iron curtain had failed. The Administration decided, as Byrnes neatly phrased the decision, that "any new appropriations by Congress for foreign relief should be allocated by the United States," not by international agencies.[22] Not even this new approach, however, seemed to work. In Czechoslovakia the State Department attempted to stop nationalization and unequal treatment of American trade by inserting special clauses in bilateral commercial agreements, but that country nevertheless continued to sink behind the Russian curtain.[23]

American policy had radically changed since Stimson's memorandum to Truman of September 11, 1945 had suggested direct, bilateral talks on a give-and-take basis with the Soviets. Exactly one year later to the day, James Forrestal flew to New York to counsel with the retired Stimson. "He said," Forrestal recorded in his diary that night, "the way things had now developed he thought we should not delay in going forward with the manufacture of all the atomic missiles we could make."[24] Such was the inheritance left by the first year of the continued, although cold, war.

---

[22] James F. Byrnes, *Speaking Frankly* (New York, 1947), p. 146.
[23] Francis T. Williamson to Laurence Steinhardt, August 15, 1946, Papers of Laurence Steinhardt, Library of Congress, Washington, D. C.
[24] *Forrestal Diaries*, p. 200.

CHAPTER III

Two Halves of the Same Walnut (1946-1948)

IN THOSE DAYS not as many Americans shared Stimson's belief that atomic missiles were the most likely instruments for bringing peace to the world. More interested in spending pent-up wartime savings than in stopping the Red Tide, these citizens began to wonder why the vaunted American economic power was not reordering the world, especially if the sole obstacle was a crippled Soviet Union. Wonder soured into frustration as crises in China, the Middle East, the United Nations Atomic Energy Commission, and Europe failed to reach neat and favorable resolutions. By the autumn of 1946, these frustrations helped break apart the New Deal coalition of Franklin D. Roosevelt, which for more than a decade had formed the political, social, and economic mold for a supposedly new America.

Ironically, a most likely heir to Roosevelt's policies was the first to split the coalition. Henry Agard Wallace had been a great Secretary of Agriculture in the early New Deal; Vice-President from 1941 to 1945; maneuvered out of the Vice-Presidency in the 1944 Convention by Southern conservatives, moderate liberals, and Roosevelt himself; and finally named Secretary of Commerce in 1945. Here he devoted himself to the cause of what he liked to call "the Common Man," by extending increased loans to small businesses and, above all, enlarging the economic pie by working for a vastly increased foreign trade. Wallace soon discovered that Truman, unlike Roosevelt, could not deliver on domestic legislation. The new President, moreover, threatened to clog the trade channels to Russia, Eastern Europe, perhaps even China, with an increasingly militant attitude toward the Soviet Union. In April 1946, Wallace strongly questioned Byrnes' attempt to obtain American air bases in Iceland, and in July began a running argument with Baruch over the Administration's position on atomic energy.

At a political rally in New York on September 12, Wallace delivered a speech, cleared personally by Truman, which focused on the necessity of a political understanding with Russia. This, Wallace declared, would require guaranteeing Soviet security in Eastern Europe. In an oblique attack on Churchill's "Iron Curtain" speech, Wallace asked that the United States assure Stalin that "our primary objective is neither saving the British Empire nor purchasing oil in the Near East with the lives of American soldiers." With such an understanding, the two systems could compete "on a friendly basis" and would "gradually become more alike." Wallace, however, added one proviso for such a happy ending: in this competition "we must insist on an open door for trade throughout the world. . . . We cannot permit the door to be closed against our trade in Eastern Europe any more than we can in China."[1] At that moment Byrnes and Vandenberg sat in Paris, painfully negotiating peace treaties with Russia. They immediately demanded Wallace's resignation. On September 20, Truman complied.

The vigor of this reaction to Wallace's speech measured the distance American policy had moved since the close of World War II. Wallace was essentially pleading for a renewal of the Administration's invitation of 1945 to the war-decimated Russian economy to join a friendly game of economic competition with the American industrial mammoth and to play the game according to American rules.[2] By mid-1946, Truman and Byrnes had moved far beyond this. They now assumed that the Russians would not accept such rules but would cooperate only when faced with the threat of superior military force. Wallace argued that such a threat would only result in expansive military establishments with less security and prosperity on both sides.

---

[1] Henry Wallace, "The Way to Peace," *Vital Speeches*, XII (Oct. 1, 1946), pp. 738–741.

[2] Ronald Radosh, "The Economic and Political Thought of Henry A. Wallace," Unpublished Masters Thesis, State University of Iowa, 1960, pp. 46–50, 130–134.

That Americans, then and later, pictured Wallace as a radical indicates the confusion engendered by Cold War tensions. Wallace revealed his devotion to New Deal orthodoxy when he appeared on an NBC radio program in July 1946 with William Clayton. A former cotton broker and Liberty Leaguer, Clayton was now dedicated to removing government as much as possible from private business activities. He had vividly shown this dedication in breaking down the Imperial Preference system while negotiating the British loan agreement. Clayton and Wallace completely agreed on economic policy. Wallace stressed that foreign trade must be open and multilateral; otherwise, he warned, the government would have to impose "economic dictatorship" to make the system run. He fully supported the British loan, and advocated that the United States immediately reorder Western Europe so that no additional state controls could threaten that part of the world.[3] Given this background and the ringing declaration of a worldwide open door, little wonder that the Communist *Daily Worker* in New York at first attacked Wallace's September 12th speech as a cover for "American imperialism." Only after Byrnes and Truman had made public their feelings did the *Worker* discover virtue in Wallace's suggestions.

Disavowed by the Administration, Wallace nevertheless voiced the concerns of many former New Dealers. On September 28 and 29, a group of labor leaders met with Harold Ickes and Henry Morgenthau, Jr., two stalwarts of the Roosevelt years, to proclaim support for Wallace's views and to issue a plea to end tests of atomic bombs. Five weeks later, voters revealed immense dissatisfaction with Truman's policies by giving the Republicans a landslide victory in Congressional elections. With this discontent fresh in their minds, the key members of the Chicago meeting reconvened in late December to begin breaking free of the Democratic Party by forming the Progressive Citizens of America. With Wallace performing as featured speaker, the PCA dedicated itself to easing relations with the Communist bloc and enlarging the New Deal at home and abroad.

---

[3] Text of NBC program, "University of the Air," July 13, 1946, Speech file, 1946, Papers of William Clayton, Truman Library.

A week later on January 3, 1947, another group of liberals met in Washington's Willard Hotel to form the Americans for Democratic Action. This group, in contrast with the PCA, pledged to continue working within the Democratic Party and to fight Communism both at home and overseas. Chairing this founding session was Reinhold Niebuhr, theologian, philosopher, historian, and perhaps the most formative contemporary influence on American liberalism. Not since Jonathan Edwards' day of the 1740s had an American theologian so affected his society, and like Edwards, Niebuhr emphasized the role of sin and sinful power in that society. He disavowed the "sentimental optimism" that shaped American thought in the 1900-to-1930 era and which again was appearing in the post-1945 world in the guise of "positive thinking." In a remarkable series of books and lectures, he had developed his central theme that because of avarice, finiteness, and inability to realize the limits of his own power, man was overwhelmed with anxieties and unable to use his freedom constructively. This anxiety led to a will-to-power and this, in turn, led to conflict. Given such "egoistic corruption in all human virtue,"[4] Niebuhr warned that reason, and particularly faith in science, could never be trusted, for both reason and science too often refused to use the religious and historical insights required to solve secular problems.

As the Cold War heightened, Niebuhr stood ready with an explanation and a solution. Communism was at once the worst and most aggressive of societies because its faithful believed they could find a perfect union among sinful men simply by minimizing the drive for property. They overlooked what Niebuhr considered more important and ineradicable, the will-to-power. Worse, Communism historically had sought to accomplish its purposes by centralizing power in one or several men instead of working out a balance of power within that society. By employing science and so-called scientific rationales, Communism had proven once again, Niebuhr believed, that science is highly serviceable and easily maneuvered in a totalitarian society.

---

[4] Reinhold Niebuhr, "The Foreign Policy of American Conservatism and Liberalism," in *Christian Realism and Political Problems* (New York, 1953), p. 66.

By 1947, Niebuhr believed that the West's only hope lay in creating the best possible balance-of-power situations. Inside the United States he thought New Deal capitalism offered the most promise. Abroad, no trust could be placed in world government. He supported instead the Baruch Plan on atomic energy (Russia must accept it or "embark upon an isolationist course," Niebuhr wrote, thus giving an interesting liberal view of the supposed alternatives[5]), and wrote article after article in 1946 and 1947 pleading for a revitalized Europe to offset the Soviet threat.

After a visit to Europe in 1946, Niebuhr fixed upon the German problem. Here again he became an important symbol, if not a strong influence, upon a central strand of American foreign policy. Niebuhr was one of the earliest to spell out in detail the spiritual, political, and economic unity of the Atlantic community, the need to preserve the European outposts of that community from Communism, and the pivotal role that Germany must play if Europe was to be saved. "Russian truculence cannot be mitigated by further concessions," Neibuhr wrote in *Life* in October 1946. "Russia hopes to conquer the whole of Europe strategically or ideologically." Then came a thrust at Wallace: ". . . it has been the unfortunate weakness of both liberalism and liberal Christianity that they have easily degenerated into sentimentality by refusing to contemplate the tragic aspects of human existence honestly."[6] In applauding the rapid development of the German steel industry in 1947, Niebuhr accepted the "explicit division between East and West which has taken place. . . . Only God can bring order out of this kind of mixture of good and evil. We must, meanwhile, keep our powder dry."[7]

Niebuhr's work provided points of departure for criticizing Wallace, condemning Communism, formulating a Europe-first policy, and rebuilding Germany. Most important, he provided a historical basis and rationale for the tone, the outlook, the unsaid, and often unconscious assumptions of this period.

Soviet actions in Eastern Europe during late 1946 offered evidence to vindicate Niebuhr's assessment. Police action system-

---

[5] *Christianity and Crisis*, VI (July 8, 1946), p. 2.
[6] *Life*, October 21, 1946, pp. 65–72.
[7] *Christianity and Crisis*, VII (Aug. 4, 1947), p. 2.

atically removed opposition parties until elections could safely return large Communist majorities in Rumania and Poland in November 1946 and January 1947, respectively. At home, Soviet theoreticians launched a new doctrinal line in October 1946 with articles encouraging Western European socialists and the "proletarians" of other nations to undertake revolutionary action. With the one exception of the Greek revolution, however, the Soviet bloc was careful not to be too overt in directly assisting such revolutionaries. Stalin seemed to be biding his time, confident that the unevenness of capitalist development, which he had explained in the February 9 speech, would cause a "general crisis" in the West and so undercut "atom-dollar" diplomacy.

The "revolutionaries," moreover, seemed to be doing very well on their own. Communist party power rose steeply in Europe, particularly in France where the first Cabinet of the new Fourth Republic contained four Communists, including the Minister of Defense. Italy had placed Communists in the Cabinet since 1945. Chaotic conditions in the former colonial areas also opened exceptional opportunities to well-organized revolutionaries. The two gems of the British Crown, India and Egypt, shattered the Empire with their drives for more freedom from British control. They were soon joined by Pakistan, Burma, Ceylon, and Nepal. France began a long, futile, eight-year war to regain power over Indochina. The Dutch faced full-scale revolution in Indonesia. The Middle East was in turmoil over the determination of a half-dozen countries to be completely independent, as well as over the influx of 100,000 Jews who hoped to establish a homeland in Palestine.

In late 1946 and early 1947, American officials gave increased attention to these newly-emerging areas. Europe could not be fully stabilized until England, France, and the Netherlands settled their colonial problems. The State Department also assumed that the American economy and the economy of the Western Community, which depended upon American prosperity, demanded a proper settlement of these conflicts. In a speech in November 1946, Clayton explained that the expansion in the domestic economy and the "depletion of our natural resources" would make the United States considerably more dependent on the importation of raw materials and minerals. Many of these came from the newly-emerging areas. Adolf A. Berle, economist, advisor to Roosevelt and Truman, and State Department official, declared in October that the Soviet Union and the United States had begun a battle for the allegiance of the underdeveloped parts of the world. "Within four years the world [will] be faced with an apparent surplus in production beyond any previously known," Berle explained; "intelligent handling of foreign economic policy" now could level off later those "cycles of 'boom and bust' which disfigured our prewar economy." Berle urged that the inevitable American surpluses be used to "take the lead in material reconstruction" of the underdeveloped areas.[8]

This correctly identified one paramount American motivation, but the policy could not be understood without comprehending as well the ideological assumptions which Niebuhr so systematically formulated, and the realization that the underdeveloped areas and Western Europe were so interlinked that they were two parts of a single policy. The "Containment" of Russia became the short, if not wholly accurate, way of describing this package of American needs and policies.

The preconditions for action were present; the package simply awaited the proper moment for the opening and the unfolding of the policies. On February 21, 1947, the British Ambassador informed the State Department that London could not provide the $250 million of economic military support needed by Turkey and Greece. As Secretary of State Marshall explained this note, "it was tantamount to British abdication from the Middle East with obvious implications as to their successor."[9] The United States was fully aware of the disastrous decline of the British economy through the winter of 1946-1947. By February 7, more than half of British industry stood quiet, electricity was severely rationed, and the Treasury neared the bottom of loans obtained from the United States and Canada.

Realizing England's growing inability to maintain the dike against Communism in the Middle East, the United States during

---

[8] Adolf A. Berle, "The Formulation of American Foreign Policy," in John Carter Vincent, et al., America's Future in the Pacific (New Brunswick, N. J., 1947).

[9] Forrestal Diaries, p. 245.

1946 had become more and more involved in Greek and Turkish affairs. The United States led the demands for an international commission to supervise the Greek elections of March 1946, in which the party of King George II won power. After revolutionaries, supported by the Communist governments of Bulgaria and Yugoslavia, initiated civil warfare against the new government, the State Department sent observers and, in January 1947, an economic mission. As early as September 1946, the Administration prepared programs of military aid for Greece and Turkey. In December, the United States supported the Security Council's decision to send a Commission of Investigation; this was led by an American who worked closely with other American officials already on the scene. Finally, hours before the British note arrived on February 21, Secretary Marshall had prepared instructions for intensifying American economic and military aid to Greece. Within a week after receiving the British note, the State Department worked out a detailed proposal for assistance. After only nineteen days, the President went to Congress with a complete program. Clearly, the formulation of the Truman Doctrine was not a sudden and drastic departure in American foreign policy.

In his message of March 12, 1947, the President explained that the new program sought to promote stability in Western Europe as well as Greece and Turkey by using $400 million of American-controlled military and economic aid to stop Communist-supported rebellions in the two nations. This speech, as well as the many conferences that shaped the doctrine, stressed the growing American concern for the underdeveloped nations. Within twenty-four hours after the receipt of the British note, the State Department's Russian expert, George Kennan, chaired a meeting of specialists on Middle Eastern and African affairs; these policy-makers were relieved that they could now act openly to halt Russia from breaking through Greece and Turkey into the Middle East, Asia, and North Africa. Five days later, Truman, Marshall, and Acheson explained the situation to important Congressmen. It was not a warm audience. The Republicans were busy cutting taxes 20 percent and chopping $6 billion from Truman's already tight budget. The legislators remained unmoved until Acheson swung into the argument that the threat was Russian Communism; its aim the control of the Middle East, South Asia, and Africa; and that this control was a central part of the Communist plan to encircle and capture the ultimate objective of Germany.[10] This argument, coupled with Truman's assurance that the United States would control not only every penny of American aid to Greece, but also run the Greek economy by controlling foreign exchange, budget, taxation, currency, and credits, won over the Congressmen.[11]

Vandenberg and others feared that most Americans, including many Congressmen, might be cool to the program because of a failure to understand the extent of the Soviet danger. Truman and his advisors therefore went to some length to oversell the doctrine ideologically. As Vandenberg advised, the President "scared hell out of the American people," by painting in dark hues the "totalitarian regimes" which threatened to snuff out freedom everywhere. Insofar as public opinion was concerned, this tactic worked well for the Administration, at least until three years later when Senator Joseph McCarthy and others turned the argument around and accused the Administration of too softly handling such a horrible danger.

Inside the State Department, however, the tactic immediately ran into opposition. On March 6, Kennan objected bitterly to the sending of any military assistance to nations such as Turkey which bordered the Soviet Union. Unlike economic aid, arms and ammunition, not to mention possible American military advisers, could be highly provocative. Kennan also protested against the harsh ideological tone and open-ended commitment of American aid in the early drafts of Truman's proposed speech.[12] These criticisms initiated a breach which soon developed into an open and highly significant break between Kennan and Acheson over the matter of military aid to supposed allies. Kennan's objections did not modify the policy that was already in motion. After Truman delivered the message, Robert Taft, the leading Senate Re-

---

[10] Joseph M. Jones, *The Fifteen Weeks* (New York, 1955), pp. 139–140.
[11] "Draft of President's Policy Statement to the Chief of the American Mission to Greece," by John Snyder, June 3, 1947; Greece and Turkey: Assistance to, Under Public Law 75, Papers of Harry S. Truman, Truman Library.
[12] Jones, *Fifteen Weeks*, pp. 154–155.

publican, accused Truman of dividing the world into Communist and anti-Communist zones, then objected to the proposed military aid with the words, "I do not want war with Russia." Western European governments joined in this criticism. Henry Wallace, then traveling in Europe, accused Truman of "reckless adventury" that would cost the world "a century of fear." Senator Vandenberg rushed to the defense of the President by calling Wallace an "itinerant saboteur."

Others expressed different, and to the State Department, more troublesome objections. Walter Lippmann led a general attack on the Administration's bypassing of the United Nations: "If the pattern of our conduct in this affair becomes a precedent," the columnist warned, "we shall have cut a hole in the Charter which it will be very difficult to repair." Other critics observed that in assisting the governments of Greece and Turkey, the United States was saving reactionary, crumbling social structures unlikely to be of much assistance in making freedom ring throughout the world.[13]

Congress finally completed action on the $400 million request on May 15, and Truman signed the measure a week later. The Soviet response was unpredictably soft. Stalin shrewdly encouraged Tito to handle the job of supporting the Greek Communists, thereby keeping the Yugoslavs and Bulgarians embroiled with the West and freeing Russia of direct responsibility. In an April interview, Stalin expressed hope that Americans and Russians could collaborate in creating a peaceful world, although he followed this with a not indirect comparison of the United States with Hitlerite Germany. During these months, Stalin devoted his major attention to "Zhdanovism," the cleansing of the minds of Soviet intelligentsia who were at odds with his internal policies. The most severe response came at the United Nations. Soviet delegate Andrei Gromyko asked why the United States insisted on acting before the United Nations investigating commission reported, and charged that the United States would destroy Greek and Turkish independence. Gromyko wondered how Turkey, which had sided with the Nazis in World War II, could qualify for such aid. Another, perhaps more significant reaction

---

[13] *Washington Post*, March 21, 1947, p. 17.

occurred in Moscow when the first explicitly Cold War, anti-American play, Konstantin Simonov's "The Russian Question" opened in early April.

The Truman Doctrine evolved naturally into the Marshall Plan. On March 5, Senator Vandenberg defined the Greek crisis as "symbolic of the world-wide ideological clash between Eastern Communism and Western Democracy."[14] That same day Acheson initiated a State Department survey to investigate the possibilities of broadening aid to nations other than Greece and Turkey. Two days later, Secretary of Navy James Forrestal sent a highly emotional memorandum to Truman, which warned that the present danger was at least as great as that during World War II. Forrestal urged the President to quit the defensive and "attack successfully" with an all-out economic effort which would revitalize Germany and Japan and stabilize the Western world before the "Russian poison" conquered Europe, "South America, and ourselves."[15]

The Doctrine itself suggested no real limitations to the scope of the American effort, but six weeks after Truman's speech, Secretary of State Marshall reoriented policy by concentrating State Department attention upon Europe. The underdeveloped countries would not come back into focus for another seven years. Returning badly shaken from a Foreign Ministers conference in Moscow, the Secretary of State insisted in a nationwide broadcast that Western Europe must receive immediate help. "The patient is sinking," Marshall declared, "while the doctors deliberate." Personal conversations with Stalin had convinced the Secretary of State that the Russians were simply waiting for Europe to collapse. Marshall looked for little help from the weak, embattled European governments. Convinced that the United States must take the lead in restoring Europe, Marshall appointed a Policy Planning Staff under the direction of George Kennan to draw up policies for such a program.

Kennan later explained the basic assumption which underlay the Marshall Plan and, indeed, the entire range of America's

---

[14] *Papers of Senator Vandenberg*, p. 340.
[15] Arnold A. Rogow, *James Forrestal; A Study of Personality, Politics, and Policy* (New York, 1963), pp. 335–337.

postwar policies between 1947 and 1955. Excluding the United States, Kennan observed,

. . . there are only four aggregations which are major ones from the standpoint of strategic realities [that is, military and industrial potential] in the world. Two of those lie off the shores of the Eurasian land mass. Those are Japan and England, and two of them lie on the Eurasian land mass. One is the Soviet Union and the other is that of central Europe . . . .

Viewed in absolute terms, I think the greatest danger that could confront the United States security would be a combination and working together for purposes hostile to us of the central European and the Russian military-industrial potentials. They would really create an entity . . . which could overshadow in a strategic sense even our own power. It is not anything, I think, which would be as easy of achievement as people often portray it as being here. I am not sure the Russians have the genius for holding all that together . . . . Still, they have the tendency of political thought, of Communist political expansion.[16]

Building upon this premise, round-the-clock conferences in May, 1947 began to fashion the main features of the Marshall Plan. Kennan insisted that any aid, particularly military aid, be limited and not given to just any area where Communists seemed to be enjoying some success. Lippmann helped solve this problem and also the question of how to minimize American interference in Europe's domestic affairs; he suggested that Europe be encouraged to take the initiative in overall planning by presenting a complete program for American consideration. The all-important question then became how to handle the Russians. Ostensibly, Marshall accepted Kennan's advice to "play it straight" by inviting the Soviet bloc. In reality, the State Department made Russian acceptance improbable by demanding that the economic records of each nation be open for scrutiny; for good measure Kennan also suggested that the Soviets' devastated economy, weakened by war and at that moment suffering from drought and famine, participate in the Plan by shipping Soviet

---

[16] U. S. Congress, Senate, Subcommittee to investigate the Administration of the International Security Act . . . of the Committee on the Judiciary, 82nd Congress, 1st Session, *The Institute of Pacific Relations* (Washington, 1951), pp. 1557–1558. (Hereafter cited as *I.P.R. Hearings*.)

goods to Europe. Apparently no one in the State Department wanted the Soviets included. Russian participation would vastly multiply the costs of the program and eliminate any hope of its acceptance by a purse-watching Republican Congress, now increasingly convinced by Truman of the need to battle Communists, not feed them.

Acheson's speech at Cleveland, Mississippi on May 8 and Marshall's address at Harvard on June 5 revealed the motives and substance of the Plan. In preparing for the earlier speech, Acheson's advisors concluded that American exports were rapidly approaching the $16 billion mark. Imports, however, amounted to only half that amount, and Europe did not possess sufficient dollars to pay the difference. Either the United States government would have to grant credits to European importers or Europe would be unable to buy American goods. The President's Council of Economic Advisers was predicting a slight business recession, and if, in addition, exports dropped in any substantial amount, "the effect in the United States," as one official wrote, "might be most serious."[17] Acheson underlined these facts in the May 8th speech.

At Harvard, Marshall urged European nations to create a long-term program that would "provide a cure rather than a mere palliative." On June 13 British Foreign Minister Ernest Bevin accepted Marshall's suggestion and four days later traveled to Paris to talk with French Foreign Minister Georges Bidault. The question of Russian participation became uppermost in their discussions. *Pravda* had labeled Marshall's speech as a Truman Doctrine with dollars, a useless attempt to save the American economy by dominating the markets of Europe. Bidault ignored this; pressured by the powerful French Communist Party and fearful that Russia's absence might compel France to join the Anglo-Saxons in a divided Europe dominated by a resurrected Germany,[18] he decided to invite Molotov. The Russian line immediately moderated.

On June 26, Molotov arrived in Paris with eighty-nine economic experts and clerks, then spent much of the next three days

---

[17] Jones, *Fifteen Weeks*, p. 207.
[18] See, for example, *The New York Times*, June 19, 1957, p. 1.

conferring over the telephone with officials in Moscow. The Russians were giving the Plan serious consideration. Molotov finally proposed that each nation individually establish its own recovery program. The French and British proposed instead that Europe as a whole create the proposal for American consideration. On June 30, the West European nations threw their support back of the Anglo-French proposal. Molotov angrily quit the conference, warning that the Plan would undermine national sovereignty, revive Germany, result in American control of Europe and, most ominously, divide "Europe into two groups of states . . . creating new difficulties in the relations between them."[19] Within a week after his return to Moscow, the Soviets set their own "Molotov Plan" in motion. The Poles and the Czechs, who had expressed interest in Marshall's proposal, now informed the Paris conference that they could not attend because it "might be construed as an action against the Soviet Union."

From July 16 until September 22, sixteen European nations hammered out a program. The absence of Russians did not mean an absence of problems. In an interesting preview of a dilemma which would haunt Western Europe in the 1960s, Britain rejected French proposals for a supranational body to supervise the Plan. Governed by her Commonwealth ties and her dependence on and ideological links with the United States, Great Britain successfully insisted upon a committee of sovereign nations. Presented with this first opportunity of fulfilling their fervent desire for a closely-knit Europe, American officials appeared confused. They were not prepared to push the British into such a Europe, yet a Europe without England opened possibilities for intra-European friction. "I always thought it odd," one European official observed, "that the descendants of the writers of *The Federalist* were content to be misty on the essentials of policy."[20]

Another problem at the conference was symbolized by the Treaty of Dunkirk, signed by Britain and France in March 1947. This pact pledged cooperation in the containment of a revived,

---

[19] Text in *The New York Times*, July 3, 1947, p. 3.
[20] Harry B. Price, *The Marshall Plan and Its Meaning* (Ithaca, New York, 1955), pp. 80, 287.

perhaps Communist, Germany. As America's closest Allies demonstrated how green were their memories of World War II, the United States determined to revive Germany quickly. In December 1946, the United States and Great Britain overrode French opposition in order to merge economically the American and British zones in Germany. Administrative duties fell into the hands of Germans. By mid-July 1947, American officials moved so rapidly to rebuild German industry that Bidault finally warned Marshall to slow down or else the French government would never survive to carry through the economic recovery program. Marshall made the Paris conference more serene by bringing the French into the discussion over Germany, but the United States carried on its program to build German nonmilitary industry to the point where Germany would be both self-sufficient and able to aid the remainder of Western Europe. On September 22, the Paris meeting completed its work, pledging increased production, tariff reductions, and currency convertibility in return for American aid. The State Department could view its successes in Germany during the summer as icing on the cake.

The European request for a four-year program of $17 billion dollars of American aid now had to run the gauntlet of a Republican Congress which was dividing its attention between slashing the budget and attacking Truman, both in anticipation of the presidential election only a year away. In committee hearings in late 1947 and early 1948, the Executive Department systematically presented its case. Only large amounts of government money which could restore basic facilities, provide convertibility of local currency into dollars, and end the dollar shortage would stimulate private investors to rebuild Europe, Administration witnesses argued. Then, a rejuvenated Europe could offer many advantages to the United States: eradicate the threat of continued nationalization and spreading socialism by releasing and stimulating the investment of private capital, maintain demand for American exports, encourage Europeans to produce strategic goods which the United States could buy and stockpile, preserve European and American control over Middle Eastern oil supplies from militant nationalism which might endanger the weakened European holdings, and free Europeans from economic problems so they could help the United States militarily.

The Administration's plan revolved around a rebuilt and autonomous Germany. As Secretary of State Marshall told Congress, "The restoration of Europe involves the restoration of Germany. Without a revival of German production there can be no revival of Europe's economy. But we must be very careful to see that a revived Germany can not again threaten the European community." The Marshall Plan offered a way to circumvent Allied restrictions of German development, for it tied the Germans to a general European program and then offered vast sums to such nations as France which might otherwise be reluctant to support the rebuilding of Germany.[21]

The Marshall Plan served as an all-purpose weapon for Truman's foreign policy. It charmed those who feared a slump in American exports and who believed, Communist threat or no Communist threat, that American and world prosperity rested on a vigorous export trade. A spokesman for the National Association of Manufacturers, for example, appeared considerably more moderate toward Communism than most government officials when he argued that Europe suffered not from "this so-called communistic surge," but from a "production problem" which only the Marshall Plan could solve.[22] Appropriately, Truman named as Administrator of the Plan Paul Hoffman, a proven administrator who, as Dean Acheson once observed, preached a "doctrine of salvation by exports with all the passion of an economic Savanarola."[23] The Plan also attracted a group, including Niebuhr, which placed more emphasis upon the containment of Communism. The Plan offered all things to all people. Or almost all, for Henry Wallace decided to oppose it in late 1947 on the grounds that only by channeling aid through the United Nations could calamitous American-Russian relations be avoided.

The Marshall Plan now appears not the beginning but the end of an era. It marked the last phase in the Administration's use of economic tactics as the primary means of tying together the

---

[21] U. S. Congress, House, Foreign Affairs Committee, 80th Congress, 1st and 2nd Sessions, *United States Foreign Policy for a Post-War Recovery Program* . . . (Washington, 1948), I, 354–359.

[22] *Ibid.*, I, 680–681.

[23] Dean Acheson, *Sketches From Life of Men I Have Known* (New York, 1959), p. 19.

Western world to stop Communist thrusts. The Plan's approach, that peaceful and positive approach which Niebuhr applauded, soon evolved into military alliances. The Americans for Democratic Action and the American business community came much closer to agreement on Soviet policy than either cared to admit, and both necessarily went along with this new and considerably less-peaceful tactic. Given commonly-shared assumptions of the Russian system, they could do little else but finally admit that the President was correct in saying that the Truman Doctrine and the Marshall Plan "are two halves of the same walnut," and they willingly acquiesced as the military aspects of the Doctrine developed into quite the larger part.

The link between the two halves was the Administration's view of what made the Russians act like Communists. George Kennan analyzed this view in a well-timed article appearing in July 1947 under the mysterious pseudonym, "Mr. X." Washington's most respected expert on Soviet affairs, Kennan had warned throughout the early 1940s against any hope of close cooperation with Stalin after the war. In early 1946 he sent a long dispatch to Washington from Moscow suggesting that at the "bottom of the Kremlin's neurotic view of world affairs is the traditional and instinctive Russian sense of insecurity." In post-1917 Russia this became highly explosive when mixed with Communist ideology and "Oriental secretiveness and conspiracy."[24] This despatch brought Kennan to the attention of Secretary of Navy James Forrestal who helped bring the diplomat back to Washington and then strongly influenced Kennan's decision to publish the "Mr. X" article.

That analysis began not by emphasizing "the traditional . . . Russian sense of insecurity," but by assuming that Stalin's policy was shaped by a combination of Marxist-Leninist ideology, which advocated revolution to defeat the capitalist forces in the outside world, and the dictator's determination to use "capitalist encirclement" as a rationale to regiment the Soviet masses so that he could consolidate his own political power. Kennan be-

---

[24] Barton J. Bernstein and Allen J. Matusow, *The Truman Administration . . .* (New York, 1966), pp. 198–212; *Forrestal Diaries*, pp. 135–140; Rogow, *Forrestal*, pp. 200–203.

littled such supposed "encirclement," although he recognized Nazi-Japanese antagonism toward the Soviets during the 1930s. (Kennan omitted mentioning specifically the American and Japanese intervention in Russia between 1918 and 1920 and the American attempt to isolate Russia politically through the 1920s.) "Mr. X" believed that these Soviet beliefs precluded the possibility that Stalin would moderate Communist determination to overthrow the Western governments. Any softening of the Russian line, Kennan warned, would be a diversionary tactic designed to lull the West. The endemic Soviet aggression could be "contained by the adroit and vigilant application of counter-force at a series of constantly shifting geographical and political points." The United States would have to undertake this containment alone and unilaterally, but if it could do so without weakening its prosperity and political stability, the Soviet Party structure would undergo a period of immense strain climaxing in "either the break-up or the gradual mellowing of Soviet power."[25]

The publication of this article initiated one of the more interesting debates of the Cold War. Walter Lippmann was one of those who did not accept the "two halves of the same walnut" argument, believing, instead, that the Marshall Plan did not exclude peaceful relations with the Kremlin. Unlike Niebuhr (whom Kennan once called "The father of us all") Lippmann could rip apart the military aspects of the Truman Doctrine while applauding the Marshall Plan because he disagreed with Kennan's assessment of Soviet motivations. In a series of newspaper articles, later collected into a book entitled *The Cold War*,[26] Lippmann argued that Soviet policy was moulded more by traditional Russian expansion than by Communist ideology. "Stalin is not only the heir of Marx and of Lenin but of Peter the Great, and the Czars of all the Russians." Because of the victorious sweep of the Red Army into Central Europe in 1945, Stalin could accom-

---

[25] "The Sources of Soviet Conduct," *Foreign Affairs*, XXV (July, 1947), pp. 566–582. Kennan much later believed the essay had been misinterpreted. George F. Kennan, *Memoirs* (Boston, 1967), pp. 364–367. But also see Lloyd C. Gardner, *Architects of Illusion* (Chicago, 1970), pp. 270–300.

[26] Walter Lippmann, *The Cold War: A Study in U.S. Foreign Policy* (New York, 1947).

plish what the Czars for centuries had only hoped to obtain. This approach enabled Lippmann to view the Soviet advance as a traditional quest for national security and, in turn, allowed him to argue that Russia would be amenable to an offer of withdrawal of both Russian and American power from central Europe. That area could then be neutralized.

Lippmann outlined the grave consequences of the alternative, the "Mr. X"-Truman Doctrine policy: "unending intervention in all the countries that are supposed to 'contain' the Soviet Union"; futile and costly efforts to make "Jeffersonian democrats" out of Eastern European peasants and Middle Eastern and Asian warlords; either the destruction of the United Nations or its transformation into a useless anti-Soviet coalition; and such a tremendous strain on the American people that their economy would have to be increasingly regimented and their men sent to fight on the perimeter of the Soviet bloc. The columnist warned that if "Mr. X" succeeded in applying counter-force to the "constantly shifting geographical and political points," the Soviets would perforce be allowed to take the initiative in the Cold War by choosing the grounds and the weapons for combat. Finally, Lippmann, like the Administration, emphasized Germany's importance, but he differed by observing that Russia, which controlled eastern Germany, could at her leisure outmaneuver the West and repeat the 1939 Nazi-Soviet pact by offering the ultimate reward of reunification for German cooperation. "The idea that we can foster the sentiment of Germany unity, and make a truncated Germany economically strong," Lippmann wrote, "can keep her disarmed, and can use her in the anti-Soviet coalition is like trying to square the circle."

Lippmann was profound, but he had no chance of being persuasive. By the end of August 1947, the State Department rejected Lippmann's proposals for disengagement in Central Europe by assuming that the "one world" of the United Nations was "no longer valid and that we are in political fact facing a division into two worlds."[27] There also appeared a second assumption that, as "Mr. X" had hinted, the Cold War had become a conflict between two superpowers in which the United States must main-

---

[27] *Forrestal Diaries*, p. 307.

tain maximum freedom of action. By the middle of 1947 the emphasis on the reciprocal trade agreements, so important to Byrnes and Truman in 1945, had been debased by Republican-inserted "escape" clauses for American producers wanting higher tariffs, and by an export control act supported by Truman with the argument that it allowed the United States to discriminate against the Soviet bloc. The State Department also renegotiated Anglo-American agreements on exchanging information on atomic energy. The United States could now develop atomic weapons without having to deal with the British. The London government decided to build its own bomb, free of American encumbrances, for as Attlee later explained, "We couldn't allow ourselves to be wholly in their hands, and their position wasn't awfully clear always."[28]

This weakening of trade arrangements and the emphasis on atomic energy indicated that the Administration was operating on a third assumption: economic development could not occur until "security" was established. This increasing concern with things military became evident in early 1948 when the United States accelerated antiguerilla operations in Greece at the expense of economic development. It also appeared in late October 1947 when Kennan suggested that the United States change its long-standing hostility to Franco's government in Spain in order to cast proper military security over the Mediterranean area. A year earlier, the United States had joined with Britain and France in asking the Spanish people to overthrow Franco by political means because his government was pro-Nazi and totalitarian. Kennan's observation marked the turn in Spanish-American relations which ended in close military cooperation after 1950.[29]

Most important, Truman finally found the opportunity to transform what he termed "the antiquated defense setup of the United States" of 1945 by passing the National Security Act through Congress in July 1947. This bill provided for a single Department of Defense to replace the three independently-run services, statutory establishment of the Joint Chiefs of Staff, a National Security Council to advise the President, and a Central

---

[28] Clement Attlee, *Twilight of Empire* . . . (New York, 1962), p. 118.
[29] *Forrestal Diaries*, p. 328.

Intelligence Agency to correlate and evaluate intelligence activities. James Forrestal, the leading advocate among presidential advisers of a tough military approach to Cold War problems, became the first Secretary of Defense. Forrestal remained in this position until he resigned in early spring 1949. Two months later on the night of May 22, Forrestal, suffering from mental and physical illness, jumped or fell to his death from the twelfth floor of the Bethesda Naval Hospital.

The new military policy of 1947 soon underwent a trial run in that long-time laboratory of United States policies, Latin America. After several postponements, the American Nations convened at Rio de Janeiro from mid-August until September 2. The United States delegation candidly laid out the rules for the conference. There would be no discussion of economic aid, Secretary Marshall explained, because European recovery took precedence over Latin American development. The conference must instead initiate steps towards a collective security arrangement. In doing so, the United States expected each nation to take some action against future aggressors, whether that action be military or otherwise. No nation, the American delegation argued, could remain truly neutral. On September 2 the delegates signed the Rio Treaty providing for collective self-defense for the hemisphere, the first such treaty formulated under Articles 51 and 52 of the United Nations Charter. The Treaty provided that an attack against one American Republic would be considered as an attack upon all, and that when two thirds of the hemispheric nations agreed to resist such an attack, all states must cooperate by contributing either troops or supplies.[30] Nine months before, Vandenberg had lamented that a "Communistic upsurge" in Latin America was dividing the hemisphere, although he provided no evidence of this "upsurge."[31] After the signing of the Rio Treaty, Vandenberg rested more easily: "This is sunlight in a dark world," he informed his Senate colleagues.

The following March the Ninth Inter-American Conference convened at Bogotá, Colombia. Again, the United States refused

---

[30] *Documents on American Foreign Relations*, IX (1947), edited by Raymond Dennett and Robert K. Turner (Princeton, New Jersey, 1948), pp. 531–543.

[31] *Papers of Senator Vandenberg*, p. 335.

to make any economic commitments. At the most, Marshall hoped that he could use the occasion to create the proper atmosphere so that Latin American laws, particularly those relating to oil resources, might be modified to be more attractive to United States capital and skill. Out of this approach came the Charter of the Organization of American States, which established administrative machinery for hemispheric consultation, and an Advisory Defense Committee for military strategy. This much the United States approved. The Latin Americans, however, stubbornly insisted upon adding a statement of the principles and standards which should govern hemispheric relations. Over American objections, this move carried. Articles 15 and 16 were incorporated in the Charter. The first stated: "No State or group of States has the right to intervene, directly or indirectly, for any reason whatever, in the internal or external affairs of any other State. . . ." Article 16 was more specific: "No State may use or encourage the use of coercive measures of an economic or political character in order to force the sovereign will of another State and obtain from it advantages of any kind." [32] The United States Senate ratified the Charter, but this was the last major inter-American conference held during Truman's presidency. The Administration had obtained the desired military arrangements and, perhaps, too many political obligations.

As the O.A.S. Charter fight revealed, successes at home and abroad for the Administration's view of the Cold War did not come cheaply. At home the terrible price became dimly apparent in 1947. Throughout 1946, J. Edgar Hoover of the Federal Bureau of Investigation, Forrestal, and Attorney-General Tom Clark attempted to convince Truman to begin a loyalty check of federal employees. The revelation of a Soviet spy ring in Canada and the even more frightening spectacle of the Republican landslide in 1946 finally forced the President to set up a commission on November 25, 1946 to work out procedures. The commission reported that an internal threat did indeed exist, but the Civil Service Commission could carry out the necessary investigations. The report met opposition from Clark, who was convinced that

---

[32] *Documents on American Foreign Relations,* X (1948), edited by Raymond Dennett and Robert K. Turner (Princeton, New Jersey, 1950), pp. 484–502.

"even one disloyal person" posed a "serious threat" to American security. With Truman's approval, Clark turned the job over to the Federal Bureau of Investigation. On March 21, 1947, Truman announced a Security Loyalty Program, the first ever established by a President, the first ever begun in peacetime. The program was so vaguely defined that political ideas and long-past associations were made suspect. Most ominously, the accused would not be given the right to face the accuser. Meanwhile, during hearings in the Senate on the appointment of David E. Lilienthal as Chairman of the Atomic Energy Commission, the first major charges of "soft on Communism" were hurled by Robert Taft because of Lilienthal's New Deal background and his opposition to the Baruch position on the veto.

Taft's action sickened Vandenberg, who compared it to "the 'Lynch law,'" but such charges were only beginning. The House Un-American Activities Committee began to intimate that Truman was certainly correct in his assessment of Communism's evil nature, but lax in eradicating it. In March 1948, the Committee demanded the loyalty records gathered by the F.B.I. Truman handled the situation badly. Unable to exploit the Committee's distorted view of the internal Communist threat, he accused it of trying to cover up the bad record of the Republican Congress. He refused to surrender the records, ostensibly because they were in the exclusive domain of the Executive, more probably because of his fear that if the Republicans saw the FBI reports, which accused some federal employees of disloyalty on the basis of hearsay, unproved allegations, and personal vendettas, November might be an unfortunate month for Truman's political aspirations.[33] Unable to discredit the loyalty program he had set in motion, trapped by his own indiscriminating anti-Communist rhetoric designed to "scare hell out of the American people," Truman stood paralyzed as the ground was carefully plowed around him for the weeds of McCarthyism.

Paradoxically, pivotal Congressional figures also began questioning the growing price of the Cold War, but for quite another reason. Truman was incapable of dealing with the loyalty issue,

---

[33] Athan Theoharis, "The Rhetoric of Politics . . ." in author's possession; courtesy of Professor Theoharis, Wayne State University.

but through the exploitation of continual international tension, this man who had arrived at the White House with minute prestige was slowly growing into one of the most powerful of all Presidents. Vandenberg ruminated on this development a few weeks after, appropriately, the Truman Doctrine speech:

The trouble is that these "crises" never reach Congress until they have developed to a point where Congressional discretion is pathetically restricted. When things finally reach a point where a President asks us to "declare war" there usually is nothing left except to "declare war." [34]

Vandenberg could offer no remedy to correct the weakening of Congress's constitutionally-granted powers nor, as this problem worsened during the next two decades, could anyone else. Congress's special powers in foreign policy lay largely in appropriating monies. As consensus developed around Kennan's view of Communism, and as military replaced economic power as the primary American diplomatic weapon, Congressional power waned while Presidential power widened.

Soviet officials took note of these developments. Their attention particularly riveted upon Germany. They interpreted the Marshall Plan to mean the American "intention to restore the economy of Germany and Japan on the old basis [of pre-1941] provided it is subordinated to interests of American capital." [35] Rebuilding Europe through the Marshall Plan and tying it closely to American economic power ended Stalin's hope of influencing, directly and indirectly, Western European policies. Incomparably worse, however, was linking that Europe to a restored Western Germany. This not only undercut Soviet determination to keep this ancient enemy weak, as well as divided, but vastly increased the potential of that enemy, tied him to the forces of "capitalist encirclement," and revived the terrible memories of two world wars.

Since the Iranian and Turkish crises of late summer 1946, the Soviets had not been active in world affairs. Molotov's departure

---

[34] *Papers of Senator Vandenberg*, p. 342.
[35] Telegram from Moscow Embassy to Secretary of State Marshall, May 26, 1947, Papers of Joseph Jones, Truman Library.

from the Paris Conference on July 2, 1947 marked the turn. Molotov quickly initiated a series of moves to tighten Soviet control within the bloc. Large amounts of Soviet aid began to flow to Poland, Czechoslovakia, and Bulgaria to push ahead industrialization and, in the process, to increase Soviet authority. A program of bilateral trade agreements, the so-called "Molotov Plan," began to link the bloc countries and Russia in July 1947. The final step came in January 1949, when the Council for Mutual Economic Assistance (COMECON) provided the Soviet answer to the Marshall Plan by creating a centralized agency for stimulating and controlling bloc development. As a result of these moves, Soviet trade with the East European bloc, which had declined in 1947 to $380 million, doubled in 1948, quadrupled by 1950, and exceeded $2.5 billion in 1952. Seventy percent of East European trade was carried on with either the Soviet Union or elsewhere within the bloc.[36]

Four days after his return from Paris, Molotov announced yet another and more ominous development in Soviet foreign policy, the establishment of the Communist Information Bureau (Cominform). Including Communists from Russia, Yugoslavia, France, Italy, Poland, Bulgaria, Czechoslovakia, Hungary, and Rumania, the Cominform provided another instrument for increasing Stalin's control. This was his answer to the Czech and Polish interest in joining the Marshall Plan. In late August, a month before the first Cominform meeting, Soviet actions in Hungary indicated the line which would be followed. After a purge of left-wing anti-Communist political leaders, the Soviets directly intervened by rigging elections on August 31. All anti-Communist opposition disappeared. Three weeks later at the Cominform meeting in Warsaw, Zhdanov formally announced new Soviet policies in a speech that ranks next only to Stalin's February 9, 1946 address as a call to Cold War.

Zhdanov's analysis of recent international developments climaxed with the announcement that American economic power, fattened by the war, was organizing Western Europe and "countries politically and economically dependent on the United States,

[36] Stanley J. Zyzniewski, "Soviet Foreign Economic Policy," *Political Science Quarterly*, LXXIII (June 1958), pp. 216–219.

such as the Near-Eastern and South-American countries and China" into an anti-Communist bloc. The Russians and the "new democracies" in Eastern Europe, Finland, Indonesia, and Vietnam meanwhile formed another bloc which "has the sympathy of India, Egypt and Syria." In this way, Zhdanov again announced the rebirth of the "two-camp" view of the world, an attitude that had dominated Russian policy between 1927 and 1934 when Stalin bitterly attacked the West, and a central theme in the Soviet dictator's speech of February 1946. In some respects, Zhdanov's announcement resembled the "two-world" attitude in the United States. This mirror image was especially striking when Zhdanov admonished the socialist camp not to lower its guard. "Just as in the past the Munich policy untied the hands of the Nazi aggressors, so today concessions to the new course of the United States and the imperialist camp may encourage its inspirers to be even more insolent and aggressive." [37]

Following Zhdanov's call-to-action, the Cominform delegates sharply criticized practices of French and Italian Communists who seemed to want a more pacific line and, once again following the disastrous practices of the 1927-1934 era, ordered all members to foment the necessary strikes and internal disorder for the elimination of independent socialist, labor, and peasant parties in their countries. The meeting was the high-water mark of the tough Zhdanov line in Soviet foreign policy. Its effect was soon felt not only in bloc and Western European countries, but inside Russia as well. Stalin cleansed Soviet economic thinking by discrediting and removing from public view Eugene Varga, a leading Russian economist who had gone against the political grain by warning that Marxists were wrong in thinking that the Western economies would collapse in the near future. "The entire experience of history teaches," *Pravda* announced, "that there does not exist and cannot exist in the world a science divorced from politics."

Other than tightening Stalin's control in the bloc and inside Russia itself, the Cominform's first meeting triggered yet a third

---

[37] Andrei Zhdanov, "The International Situation," reprinted in *The Strategy and Tactics of World Communism*, Supplement I (Washington, 1948), pp. 212–230.

development in Russian policy. Zhdanov urged that "All anti-imperialist forces of the various eastern countries," accelerate "their struggle" for "the liberation of more than a billion oppressed peoples of the East." This growing Russian emphasis on the underdeveloped world occurred at the same time that the United States fully subordinated its Asian and Latin American policies to its European interests. Within six months, native Communists began intensive application of the new hard-line doctrine in India, Pakistan, Burma, Malaya, the Philippines, and Indochina.

These new Soviet tactics did not change American priorities. The State Department did move to mediate Indonesia's revolt against Dutch rule and attempted to moderate Indonesian demands with promises of economic assistance. By early 1948, however, Congress dawdled in its consideration of Marshall Plan legislation. The Plan was coming under increased criticism. Taft proclaimed that good American money should not be poured into a "European TVA." On the opposite side of the political spectrum, Henry Wallace attacked it as a "Martial Plan." And then came the fall of Czechoslovakia.

The Communist Party and its leader Klement Gottwald first appeared as a political force in Czechoslovakia during the parliamentary elections of May 1946, by obtaining 38 percent of the vote, the largest total given any party. President Eduard Beneš and Foreign Minister Jan Masaryk, one of the foremost diplomatic figures in Europe, attempted to maintain a balance between East and West throughout 1947. State Department officials, however, became increasingly pessimistic that Beneš would succeed, particularly after Stalin effectively vetoed Czech membership in the Marshall Plan. The final blows began to fall when the Cominform instructed Communists to cement their power by eliminating independent parties. In mid-February 1948, as Soviet armies camped on the Czech borders, Premier Gottwald refused to cooperate with Beneš' plans to reorganize the police. The Cabinet broke up, and as Gottwald issued an ultimatum for a new government under his power, a Soviet mission led by top Foreign Ministry officials flew to Prague to demand Beneš' surrender. On February 25, the President capitulated and the Communists assumed complete control. Two weeks later Masaryk either committed suicide or, as Truman believed, was the victim of "foul play."

Truman correctly observed that the *coup* "sent a shock throughout the civilized world." A year before, Hungary had been the victim of a similar if less dramatic squeeze. Within two months, new opportunities would beckon to the Cominform when the Italian election was held. On March 5 a grave telegram arrived from General Clay in Germany. Although "I have felt and held that war was unlikely for at least ten years," Clay began, "within the last few weeks, I have felt a subtle change in Soviet attitude which . . . gives me a feeling that it may come with dramatic suddenness." For ten days, government intelligence worked furiously investigating Clay's warnings and on March 16 gave Truman the grim assurance that war was not probable within sixty days.[38] Two days before, on March 14, the Senate endorsed the Marshall Plan 69-17. As it went to the House for consideration, Truman, fearing the "grave events in Europe [which] were moving so swiftly," decided to appear before Congress.

In a speech remarkable for its single-minded emphasis on the "increasing threat" to the very "survival of freedom," the President proclaimed the Marshall Plan "not enough". Europe must have "some measure of protection against internal and external aggression." He asked for Universal Military Training, the resumption of Selective Service (which he had allowed to lapse a year earlier), and speedy passage of the Marshall Plan.[39] Within twelve days the House approved authorization of the Plan's money.

With perfect timing and somber rhetoric, Truman's March 17th speech not only galvanized passage of the Marshall Plan, but climaxed a change in American foreign policy that had been heralded as early as the previous summer. Congress stamped its approval on this new military emphasis by approving a Selective Service bill. Although Universal Military Training, one of Forrestal's pet projects, found little favor, a supposedly penny-proud Congress replaced it with funds to begin a seventy-group Air

---

[38] *Forrestal Diaries*, pp. 387, 395.
[39] *Documents on American Foreign Relations*, X (1948), pp. 5–9.

Force, 25 percent larger than even Forrestal had requested. Perhaps the most crucial effect of the new policy, however, appeared in the Administration's determination to create great systems which would not only encourage military development, but compel the western world to accept new political alignments as well. The first of these efforts had been the Rio Pact. The second, somewhat different, and vastly more important effort was the North Atlantic Treaty Organization.

CHAPTER IV

New Coalitions (1948-1950)

D URING THE SPRING OF 1948 a united Administration, enjoying
strong support on foreign policy from a Republican Congress, set off with exemplary single-mindedness to destroy the
Communist threat which loomed over Western Europe. Within
two years this threat had been scotched, but the officials who
created the policy had split, the Congress that ratified the policy
had turned against the Executive, the Administration itself fought
off charges that it had been infiltrated by Communists, and the
United States found itself fighting a bloody war not in Europe
but in Asia. These embarrassments did not suddenly emerge in
1950, but developed gradually from the policies of 1948 and
early 1949.

During the same month that Congress approved the Marshall
Plan, the British, French, and the Benelux signed the Brussels
Treaty. In this defense arrangement, each signatory promised
to aid the other parties in the event of attack with all military
and other aid "in their power." President Truman applauded the
treaty, and soon Senator Vandenberg and Robert Lovett, Acheson's successor as Under Secretary of State, were spending long
evenings in Vandenberg's Wardman Park Hotel suite drawing
up a congressional resolution to pave the way for American entry
into the new European association. Presented to the Senate on
May 19, the Vandenberg Resolution genuflected briefly before
the United Nations Charter, then passed on to the more important business of requesting a regional arrangement, under
Vandenberg's pet Article 51, in which the United States would
participate militarily on those conditions given in the Marshall
Plan: "continuous and effective self-help and mutual aid." This

breezed through the Senate on June 11 by a 64-4 vote, and Lovett began a three-month long series of conferences with European leaders to draft a final treaty. These discussions had barely begun when they were shaken by two events. In Europe the Berlin blockade severely tested the unity that was to form the basis of NATO. In the United States a foreign policy debate erupted during the presidential election.

The Berlin blockade had its beginnings in those moments of 1945 and 1946 when the breakdown of the Four Power Allied Control Council made impossible the reunification of Germany. The Soviets continued to hope they could create a unified but demilitarized Germany under their own control, or, as Molotov told Byrnes in 1946, a united Germany which could be neutralized after Russia received adequate industrial reparations. As Marshall stressed, however, the prosperity of Western Europe depended upon German industrial recovery. If it could not reunify Germany, the West could develop the western, industrial portions controlled by France, Great Britain, and the United States, and integrate the areas into a new European community. These three powers plus the Benelux reached agreement on this approach during intermittent meetings in London from February into June. As outlined in a communiqué of March 6, the London Conference determined to bring Germany within the "economic reconstruction of western Europe." The basis for a "federal form of government" would also be shaped through a fusion of the three Western zones. The Ruhr's great resources were to be brought under joint control of the Western powers.[1] The Conference then decided upon a currency reform to repair the inflation and widespread black market activities caused in Germany by the weak Reichsmark.

On April 1, the Russians responded to these announcements by temporarily restricting military supplies moving from the Western areas through the Russian zone into Berlin. On June 4, the West gave the green light to the Germans for initiating constitutional processes leading to a German Federal Republic. Two weeks later, the West began issuing the new currency in their

---

[1] U.S. Congress, Senate, Committee on Foreign Relations, 87th Congress, 1st Session, *Documents on Germany, 1944–1961* (Washington, 1961), pp. 87–88.

own zones, although not in Berlin. Protesting that the reform would result in the dumping of the worthless old Reichmarks in their sector, the Soviets began a separate currency reform for Berlin. On June 23, the London powers extended their new marks to the Western sectors of the former capital.

For the Soviets the crisis was at hand. The Western moves were obviously designed to accept and exploit the *status quo* in Germany. The Soviets, however, predicated their European policy upon a weakened non-Western Central Europe, and they now faced imminent, perhaps total, defeat of that policy. Worse, Stalin confronted the prospect of a rebuilt West Germany and a West Berlin deep inside the Soviet zone which could utilize this new power. Then, suddenly, Stalin's authority was challenged from within the bloc itself.

Josip Broz Tito was quite unlike Stalin's other followers in Eastern Europe. As a guerilla leader he had liberated his own nation without aid from the Red Army, and in doing so had created a mass basis of support at a time when Stalin and other Communist leaders increasingly rested their power on elite groups. His country, unlike Czechoslovakia, did not border on the Soviet Union and enjoyed access to the Mediterranean area. Tito's belief in Communism had never been in question; he was the only bloc leader who fully supported Stalin's and Zhdanov's creation of the Cominform. Tito's nationalism, however, had never been questioned either. When Stalin began to demand full Yugoslav adherence to the Comecon and the mutual assistance pacts, Tito balked. Enraged, Stalin claimed, "I will shake my little finger—and there will be no more Tito."[2] The Yugoslav's secret police, however, proved superior to Stalin's, and after the Soviet dictator tried in vain to overthrow Tito with an internal *coup*, Stalin called a special Cominform meeting in June 1948 to expel Yugoslavia from the bloc for "taking the route of nationalism." Tito not only successfully challenged Stalin's power, but disproved Stalin's key assumption that the world was divided into "two camps," with any so-called third force only a cover for

---

[2] Nikita S. Khrushchev, *The Crimes of the Stalin Era* . . . , Annotated . . . by Boris I. Nicolaevsky (New York, 1956), p. 48. This copy from *The New Leader* is well annotated.

capitalism. Having shaken both Stalin's power and theory, Tito's example threatened Soviet control throughout Eastern Europe. At that moment in mid-June when Stalin was preparing to bring Tito's many sins into the open, the Allies challenged Soviet policies in Germany. Stalin's first reaction was the ordering of bloody purges in Eastern Europe to exterminate nascent Titos. During the next two years, probably one out of every four Communist members in the bloc fell from power.

He next attempted to sever the West from the 2,400,000 West Berliners. On June 24, the Soviets stopped all surface traffic between Berlin and the Western zones. The Western powers had never negotiated a pact guaranteeing these rights; the Soviets now rejected arguments that occupation rights in Berlin and the use of the routes during the previous three years had given the West legal claim to unrestricted use of the highways and railroads. On June 28 came the American response. Without consulting anyone but a few Cabinet advisors, Truman decided, as Forrestal recalled the President's words, "We [are] going to stay period." Secretary of State Marshall later placed this decision within a context which bore a strange resemblance to the framework within which Stalin was working: ". . . we had the alternative of following a firm policy in Berlin or accepting the consequences of failure of the rest of our European policy."[3] The domino theory could work, apparently, on both sides of the Iron Curtain, and Germany had become the first domino.

The United States began a massive airlift, ultimately lasting 324 days, which soon delivered 13,000 tons of supplies a day. The success of the airlift forced Russia to discuss the problem in July. The Soviets indicated their paramount objective by tying a settlement on Berlin to "the general question of four-power control in regard to Germany." No progress could be made along these lines, but the note demonstrated that Stalin was playing for high stakes. So was Truman. In mid-July, he transferred to England two groups of B-29 bombers, the planes designated to carry atomic bombs. Truman's action demonstrated how the monopoly of these bombs allowed the Administration to balance the budget and cut back conventional army forces, yet at the

---

[3] *Forrestal Diaries*, pp. 454–455.

same time not diminish its capacity or willingness to brandish military force. The President assured Forrestal and Marshall that although he prayed the bomb would not have to be used, "if it became necessary, no one need have a misgiving but what he would do so." The evening after Truman made this remark, a meeting of leading newspaper publishers agreed that if war occurred over Berlin, the American people would expect the bomb to be used. Taking these words at face value, the Pentagon requested that control of the bomb be transferred from the President to the military so that the latter might make proper preparations for its use. Here Truman drew the line: he did not intend "to have some dashing lieutenant colonel decide when would be the proper time to drop one." This decision became more significant when Lovett brought word back to Washington that General Clay, the American comander in Berlin, "was now drawn as tight as a steel spring."[4] Truman's use of or a public threat to use atomic weapons during this crisis would have been grim evidence of presidential power during the Cold War. Truman committed the nation to the defense of Berlin, perhaps to waging war with the Soviet Union, without apparently consulting the representatives of the American people. He could also have used atomic weapons without consulting Congress.

In mid-May 1948, Truman gave further evidence of that power, although this occurred less in the context of possible atomic war against the Soviets than inevitable political war against Republicans. Shortly after 6:00 p.m. on May 14, the President recognized the newly-proclaimed state of Israel. Truman did this after rejecting the advice of both his military and diplomatic advisors. For months Forrestal had warned that such action would lead to the loss of vital Middle Eastern oil resources in the Arab states or, possibly, to an Israeli-Arab war from which only the Soviets might profit. The President received similar advice from State Department officials. Truman's action left the American delegation to the United Nations dumbfounded, for at that moment the delegation was trying to overcome both Jewish and Arab opposition to a partition plan in which the United Nations trusteeship would replace British power in the disputed Palestine area.

---

[4] *Ibid.*, pp. 487–489, 460–461, 480–481.

In the decisions on Berlin and Israel, Truman enjoyed such strong Congressional support, (although the Congress had not been formally consulted in either instance), that foreign policy never became a major issue between Truman and the Republican nominee, Thomas E. Dewey of New York, during the 1948 presidential campaign. Reinhold Niebuhr summarized the basic viewpoint of most Republicans and Democrats when he wrote in *Life* magazine in September 1948, "For peace we must risk war." The Soviets were weaker and would not fight, Niebuhr declared. "We cannot afford any more compromises. We will have to stand at every point in our far-flung lines."[5] These views underlay the foreign policy planks of both parties, although the platforms did not agree in every particular. In contrast to the Democrats, the Republicans emphasized the need to save China, lauded bipartisanship, placed heavier emphasis on building the military, and accused the President of not comprehending the real nature of the Russian peril. The Democrats answered the latter charge by inserting a plank (which had no counterpart in the Republican platform) condemning Communism "overseas and at home," and pledging strong enforcement of laws against subversive activities.

The Cold War against Communism at home and abroad did transform the campaign into a bitter struggle over foreign policy, but not between the two major parties. The clash occurred between the Democrats and Henry Wallace's new Progressive party. As the Progressives began to cry that the "old parties" did not really want a settlement with Russia, Wallace, along with many of his non-Communist supporters, became fair game to those Americans committed to fighting the Cold War with no holds barred. Apparently because of his political views, one Wallace supporter was stabbed to death in Charleston, South Carolina. At Evansville College, Bradley University, Northwestern, the University of Georgia, the University of Miami, and the University of New Hampshire, Progressive party adherents were either fired or made to suffer in other ways for their political

---

[5] Reinhold Niebuhr, "For Peace We Must Risk War," *Life*, XXV (September 20, 1948), pp. 38–39.

convictions.[6] The Americans for Democratic Action, fearing that Wallace might split the liberal vote and thus hand the victory to Dewey, tried to use guilt-by-association tactics by printing in major urban newspapers the names of the Progressive party's principal contributors and then listing the organizations on the Attorney General's list of subversive groups to which these contributors belonged—or had belonged.[7]

The Berlin blockade and Truman's shift to the left on domestic issues killed off any hopes the Progressives nursed of determining the election. Wallace received only 1,157,326 votes; half of these came from New York. Overcoming handicaps imposed by defections to the Wallacite left and the Dixiecrat right and by public opinion polls which showed him trailing Dewey, Truman lustily enjoyed scoring the greatest upset in twentieth-century American politics. The Progressive party rapidly declined, Wallace finally quitting in 1950 when he supported Truman's actions in Korea. In Europe, negotiations resumed on the NATO treaty.

These negotiations moved to the front of American diplomatic activity. In his Inaugural Address of January 20, 1949, Truman made a slight effort to restore some balance when in outlining the four major points of his foreign policy, he suggested as the so-called Point Four, "a bold new program" to spread scientific and industrial knowledge to the underdeveloped areas. The President and Congress moved very slowly in implementing this glamorous concept. The business community, on which Truman depended for the passage and implementation of any large aid program, attacked the probability of more governmental interference in the underdeveloped areas, asking instead that Truman negotiate with these nations treaties assuring fair and equitable treatment of private investment and personnel. For a year and a half Truman could obtain no Point Four legislation. In the summer of 1950, Congress finally passed a token appropriation of $27 million to begin a technical aid program in conjunction with the United Nations. Even the method was attacked by Senator Tom Connally, Democratic Chairman of the Foreign Relations Com-

---

[6] Karl M. Schmidt, *Henry A. Wallace: Quixotic Crusade, 1948* (Syracuse, 1960), pp. 86–88.
[7] *Ibid.*, pp. 159, 252.

mittee: "I don't see why in the world we need to turn this over and let . . . the United Nations run it and . . . mess it all up." [8] Connally's feeling ran somewhat at variance with Point One of Truman's Inaugural—full support of the United Nations.

Others questioned the relevance of such an aid program even to a neighbor like Latin America. In 1949 President Juan Perón of Argentina was accused by United States observers of using the tactics of the early Mussolini, Chile was under constant threat of a right-wing plot, Peru fell to a military junta, Venezuela lost its reform program after a military regime took control, and dictators Rafael Trujillo of the Dominican Republic and Anastasio Somoza of Nicaragua attempted to spread their own type of stability by conducting armed attacks on their neighbors. The underdeveloped world seemed treacherous ground, not at all resembling that of Western Europe under the Marshall Plan. The United States could find solace only in the OAS Charter, which theoretically opposed the violence erupting in Latin America, and in the especially comforting thought that at least Communism was not involved.

The other two points of the President's Inaugural—the encouragement of European recovery and the pledging of aid to help nations defend themselves—seemed more plausible. Here he dealt with the familiar cultures and policies of Europe. He also worked with a new Secretary of State who knew Europe intimately. The foremost American policy-maker in the post-World War II era, Dean Acheson founded his foreign policy upon those Atlantic ties which conservative statesmen in Europe traditionally considered the last hope of Western civilization. Acheson himself splendidly exemplified such conservatism. As a young, brilliant lawyer whom Roosevelt had plucked out of Washington's most august law firm, Acheson had resigned from the early New Deal because he considered Roosevelt's monetary policies rather weird. In 1936 he dramatized this break by attending a Liberty League rally. The approach of the war, however, drew Acheson back into government, and between 1941 and 1947 he

---

[8] Quoted in Richard P. Stebbins, *United States in World Affairs, 1950* (New York, 1951), p. 98.

devoted himself to the European policies which climaxed in the Marshall Plan.

As a good conservative, Acheson's allegiance to the Western partnership, in which he correctly viewed the United States as senior partner, overcame his few qualms about the later New or Fair Deals. His fear, moreover, of the growing Soviet menace satisfied even Senator Vandenberg: Acheson "is so totally anti-Soviet and is going to be so *completely* tough," the Michigan Senator wrote from a Foreign Ministers Conference in May 1949, "that I really doubt whether there is any *chance at all*" for an agreement.[9] Nor did Acheson allow the wishes of the multitude to disturb his outlook. The growing popularity of public opinion polls, he remarked in 1946, signifies that "we have become . . . of a somewhat hypochondriac type, and ascertain our state of health by this mass temperature taking. Fortunately this was not one of the hardships of Valley Forge." As for the United Nations, "in the Arab proverb, the ass that went to Mecca remained an ass, and a policy has little added to it by its place of utterance." Acheson preferred to place his confidence in power, since, as he once informed a group of distinguished lawyers, "law simply does not deal with such questions of ultimate power—power that comes close to the sources of sovereignty."[10] His war against Communism, his trust in power, particularly military power, and the veneration he held for traditional Europe admirably suited Acheson for the new era to be opened by the NATO pact.

The world in which NATO was to be born in early 1949 was undergoing rapid change. Nowhere was this more evident than in the Soviet Union. The successful Allied response to the Berlin blockade and Tito's defiance of the Cominform forced Stalin to question Zhdanov's fanaticism. By the end of July 1948, Zhdanov was dead, perhaps poisoned, more likely the victim of a heart attack after violent arguments with Stalin. Zhdanov's supporters

---

[9] *Papers of Vandenberg*, p. 485.
[10] Dean Acheson, *Pattern of Responsibility; Edited by McGeorge Bundy From the Record of Secretary of State Dean Acheson* (Boston, 1952), pp. 17, 21; the quotation on law is given in Richard J. Barnet and Marcus G. Raskin, *After 20 Years: Alternatives to the Cold War in Europe* (New York, 1965), p. 299.

now disappeared in a mass purge, and Georgi Malenkov and Nikita Khrushchev, both of whom wanted Stalin to devote more attention to internal economic problems, moved up the rungs of the ruling elite.

Stalin needed time to rearrange the hierarchy and to allow the dialectic of Marxism-Leninism to take its course in the United States, for in early 1949 Stalin believed the long-predicted American depression was finally beginning to close its grip. As unemployment rose to 3,500,000 in 1950, the Soviet press devoted increasing space to the impending crash. Stalin did little, moving only to tighten his control within Russia and the satellites. In April, the Soviets began lifting the Berlin blockade. In Western Europe, which NATO was to undergird, Communists in Italy and France lost considerable ground, and despite a recession caused by the American economic downturn, overall industrial production exceeded the 1938 level by 15 percent, while grain production rose more than 50 percent above the 1947 yield. As Truman's chief diplomatic troubleshooter W. Averell Harriman testified, fear in Europe "no longer exists as it existed 18 months ago."[11]

In this changing, quieter international environment, the Senate began hearings on the NATO pact. Twelve nations had signed it: the United States, Canada, Denmark, France, Iceland, Italy, Portugal, Norway, Great Britain and the Benelux. They pledged to use force only in self-defense, and to develop "free institutions" particularly through the encouragement of "economic collaboration between any or all" of the parties. Article 5 was central:

The Parties agree than an armed attack against one or more of them in Europe or North America shall be considered an attack against them all; and consequently they agree that, if such an armed attack occurs, each of them . . . will assist the Party or Parties so attacked by taking forthwith, individually and in concert with the other Parties, such action as it deems necessary, including the use of armed force . . . .

---

[11] U.S. Congress, Senate, Committee on Foreign Relations, 81st Congress, 1st Session, *Hearings . . . On . . . The North Atlantic Treaty* (Washington, 1949), p. 203.

Article 11 modified this commitment by adding that the pact's provisions shall be carried out in accordance with each nation's "constitutional processes." Vandenberg and Connally had inserted this clause in an attempt to curb Executive powers. Article 9 established a Council to implement defense policies. Articles 12 and 13 provided for a review in ten years; after twenty years any member could quit after giving one-year notice.

At first the hearings went well. Acheson calmed the fears of Senator Henry Cabot Lodge by emphasizing that no one "at the present time" contemplated following NATO with "a Mediterranean pact, and then a Pacific pact, and so forth." Everyone present agreed that the defense of Europe could not be entrusted to the United Nations. A consensus formed on the proposition that NATO "is to create not merely a balance of power, but a preponderance of power." This fitted into Truman's and Acheson's policies of dealing with the Russians from "positions of strength." The West, however, already enjoyed such a "preponderance" because of its possession of the atomic bomb. NATO promised to add little more. This led to a line of questioning which soon revealed that, indeed, even Administration witnesses had difficulty discovering the military importance of the pact.

At the time the West's dozen, underequipped divisions faced twenty-five fully-armed Russian divisions stationed in Central Europe. When asked whether the Administration planned to send "substantial" numbers of United States troops to shore up European defenses, Acheson and General Omar Bradley, Chairman of the Joint Chiefs of Staff, assured the Senate, in Acheson's words, "The answer to that question, Senator, is a clear and absolute 'No.' " Continuing their search for the manpower that would fill NATO, the Committee then asked Acheson whether the Administration contemplated putting Germans back into uniform. "We are very clear," Acheson replied, "that the disarmament and demilitarization of Germany must be complete and absolute."[12]

The questioning necessarily took another line. If NATO did not possess the manpower to quell a conventional attack, and if United States control of atomic weapons was not modified by

---

[12] *Ibid.*, pp. 54, 57, 47, 183, 144.

the pact, was NATO then aimed at preventing internal subversion in Western Europe? Acheson, believing that such successful subversive activities in Europe were "remote," thought the sole American reaction to such a *coup* would be the less-than-drastic response of allowing the victim to leave the NATO alliance. Another dimension of the problem was noted by Senator Arthur Watkins, a strong opponent of the treaty. Because of the "constitutional processes" clause, Watkins observed, an opponent could strike and take much of Europe before "we could ever get the Congress together to declare war."[13] Clearly the treaty's military significance was not overwhelming.

The key to the American view of the treaty emerged when Harriman remarked that if NATO was not carried through, "there would be a reorientation" in Europe climaxing in "a re-strengthening of those that believe in appeasement and neutrality." In a similar vein, Acheson commented in hearings a year later, "Unity in Europe requires the continuing association and support of the United States. Without it free Europe would split apart." Now that the Marshall Plan was reviving Europe economically, the United States, in the full splendor of its postwar power, was attempting to strengthen its ties with, and influence over, Europe by creating military institutions which would provide fresh channels for American aid and policies. Senator Connally phrased this succinctly in the Senate debate: "The Atlantic Pact is but the logical extension of the principle of the Monroe Doctrine."[14]

The Senate ratified the treaty 82-13. On the day he added his signature, July 23, 1949, Truman sent to Congress a one-year Mutual Defense Assistance Bill providing for about $1.5 billion for European military aid. This was the immediate financial price of the NATO commitment. A memorandum circulating through the Executive Department outlined the purpose of MDA: "to build up our own military industry," to "create a common defense frontier in Western Europe" by having the Allies pool "their industrial and manpower resources," and, particularly, to

---

[13] *Ibid.*, pp. 25, 310, 317.
[14] *Ibid.*, p. 231; Acheson, *Pattern of Responsibility*, p. 55; Tom Connally, *My Name is Tom Connally* . . . (New York, 1954), p. 231.

subordinate "nationalistic tendencies."[15] Vandenberg endorsed such laudable objectives, but he launched a strong attack on the bill in committee. "It's almost unbelievable in its grant of unlimited power to the Chief Executive," he wrote his wife. "It would virtually make him the number one war lord of the earth." He added that Senators William Fulbright, Walter George, and Henry Cabot Lodge gave bipartisan support to these views. The Michigan Senator also expressed concern that in having the United States distribute this money unilaterally, Acheson was bypassing the NATO council, which had been created to handle such military aid.[16] Vandenberg proceeded to cut presidential power slightly by giving Congress authority to shut off arms shipments at any time. Acheson, however, succeeded in keeping the funds in American hands. In the House, the bill encountered tough opposition from Congressmen determined to slice drastically all governmental expenditures. On September 22, President Truman announced the exploding of an atomic bomb by the Soviet Union. Within six days, the NATO appropriations raced through the House and went to the President for approval.

Although publicly playing down the significance of the Russian test, the Administration fully and painfully realized that, in Vandenberg's words, "This is now a different world." Few American officials had expected the Soviet explosion this early. Now that it had occurred at the same time that Communists completed their conquest of China, the American diplomatic attitude stiffened. As Leo Szilard, one of the foremost scientists in the development of the American bomb, explained, "the Russians can affect the political attitude of Western Europeans just by threatening to bomb them."[17] For American policy-makers, the battle for Europe had reopened. Having chosen NATO as their weapon, Administration officials searched for a way to sharpen that instrument now that the Soviets threatened to balance

---

[15] "Effect of the MAP on U.S. Security," draft from Foreign Assistance Coordinating Committee, June 22, 1949, Papers of David D. Lloyd, Truman Library.
[16] Papers of Vandenberg, pp. 503–504.
[17] Leo Szilard, "A Personal History of the Bomb," in "The Atlantic Community Faces the Bomb," University of Chicago Roundtable, September 25, 1949, p. 4.

American atomic power. Truman took a first step when he ordered that the development of the hydrogen bomb be accelerated. The second step began when American military authorities determined to build a large conventional European army which would include German military units.

During the NATO hearings in the spring and later in June 1950, Acheson assured Congress that Germany would not be rearmed. In those fourteen months, however, as Vandenberg noted, the world had become "different," and Germany both East and West underwent dramatic change. The first elections in West Germany for a national parliament occurred on August 14, 1949 and gave Konrad Adenauer's Christian Democratic Union a plurality of 31 percent of the votes. A vigorous seventy-three years of age, Adenauer had spent his early political life in Cologne city government and then, from 1933 to 1945, in Nazi prisons. Although one of the founders of the CDU and a prominent official in the British zone, Adenauer's postwar rise to power resulted more from ruthless political infighting than from charisma. He personally enjoyed little national support. This placed him at a disadvantage in meeting the CDU's opposition, Kurt Schumacher's Social Democrats, which had obtained 29.2 percent of the popular vote. Schumacher advanced a vigorous nationalist program demanding the return of the eastern German territories newly annexed to Poland. The words "Sudetenland" and "Saar" once more began to haunt German politics. Adenauer countered Schumacher by asserting "full legitimacy" to the eastern territories and demanding from the Western Allies complete German independence, but at the same time he tried to thwart the extreme demands of the Social Democrats. The Soviets meanwhile continued their closely controlled reconstruction of the East German Democratic Republic, protesting all the while that the West was forcing them to divide Germany.

The partitioning, West Germany's first elections, Adenauer's demands for independence, and the announcement of the Soviet bomb all occurred within a six-week period between August and October 1949. By November a branch of the Operations and Plans Division of the United States Army completed a program for German remilitarization and launched a campaign to procure NATO's acceptance. The State Department, however, demurred, arguing that an immediate move to build a German army could produce such dangerous repercussions as detrimental political reaction at home, strong hostility in France, and unpleasant responses from Poland and Russia. Truman supported these views. But the State Department was not united. After 1944, German affairs in the Department had been handled by a succession of major generals who held the rank of Assistant Secretary of State for Occupied Territories. This, in part, explains why General Clay and the State Department cooperated so well in getting Germany rapidly on its feet after the war. When the Administration created the Office of German Affairs in 1949, Henry Byroade, a regular Army brigadier general, became its chief. Byroade became doubly important when a feud between Acheson and Secretary of Defense Louis Johnson reached the point where Johnson would allow no officials in the Pentagon to talk to those in the State Department without his permission. Byroade, however, moved freely between the two departments and became a link between State Department and Pentagon plans for Germany. The Army's cause received further help when NATO studies, revealing a huge gap in manpower, generated new demands for a German army from British Commander Field Marshall Montgomery, General Clay, and John J. McCloy, United States High Commissioner in Germany. On April 30, 1950, the Joint Chiefs of Staff approved the rearmament plans, but they decided to await a more opportune moment before asking for Truman's approval.[18]

The French probably knew little about this Washington infighting, but they fully comprehended the threat that overpowering American influence in NATO posed to their own independence and their general policies for Europe. They attempted to deal with this threat by requesting that the Anglo-American Combined Chiefs of Staff, which had been conferring jointly on strategic decisions since early in World War II, now include a French officer. The United States responded by disbanding the Combined Chiefs of Staff.[19] As she had in the past and would

---

[18] Laurence W. Martin, "The American Decision to Rearm Germany," in Harold Stein (ed.) *American Civil-Military Decisions: a Book of Case Studies* (Birmingham, Alabama, 1963), pp. 646–651.

[19] *The New York Times*, August 28, 1966, p. 20.

in the future, France retaliated with a device calculated to increase French power on the continent at the expense of the Anglo-American coalition.

Foreign Minister Robert Schuman proposed in the spring of 1950 that "Little Europe" (France, Germany, Italy, and the Benelux) combine their heavy iron, coal, and steel industry. Like the American plans for German rearmament, the "Schuman Plan" also would produce large-scale political repercussions: Germany's basic industry would be integrated into Western Europe; the Ruhr would essentially become internationalized, thus hopefully destroying German military capacity while giving France entry to the area's rich coal deposits; the combining of basic industries would shortly force transport and agriculture to follow in a movement of spectacular European integration; and, not least, the exclusion of Great Britain and the United States from the plan would increase the ability of France to control continental Europe.

The State Department fully supported this plan, but officials did not agree on the question of how the alliance might develop militarily. As chief of the Policy Planning Staff, George Kennan watched the burgeoning of NATO with increasing displeasure. He had concluded that Russia could be contained, yet Cold War tensions eased, through some kind of neutralization plan for Germany and Central Europe. Kennan considered the Marshall Plan to be consistent with this approach, but NATO was not, particularly if it permanently divided and rearmed Germany. Three weeks before the announcement of the Russian bomb, Kennan observed that the world no longer resembled that of 1947, but had entered a period of "transition" in which "long-term problems and challenges of a new period are beginning now to come to the surface."[20] "Mr. X" also began placing different emphases in his views of Russian motivations. There is a Russia, he told a Columbia University audience in May, 1950, "touched by the stream of western civilization, reacting to that stream with . . . incredible freshness and sincerity." Bolshevik

---

[20] George F. Kennan, "The International Situation," *Department of State Bulletin*, XXI (September 5, 1949), pp. 323–324.

concentration camps represented only an "apparent collapse" of that tradition.[21]

When Kennan presented these views of NATO and the changing Soviet scene inside the State Department, he encountered strong opposite from Acheson.[22] The Secretary of State preferred the old to the new "Mr. X." But the explosion of the Russian bomb deepened Kennan's convictions. In early 1950, he announced he was leaving the State Department for a year of study at Princeton. So ended another "disengagement" debate within the State Department.

Kennan's planned departure did not free Acheson from criticism. The Army wanted him to go faster. Powerful Congressmen demanded that he devote equal time and resources to China. The Secretary of State temporarily fended off attacks from the Pentagon, but as a strong Europe-first advocate, and as Secretary of State during the period when Chiang Kai-shek lost China, he could not placate the China bloc. When the China enthusiasts argued that increased American assistance could save the Nationalists, Acheson responded that lack of assistance was not causing Chiang's headlong retreat. The chief of the American Advisory group in China reported in mid-November 1948 that these "military debacles in my opinion can all be attributed to the world's worst leadership and many other morale destroying factors that lead to a complete loss of will to fight."[23] By February 1, 1949, the Nationalists had lost nearly half their troops, mostly by defection. Eighty percent of the American equipment given Chiang had fallen into Communist hands. On April 21 the Communists clinched their victory by successfully crossing the Yangtze and beginning a sweep across South China. The Administration finally moved to terminate aid. This aroused the full fury of the China bloc. Supported by Walter Judd, William Knowland, Owen Brewster, and Kenneth Wherry (who earlier had uttered the immortal words, "With God's help we will lift

[21] George F. Kennan, *Russia and the United States* . . . (Stamford, Connecticut, 1950).

[22] *U.S. News and World Report*, XLIV (January 17, 1958), p. 63.

[23] Tang Tsou, *America's Failure in China*, pp. 482–483.

Shanghai up and up, ever up, until it is just like Kansas City,"),[24] Senator Pat McCarran proposed a grant of $1.5 billion dollars to be expended by American officers in the field which would be repaid through American control of Chinese customs ports. Acheson quickly stopped this move. The critics retreated to verbal attacks on the Administration, for they had no other alternatives to offer. As Knowland candidly remarked in June 1949, no responsible opponent of the Administration's policy had ever proposed sending an American army to fight in China.

On August 5, Acheson tried for the knockout blow by releasing the so-called "White Paper," a 1054-page compilation of documents to support the Administration's thesis that, as Acheson wrote in a long introduction, "The unfortunate but inescapable fact is that the ominous result of the civil war in China was beyond the control of the government of the United States. . . . It was the product of internal Chinese forces, forces which this country tried to influence but could not." The only alternative policy would have been a "full-scale intervention" of American troops, which "would have been resented by the mass of the Chinese people, would have diametrically reversed our historic policy, and would have been condemned by the American people." He looked forward to the time when the Chinese people would throw off the "foreign yoke" of Communism, but Acheson warned that if China lent "itself to the aims of Soviet Russian imperialism," the United States would consider this a violation of the United Nations Charter and, he implied, move to stop any aggression.[25]

The China bloc called the White Paper a "whitewash of a wishful, do-nothing policy which has succeeded only in placing Asia in danger of Soviet conquest."[26] The bloc then tried to pass another bill granting military aid to Chiang. Congress began to divide on the issue largely along party lines. Vandenberg, watching his prized bipartisanship being dragged down with the

---

[24] Quoted in Eric Goldman, *The Crucial Decade and After, 1945–1961* (New York, 1960), p. 116.

[25] Dean Acheson, "Letter of Transmittal, July 30," in *United States Relations With China . . . 1944–1949* (Washington, 1949), pp. xiv–xvii.

[26] Quoted in H. B. Westerfield, *Foreign Policies and Party Politics . . .* (New Haven, 1955), p. 356.

sinking cause of the Nationalists, finally worked out a compromise on this bill. Acheson then somewhat pacified the bloc by announcing on October 12 that, because it had not met traditional American conditions, the new Communist Chinese government, proclaimed on September 30, could not be recognized by the United States.

During the next two months the Administration grappled with the problem posed by Chiang's establishment of a rival Chinese government on Formosa. In late December, the Joint Chiefs and the State Department agreed that because Mao would probably conquer Formosa sometime in 1950, the United States should not issue military aid to the Nationalist regime.[27] Chiang's supporters again angrily prepared for battle in Congress, forcing the Administration to compromise when they threatened to cut off aid to Korea if some assistance was not immediately sent to Formosa. The battle was intensely bitter, and Vandenberg, seriously ill in Michigan, could not heal the wounds inflicted on bipartisanship. This fight, waged just five months before the outbreak of the Korean war, left bipartisanship an ideal and no longer a practice.

Truman and Acheson were determined to move slowly in the revolutionary Asian situation. American experts were not certain whether a common allegiance to Marxism-Leninism would suffice to link China and Russia in a friendly partnership. Stalin remembered the debacle of his China policies in the 1920s. The Chinese Communists recalled how Stalin had agreed to cooperate with Roosevelt in recognizing Chiang's government and had kept a Soviet Ambassador with the Nationalists in 1949 after most Western governments had deserted Chiang. Perhaps, however, common ideology would blot out unhappy memories. The more fundamental question soon arose, however, of who would define that ideology. In a widely-publicized interview in 1946, Liu Shao-ch'i, Mao's chief theoretician, announced that Mao had given Marxism "a new development. He has created a Chinese

---

[27] U.S. Congress, Senate, Committee on Armed Services and Committee on Foreign Relations, 82nd Congress, 1st Session, *Hearings to Conduct an Inquiry Into the Military Situation in the Far East* . . . (Washington, 1951), pp. 1770–1771; cited hereafter as *Military Situation in the Far East.*

or Asiatic form of Marxism. . . . There are similar conditions in other lands of southeast Asia. The courses chosen by China will influence them all." In November 1949, just days before Mao left for Moscow to negotiate personally with Stalin, the Chinese revived Liu's 1946 interview.[28] Within the Politburo itself, Stalin's policies were also being questioned.

A debate evidently erupted among top Soviet officials over the question of whether the possession of the atomic bomb and the victory of the Chinese Communists had so weakened the threat of "capitalist encirclement" that internal repression could be eased and domestic consumer production increased. On November 6, Georgi Malenkov, one of Stalin's closest associates since the early 1930s, delivered a speech which subtly advanced the thesis that "capitalist encirclement" was crumbling. He stressed the unity of the Russian peoples and the security of Soviet borders. Boasting that the Five-Year Plan was ahead of schedule, Malenkov challenged the West to "peaceful competition with socialism." Within this general context, he made two significant points. First, he admonished the Soviets to prepare for this competition by removing further "difficulties and obstacles" that hindered production. The shackles of Stalinist discipline could have easily been construed by Malenkov to comprise such "difficulties." Second, he argued that the economic recession in the West bore the "signs of an approaching crisis" for which the Soviets had long been waiting. This line of argument implied that Stalin no longer had to apply pressures, for the West was collapsing of its own internal contradictions.[29]

Old-line Stalinists lashed back in a speech made to the Cominform in late November. Mikhail A. Suslov, Chief of the Department of Agitation and Propaganda, took Malenkov's premises and neatly turned them around to the opposite conclusion: the rising successes of Soviet power increased the immediate danger of armed conflict. Suslov argued that because the Soviets had scored such great economic and political victories, the United States had decided to create NATO and begin work on the hy-

---

[28] Quoted in Donald S. Zagoria, *The Sino-Soviet Conflict, 1956–1961* (Princeton, 1962), pp. 14–15.
[29] *Current Digest of the Soviet Press*, I (Nov. 22, 1949), pp. 3–10.

drogen bomb. Such "war-mongering" attempts to change the balance of power, now tipping slowly in favor of the Soviets, could, Suslov warned, lead to Western attacks on Eastern Europe, Communist China, and North Korea.[30]

Stalin himself reacted more indirectly. Five days before the Korean War began, he countered growing arguments that Russia was now prepared for a sudden, explosive break that would force the withering away of the socialistic, that is, Stalinist, state, and give birth to the long-promised utopia of communism. Explaining in an article on linguistics that language develops gradually, not through "explosions," Stalin suddenly turned on "comrades who are engrossed in explosions" and informed them that neither is the theory of sudden transition "always applicable to other social phenomena."[31] Two days later he again revealed his hand by resurrecting Pavlov's "conditioned reflex" theory which stated that man could be controlled through certain laws of conditioning. On June 22, 1950, Stalin ordered Soviet scientists to study Pavlov's theories. Textbooks were rewritten to construct a state-controlled educational system which would mould the New Soviet Man and, more important, keep him under control. Stalin wanted control, not revolution. Although brandishing the vocabulary of Marx and Lenin, he had become not only conservative, but reactionary, retreating to the beliefs and tactics of the 1930s in an attempt to secure himself and his policies against the challenges of Mao and Malenkov.

The challenge from the East became apparent in discussions between the Chinese and Russian leaders which began in December. More than two months of hard bargaining ensued. The Russians obtained Sino-Soviet joint-stock companies to exploit resources in Sinkiang, and managed to restrict credit arrangements through which China could buy Soviet exports to the value of $300 million spread over five years. The Soviets later cut the value of the loan about one fifth by devaluating the ruble. China did succeed in making the treaty one of "mutual assis-

---

[30] Marshall D. Shulman, *Stalin's Foreign Policy Reappraised* (Cambridge, Massachusetts, 1963), pp. 118–119.

[31] Robert C. Tucker, *The Soviet Political Mind* . . . (New York, 1963), pp. 24–25, 100–114.

tance": Russia would consult with China in the event that Japan "or any other state that should unite" with Japan threatened aggression against China. Perhaps of greatest significance to the Chinese mind, the Soviets promised to surrender their special rights in Dairen, Port Arthur, and the Manchurian railway system. While these points were thrashed out, Stalin moved unsuccessfully back of the scene to loosen the allegiances of Manchuria and Inner Mongolia to Peking. The "fraternal alliance" was enduring an uncommon amount of horse trading and attempted backstabbing.

The slow pace of these negotiations seemed to justify the State Department's caution in dealing with the evolving Sino-Soviet bloc. George Kennan privately explained the Department's view that the Soviets "will be extrémely cautious" in spreading Marxism around Asia "because they are very, very well aware of the fact that if you cannot overshadow a country militarily, ideology is in itself an untrustworthy means with which to hold them." He recalled "Stalin one time snorting rather contemptuously and vigorously because one of our people asked them what they were going to give to China when [the war] was over and he said in effect, 'What the hell do you think we can give to China.' He said, 'We have a hundred cities of our own to build in the Soviet Far East. If anybody is going to give anything to the Far East, I think it's you.' And I think," Kennan added, "he was speaking quite sincerely." [32]

On January 12, 1950, as the Mao-Stalin talks edged along, Acheson developed some of Kennan's basic points before the National Press Club in Washington. He viewed the Soviet attempt to control Outer and Inner Mongolia, Manchuria, and Sinkiang, as "the single most significant, most important fact" in the Asian situation; such attempts would prove to Mao that the Soviets wished not to help but to dominate. Acheson stressed that nationalism, not Communism, had become the dominant characteristic of postwar Asia, and that consequently the United States, not Russia, would prove to be the best friend of those Chinese who want "their own national independence." In this context Acheson issued his famous declaration that the Pacific

---

[32] *I.P.R. Hearings*, pp. 1558–1563.

"defensive perimeter" of the United States ran from the Aleutians to Japan, the Ryukyus, and down to the Philippines. (This was not a newly-announced policy; in March 1949, General MacArthur defined the perimeter as encompassing exactly the same area.[33]) Acheson doubted that the Far East was threatened as much by military aggression as by "subversion and penetration." He singled out South and Southeast Asia as particularly susceptible to subversion, warning that men who "sit around in Washington, or London, or Paris" cannot "determine what the policies are going to be in those areas." The Secretary of State, however, carefully made two exceptions to these general policies: first, in both Japan and Korea, the United States had special economic responsibilities; second, if attack occurred west of the defense perimeter, the "entire civilized world under the Charter of the United Nations" would aid "people who are determined to protect their independence."[34]

Acheson had issued a fascinating document, acute in its view of Asian nationalism, accurate in its pinpointing of some Sino-Soviet problems, precise in its sorting out of Japan and Korea as of paramount importance to American policy, and wrong in its assumption that military aggression in the area was not imminent. The Secretary of State left many options open for policy maneuvers. Within two days, these options were severely cut. On January 13, Yakov Malik, the Soviet delegate to the Security Council, walked out after his proposal to unseat the Nationalist Chinese in favor of the Communists lost 6-3. The next day, the Communists raided American Consulate grounds in Peking. The United States view toughened. A month later on February 14, the Sino-Soviet treaty became public. Acheson interpreted the agreement as confirmation of his fears that Mao was selling out the Chinese people to the Russians. Extending his sympathy to the Chinese, he warned them against being "led by their new rulers into aggressive or subversive adventures beyond their borders."[35]

---

[33] *The New York Times*, March 2, 1949, p. 22.
[34] Dean Acheson, "Crisis in Asia," *Department of State Bulletin* XXII (January 23, 1950), pp. 111–117.
[35] Dean Acheson, "United States Policy Toward Asia," *Department of State Bulletin*, XXII (March 27, 1950), pp. 4–8.

The Sino-Soviet pact, the explosion of the Russian bomb, the divisive arguments over NATO, the whimpering end of bipartisanship added up to an unpleasant winter for the Truman Administration. A grim President demanded a wide-ranging reevaluation of American Cold War policies. In January 1950, the National Security Council began work on a highly secret document that would soon be known as NSC-68. Truman examined the study in April, and it was being implemented by the Administration when Korea burst into war. NSC-68 viewed the international arena as split, with the United States and the U.S.S.R. at either end. The Soviet bloc not only was dedicated to preserving its own power and ideology, but to extending and consolidating its power by absorbing "new satellites" and weakening any "competing system of power." To contain this threat, the United States would enjoy superiority in nuclear weapons until about 1954. Industrially, the document viewed the Communists as inferior but possessing a much greater conventional warfare capacity. The overall picture was one of "an indefinite period of tension and danger." The study urged the United States to undertake "a bold and massive program" of rebuilding the West until it far surpassed the Soviet bloc, and to meet "each fresh challenge promptly and unequivocally." In these efforts, the United States must stand at the "political and material center with other free nations in variable orbits around it." No longer, the study warned, could the United States ask " ' How much security can we afford?' " nor should it any longer attempt to "distinguish between national and global security." The United States could survive only in a world at peace and free from Communist expansion. In creating such a world, NSC-68 urged Truman to remember that the country was so rich that it could use twenty percent of its gross national product for arms without suffering national bankruptcy. This would allow a defense budget of $50 billion per year. Truman was preparing a budget of $13.5 for defense purposes as the study was completed.[36]

NSC-68 is one of the key historical documents of the Cold War. It asked the United States to assume unilaterally the de-

---

[36] A summary of the document is in Cabell Philipps, *The Truman Presidency* . . . (New York, 1966), pp. 306–308.

fense of the free world at a tremendous price and with no hesitation. It did so on the basis of its definition of Soviet foreign policy. Completed before officials had any inkling of possible trouble in Korea, NSC-68 provided a clear illustration of what effect the winter of 1949-1950 had on the Truman Administration. Peace would not be found soon; indeed, it was not to be found at all. Americans, who like other peoples, prefer their wars short and favorable, wondered why.

One answer had already been suggested on July 30, 1948, as the nation felt the reverberations of the Czech *coup* and the Berlin blockade. Elizabeth Bentley and Whitaker Chambers, a self-confessed former Communist Party member, claimed before the House Un-American Activities Committee that Communists had infiltrated the State Department a decade before. Chambers specifically accused Alger Hiss of being a Party agent. Hiss had worked in several Executive Departments after 1933, including the State Department where in 1944 he had helped lay the groundwork for the United Nations. His friends included Dean Acheson and John Foster Dulles. Hiss replied to Chambers with a libel suit for $75,000. Chambers then took federal agents to his Maryland farm and picked from a hollowed-out pumpkin microfilms of State Department documents which Chambers claimed Hiss had passed to him in 1938. The typing irregularities on the microfilms seemed to match those of one of Hiss's old typewriters. Leading American liberals, including Supreme Court Justice Felix Frankfurter and Illinois Governor Adlai Stevenson, testified on behalf of Hiss. Acheson supported the former Harvard Law School graduate in the strongest terms. After one hung jury, Hiss was finally convicted of perjury on January 21, 1950. Many Americans now believed they understood why the Cold War was not ending quickly and happily.

Hiss's fall carried with it much of the reputation of the Eastern liberal-intellectual group which had become identified with the battles and reforms of the New Deal. Wallace's defection and resounding defeat, Truman's failure to pass the new and more liberal features of his Fair Deal domestic program, and Hiss's conviction illustrated how Roosevelt's remark during World War II that "Dr. Win-the-War" had replaced "Dr. New Deal" remained relevant far into the Cold War era. The mood emerging in late 1949 was not founded upon reform but upon conservatism and consensus.

Perhaps nowhere was this more noticeable and explicit than in the writing of American history. In 1948, Charles Beard, the greatest of those historians who between 1910 and 1940 had emphasized and applauded reform and class and political divisions in American history, published *President Roosevelt and the Coming of the War.* Charging that Roosevelt had knowingly broken the constitutional boundaries imposed upon the Executive branch so he could take the nation into war, Beard warned that this tragedy could be repeated in any new campaign undertaken by the United States to bring peace to "the whole world." Such a campaign would undermine the Constitution, Beard argued, for the President would possess "limitless authority publicly to misrepresent and secretly to control foreign policy, foreign affairs, and the war power." As he had throughout his life, Beard used James Madison and *The Federalist* as his primary reference.

Such dissent from waging the Cold War was not the fashion in 1948 and 1949. Samuel Eliot Morison, Boston Brahmin, Rear Admiral (appointed by Roosevelt), and President of the American Historical Association, attacked Beard's legacy in an article subtitled, "History Through a Beard." The year after Morison's article appeared, Arthur Schlesinger, Jr., whose intellectual debt to Niebuhr was great, published a primer for the new liberals, which viewed their role not to the left, where Beard had wanted it, but in *The Vital Center.*[37] Like the historians, President Truman took pride in his ability to search the past for present policies, but he looked elsewhere as well. "We are on the right track, and we will win," he announced in early 1950, "because God is with us in that enterprise."[38]

The Anti-Christ nevertheless seemed to be everywhere, even in an age that venerated consensus. On January 14 the Chinese Communists attacked the American Consulate offices, a week

---

[37] Samuel Eliot Morison, "Did Roosevelt Start the War; History Through a Beard," *Atlantic Monthly*, CXLII (August 1948), pp. 91–97; Arthur Schlesinger Jr., *The Vital Center* (Boston, 1949, 1962).
[38] *Public Papers of Truman, 1950,* p. 344.

later Hiss was convicted, on the 31st the White House announced that the United States would make a hydrogen bomb ("annihilation of any life on earth has been brought within the range of technical possibilities," Albert Einstein reported over national television), and on February 3, London announced that a British spy ring headed by German-born, British-naturalized Klaus Fuchs had been discovered relaying atomic secrets to Soviet agents. Six days later at Wheeling, West Virginia, the junior Senator from Wisconsin, Joseph McCarthy, announced that he held in his hand proof that the Department of State was riddled with Communists. The paper he waved could prove nothing even faintly related to his charges, but no matter. The timing was perfect.

The junior Senator had not previously been known for such ideological zeal, but for an uncommon amount of political savvy. In 1946, he overcame a reputation as one of the worst Circuit Court Judges in Wisconsin history to win the Senate seat from the popular Robert M. La Follette, Jr. McCarthy accomplished this in part by running on the slogan, "Congress needs a tail-gunner," which he had never been, and by apparently destroying the legal records that reflected unfavorably on his judiciary abilities. By early 1950, with another election fight in Wisconsin only two years away, he began searching for an issue. During a conversation with a Washington attorney and two political scientists from Georgetown University, McCarthy first dismissed the St. Lawrence Seaway project as a possibility; then, with the Hiss case in the headlines, he eagerly seized upon the Communist issue. After the Wheeling speech, he became the center of some of the wildest scenes in Senate history. As his fellow legislators tried to pinpoint what he had charged, McCarthy's figures whirled from the 205 Communists, at Wheeling, to 57 the following night, 81 on February 20, and when brought before a special Senate committee headed by the highly-respected Millard Tydings, Democrat of Maryland, his figures changed again to 10, then to 116, and finally to 1. The one was Owen Lattimore, a specialist on Far Eastern studies at Johns Hopkins University. On Lattimore's conviction, McCarthy said, he would "stand or fall." When pressed for evidence, McCarthy responded in part by reverting to Truman's refusal to allow Congress to examine the loyalty files. The Executive, McCarthy claimed, was keeping the evidence locked up. The Tydings Committee finally dismissed McCarthy as a fraud and exonerated Lattimore; but it also mistakenly dismissed any idea that "security risks" could lurk in the State Department.[39]

Mao, Malenkov, the China bloc, McCarthy. As June 1950 approached, Stalin and Truman had learned that forming a consensus on the Cold War was not free of complications.

[39] Richard N. Rovere, *Senator Joe McCarthy* (New York, 1959), pp. 6, 54, 99–100, 120–122, 130, 140–160.

CHAPTER V

Korea: The War for Both Asia and Europe (1950-1951)

IN JUNE 1950, Korea was a Cold War-wracked country which lacked everything except authoritarian governments, illiteracy, cholera epidemics, and poverty. For nearly a century, it had been a pawn in Far Eastern power plays. In 1905, Japan, after using force to stop a Russian thrust, had established a protectorate over Korea and in 1910 annexed that country. When the Japanese surrendered Korea in 1945, it became a testing ground in the renewed battle between Russia and the United States. After setting up dependent but Korean-led governments in zones seized from the Japanese, Russia and the United States evacuated their occupation armies in 1948 and 1949, respectively. In March 1949, North Korea and the Soviets signed an agreement for economic cooperation. Russian military advisers and aid strengthened a formidable 100,000 man army. American military advisers also remained in the south, but President Truman encountered difficulty sending large amounts of aid to Syngman Rhee's government. At the end of June 1950, about $60 million of an allotted $110 million in economic aid had been shipped. Military assistance had scarcely begun. As at the turn of the century, Korea was a prize in the struggle between Russia and countries to the West; and, as in 1904, China, although now a very different China, stood apart from the conflict. Mao's regime devoted itself to internal reconstruction and drawing up plans for a probable invasion of Formosa sometime during 1950.

Mao had little cause to linger over Korean problems; South Korea itself posed no threat to his new government or, apparently, to the remainder of the Communist bloc. MacArthur and

Acheson had defined Korea as beyond the perimeter of American military defenses, although not outside the realm of United Nations responsibility. It seemed possible, moreover, that without either Chinese or Russian overt pressure, the South Korean government might crumble. South Korea suffered under Rhee's authoritarian government until the State Department publicly protested his disregard of constitutional rights in early 1950. In an election in May, President Rhee's party collected only forty-eight seats as opposed to one hundred and twenty seats for the other parties; this defeat occurred despite Rhee's arrest of thirty political opponents in "anti-communist" raids just before the election was held. The Korean President pieced together a coalition government that began what promised to be a precarious, perhaps short, struggle to hold power.

On June 7 the northern government of Kim Il Sung attempted to exploit Rhee's problems by initiating an all-out campaign for peaceful reunification of the country through general elections. Rhee attempted to stop the news of this offer from circulating in the South. With that encouragement, the northern government reiterated the proposal on June 19 and intensified its political offensive.

This North Korean initiative apparently fitted within a general strategy which Stalin was designing to counter two threats. In mid-May, Truman announced that discussions on a 'Japanese peace treaty would receive high priority. The negotiations would particularly consider Japanese independence and the establishment of American military bases on Japan's soil under long-term agreements. The talks, American officials observed, would not be burdened with Russian representation. For Stalin this announcement opened the unhappy prospect of unity between the two greatest industrial nations in the Pacific, perhaps even the extension of a NATO-like organization on the Asian periphery of the Soviet Union. The Sino-Soviet pact in February had singled out Japan as a potential threat to Asian Communism, and this had been followed by the Soviet press accusing Truman with attempting to "draw the Asiatic and Pacific countries into aggressive military blocs, to entangle those countries in the chains of some 'little' Marshall Plan for Asia."[1] On May 30, the

---

[1] *Current Digest of the Soviet Press,* II (April 22, 1950), p. 19.

Japanese Communist party climaxed weeks of demonstrations with attacks on United States military personnel in Tokyo. If North Korea could unify the country, peacefully or otherwise, the threat of a militarized, western-oriented Japan would be blunted, perhaps neutralized.

The second threat might well have caused Stalin even more concern. Mao's success had not created but probably encouraged revolutions throughout Asia, particularly in Indochina, the Philippines, and Indonesia. The possibility that some of these revolutions might triumph, perhaps following the pattern set by Mao, could weaken Stalin's two-camp premise and loosen his direction over the world Communist bloc. Stalin's view of world matters had become so rigid that he could not accept the nationalist content of these revolts without wrecking his own doctrines and tempering his grip on Soviet and satellite affairs. Malenkov had added to these troubles with his November speech, but by the spring of 1950 (that is, after the Chinese had shown their obstinacy in the Sino-Soviet negotiations and the revolutionary situation had intensified in Asia), Malenkov came back into line. In a speech in March, he no longer talked about the "friendly" nations surrounding Russia, but about a Europe, and especially Germany, which "fascist and revanchist forces," led by the United States, planned to turn into "a military-strategic bridgehead of American aggression." A speech by Molotov the same month was equally aggressive.[2] Stalin had confined the domestic debate; a short and successful war by a Russian-controlled North Korea could intimidate Japan and check the expansive aims and reputation of Mao. On June 25, large numbers of North Korean troops moved across the 38th parallel which divided the country. They followed Soviet-built tanks which had been shipped to Korea during the previous two months.

Attending to family business in Independence, Missouri, when the attack occurred, Truman immediately returned to Washington. He and Acheson assumed the invasion was Russian-directed, perhaps the beginning of an extensive Sino-Soviet thrust. Their initial reaction, however, was carefully measured. They ordered MacArthur in Tokyo to dispatch supplies to the South Korean troops. Then, moving to contain the action, Truman ordered the

---

[2] *Ibid.*, II (April 29, 1950), pp. 3–9.

CONFLICT IN KOREA, 1950-1953

RUSSIA

Vladivostok

CHINA   MANCHURIA

Yalu R.

Farthest penetration of U.S.
northward, Nov. 24, 1950

NORTH

Chosin
Reservoir   KOREA

JAPAN

SEA

Pyongyang

Armistice line, July 27, 1953

38th parallel

Inchon   Seoul

SOUTH

KOREA   Pusan perimeter
(farthest penetration
of North Korea southward)
Sept. 15, 1950

YELLOW

SEA   Pusan

Tokyo

JAPAN

PACIFIC

OCEAN

American Seventh Fleet to sail between China and Formosa, and
sent additional assistance to counter-revolutionary forces in the
Philippines and Indochina. In a hurriedly called session of the
United Nations Security Council, an American resolution brand-
ing the North Koreans as aggressors, demanding a cessation of
hostilities, and requesting a withdrawal behind the 38th parallel,
passed 9-0 with Yugoslavia abstaining. The Soviet Union was
not represented, for Yakov Malik continued his boycott to protest the exclusion of Red China. Two days later, as the military
situation worsened, Truman ordered American air and naval
units into action. That same day, the 27th, the United Nations
passed a resolution recommending that its members aid South
Korea in restoring peace. This passed 7-1 with Yugoslavia op-

posing and Egypt and India abstaining. Malik still had not appeared; the rapidity and extent of Truman's reaction had taken the Soviets by surprise.

The day after American units had been committed, the President conferred with Congressional leaders for the first time to inform them of his action. The only strong objection was voiced by Senator Taft who approved of Truman's action but disliked the sending of Americans to war without consulting Congress. Neither then nor later did the President discuss Taft's objection with the full Congress. Two days later, on June 30, Truman made the final commitment. The South Korean army of 65,000 men had suffered heavy losses in the first week of fighting. The President decided that only American ground units could stop the southward flood. In sending these troops Truman emphasized that the United States aimed only "to restore peace there and . . . restore the border." Supporting air attacks were similarly to be limited to the area around the 38th parallel.

Throughout the first week of the war the President carefully refrained from publicly linking the Russians to the attack. He hoped thereby to enable them to stop the aggression without loss of public face. On June 27 Truman dispatched a note to Moscow assuring Stalin that American objectives were limited; the President expressed the hope that the Soviets would help in quickly restoring the *status quo ante bellum*. Truman's immense concern about potential Russian involvement motivated the American statement on June 30 that the United Nations wanted only to restore the parallel as the dividing line, and also resulted in Truman countermanding Air Force directives of July 6 which ordered high-level photo reconnaissance over Russian ports.[3] The Soviets initially responded to Truman's overtures by accusing South Korean forces of invading North Korea. Within ten days this view underwent considerable change. The war was a "civil war among the Koreans," Deputy Minister of Foreign Affairs Andrei Gromyko claimed on July 4. Under these circumstances, Gromyko concluded, the Soviet Union could take no action.[4]

---

[3] Truman, *Memoirs*, II, pp. 341, 346.
[4] Max Beloff, *Soviet Policy in the Far East, 1944–1951* (London, 1953), p. 186.

Privately in June and publicly during the late summer, the Truman Administration became less restrained in defining the Soviet role. "In Korea the Russians presented a check which was drawn on the bank account of collective security," Acheson claimed. "The Russians thought the check would bounce. . . . But to their great surprise, the teller paid it."[5] The terms "collective security" and "U.N. action" became the catch-words which supposedly explained and justified Truman's decisions in late June. Both terms were misleading. The United States had no collective security pact in the Pacific in 1950. If the Japanese occupation served as an example of how collective security worked in the abstract, the American exclusion of Australia and Great Britain from control of Japan between 1945 and 1950 twisted collective security to mean unilateralism. As Acheson used the term "collective security," it meant the United States would both define the extent of the "collective" and unilaterally, if necessary, furnish the "security." Nor is there any indication that the President consulted his European or Asian allies before committing American air and naval units on the 27th.[6] This was not the first nor would it be the last time the United States would take unilateral action in an explosive situation without consulting its Western European partners.

As for the sudden American concern to bolster the United Nations, this had not been apparent when the United States acted unilaterally or with some Western powers to establish the Truman Doctrine, the Rio Pact, the Marshall Plan, and NATO. American actions in Korea were consistent with this history, for the United States used the June 27th resolution to establish a military command in Korea that took orders not from the United Nations but from Washington. "The entire control of my command and everything I did came from our own Chiefs of Staff," MacArthur later recalled. "Even the reports which were normally made by me to the United Nations were subject to censorship by our State and Defense Departments. I had no direct connection with the United Nations whatsoever."[7] Sixteen nations

---

[5] Acheson, *Pattern of Responsibility*, p. 254.
[6] For example, Truman, *Memoirs*, II, pp. 330–340.
[7] *Military Situation in the Far East*, p. 10.

finally contributed to "United Nations" forces, but the United States provided 50 percent of the ground forces (with South Korea providing most of the remainder), 86 percent of the naval power, and 93 percent of the air power. In October during the Truman-MacArthur conference at Wake Island, a dozen American officials prepared plans for the reconstruction of *all* Korea without consulting anyone, not even the United Nations or Syngman Rhee.

The American attitude toward the United Nations was exemplified on November 3, 1950 when American delegate John Foster Dulles successfully pushed through the General Assembly a "Uniting for Peace" proposal giving the Assembly the right to make recommendations to United Nations members for collective security measures, including the use of force, if the use of the veto stopped the Security Council from taking action. The resolution also established a permanent "Peace Observation Commission" to report on trouble spots around the world and, finally, invited members to contribute troops that could be used in a United Nations force. This resolution transfigured the United Nations. The organization no longer rested on agreements among the great powers, without which neither the United Nations nor world peace could be viable. Instead power was thrown into a body where Costa Rica had voting power equal to that of the United States or the Soviet Union. Weakening the Soviet veto, the United States also weakened its own. Assuming, however, that it could control the General Assembly, the Administration had taken a calculated risk; it had, to paraphrase Acheson, issued a blank check on the future. After a decade of increased neutralist feelings among the multiplying underdeveloped nations, that check would appear increasingly rubberized.

The United States suffered 142,000 casualties in Korea not for the sake of "collective security" or the United Nations, but because the Executive branch of the government decided that the invasion signaled a direct threat to American interests in both Asia and Europe. Europe, indeed, remained uppermost in the minds of high State Department officials. As the fighting raged in Korea, Acheson devoted increasing amounts of time to the European situation. The State Department had long defined Europe as having first importance. Acheson, moreover, had gotten burned politically and diplomatically when the Korean attack raised questions about his January 12th speech which termed the Communist threat in Asia one of "subversion and penetration," and not "military." This was a rare, probably traumatic, departure from his usual reliance upon military "positions of strength," and he moved quickly to improve the military balance in Europe. He did so, however, not solely for military objectives.

Acheson never believed that the military, political, or economic aspects of a problem could, in his words, "be separated in the intellectual equivalent of a cream separator." When General Omar Bradley, Chairman of the Joint Chiefs, once began discussing a problem with the words, "Well, from a purely military point of view. . . ," Acheson interrupted to ask that this phrase and its correlatives be taboo in all future meetings.[8] Viewing Europe in the summer of 1950, Acheson ranked the political problems ahead of the military concerns, although he used military means to obtain his political objectives. He knew that intelligence reports interpreted the Korean invasion as a "local affair" which did not apparently foreshadow a Communist attack in Europe; this interpretation was publicized by both Acheson and General Alfred Gruenther soon after the Korean attack.[9] Acheson consequently discussed Soviet capabilities, not what the Russians were about or even liable to do. When pressed on this point in February 1951, he candidly replied, "It is not only the threat of direct military attack which must be considered, but also that of conquest by default, by pressure, by persuasion, by subversion, by 'neutralism,' . . ."[10] He argued that future European political problems, which he defined as those threatening America's view of the world, be solved through the use of military policies. It was in this context, not in that of an imminent Russian invasion which very few expected, that Acheson proposed to horrified British and French officials that Germany be rearmed.

The Joint Chiefs had approved a German rearmament plan as early as April 1950. After the Korean outbreak, State Depart-

---

[8] Acheson, *Sketches From Life*, p. 103.
[9] Barnett and Raskin, *After 20 Years*, p. 29.
[10] Acheson, *Pattern of Responsibility*, pp. 90–94.

ment officials restudied the problem. During long and bitter discussions, the State and Defense Departments worked out a packaged deal in September. Germany would be rearmed and Western European qualms quieted with three devices: more American money to aid Europe with its financial problems, four to six divisions of American troops to assure Europe of American aid in case of future Russian or German aggression, and an integrated military command headed by an American general. Acheson had demanded military integration first, then German rearmament; he did not relish the task of selling German militarization to the British and French without the military command structure established. Secretary of Defense Louis Johnson sharply dissented; he wanted Germany first rearmed so that the necessary manpower would be available for the new command. Johnson temporarily won the argument just before Bevin and French Foreign Minister Robert Schuman sailed from Europe to meet Acheson at the Waldorf-Astoria Hotel in New York City for the September NATO Council meetings.[11]

On September 12, Acheson dropped, as one official called it, "the bomb at the Waldorf." To the unbelieving British and French he proposed the creation of ten German divisions. Bevin finally went along, believing that the French would never accept the plan anyway. Vandenberg recalled that when Congress had once proposed an international army with France in a subordinate position, it had "raised unshirted hell" among the French. The same response now erupted from Paris, only doubled by the additional proposal of a German army. Strong American determination to rearm the Germans, however, forced the French to retreat slightly. On October 25, 1950, Prime Minister René Pleven proposed to the French Assembly a plan for a European army in which men from all participating nations, including Germany, would be integrated at the lowest possible level, the regiment. The army would be part of the NATO command, but under the direct control of a European defense minister and political authority. Combined with the Schuman plan, Pleven explained, this would assure proper control of Germany. The

---

[11] Martin, "American Decision to Rearm Germany," in Stein, *Casebook*, pp. 653–659.

Assembly supported his proposal 349-235, but then revealed its true feelings by passing a resolution against German rearmament 402-168.

In December, the NATO Foreign Ministers discussed a compromise: German troops at the regimental level would be incorporated into the NATO establishment but not constitute more than 20 percent of its strength. Despite strong, last-minute Soviet protests which some officials believed threatened war if Germany was rearmed, the Foreign Ministers finally accepted in principle German participation, but they could not agree on details. The Ministers did approve an integrated force under a supreme commander. President Truman appointed General Dwight D. Eisenhower to this post on December 19. These agreements essentially represented the State Department's position of early September. The Defense Department now cooperated; the replacement in mid-September of Louis Johnson by General George Marshall as Secretary of Defense restored good relations with the State Department and made the Pentagon more responsive to the realities of European politics.

Truman and Acheson next sent four divisions of American soldiers to Europe in September. This immersed the Administration in deep political trouble. During Congressional hearings in April 1949, Acheson had assured touchy Senators that he expected no large numbers of American troops would be sent to the NATO command. Republican Senators had tried unsuccessfully to write legislation obligating the Executive Department to obtain Congressional authorization before troops could be sent. In early 1950, however, NSC-68 had proposed rapid and costly rebuilding of western defenses. The Korean conflict provided the opportunity to move ahead. Congress cooperated with Truman's request in July for an additional $4 billion of defense funds and a rapid buildup of the Army. The President announced on September 9 that this buildup would be followed by "substantial increases" in the number of American troops in Europe. To have the Administration that had "lost" China send troops to Europe while war was waging in Asia was too much for Republican and some Democratic politicians.

On January 5, 1951, Taft accused Acheson of misleading the American people with his April 1949 statement. Taft's timing was excellent; Chinese intervention had turned Korea into a nightmare for American officials, and just the month before, the French and British had proven most obstinate in cooperating with the United States plans for NATO. Truman hurriedly sent Marshall and Eisenhower among the rebellious Congressmen to explain that the serious European situation demanded four divisions but no more. After hearings in which Acheson described the troops as serving political as well as military objectives, the Senate on April 4 approved by a 69-21 vote a resolution proposed by John L. McClellan, a Democrat from Arkansas. This measure endorsed the Administration's proposals for NATO, including the integrated command; urged the military utilization of Germany, Italy, and Spain in order to protect Europe; and approved the sending of the four divisions but asked the President to send no more without consulting Congress. The Administration had successfully used the Korean War to create the framework within which European and general East-West problems would be discussed during the next decade.

This debate over the commitment to NATO did not occur in an atmosphere of congenial Executive-Legislative relations. The junior Senator from Wisconsin had just launched a new onslaught against "Communists," especially those in the State Department. The Tydings Committee report had quieted McCarthy somewhat until Korea exploded. As Cold War passions rise, rational public debate correspondingly sinks, and as the Korean War intensified, McCarthyism received a second life. "Today American boys lie dead in the mud of Korean valleys. Some have their hands tied behind their back, their faces shot away by Communist machine guns," the Senator wrote the President in mid-July 1950. These horrors occurred, McCarthy charged, because the Congressional program for Korea "was sabotaged."[12] He was not clear on the substance of that program, but during the following months he did not hesitate in condemning the man he believed to be the chief saboteur. George Catlett Marshall, former Army Chief of Staff, architect of military victory over Germany and Japan, Secretary of State,

---

[12] Joseph R. McCarthy to President Truman, July 12, 1950, Office File 20, Truman Mss., Truman Library.

now Secretary of Defense, was, McCarthy claimed, part of a "conspiracy so immense and an infamy so black as to dwarf any previous such venture in the history of man." Because Henry Stimson, a man with impeccable credentials as an anti-Communist and a conservative, had ranked Marshall only with George Washington, McCarthy felt compelled to have his aides document his accusations with a book on Marshall. The Senator himself probably never read the book through; if he did, he found no evidence to substantiate his charges.

Truman also considered Marshall one of the greatest Americans who ever lived, and the President began replying to McCarthy's charges by calling the Senator, among other things, the Kremlin's greatest asset. In the ensuing war of slanderous personal abuse, Truman did not stand a chance. McCarthy's use of the "multiple lie" (an accusation so long and containing so many untruths that no one could ever pin down all the lies at one time), and his repeated emphasis on so-called "facts" and "documents" in a society which easily accepts the superficial appearance of truth for the truth itself, made McCarthy invulnerable to Truman's retaliation.[13] Nor had Truman helped his cause by advancing his own conspiratorial view of Soviet activity and creating a noxious loyalty program. In 1949 and 1950 his Attorney-General, J. Howard McGrath, crossed the country protesting against professors of dubious political beliefs who infected student minds, pressed the need to bring increased numbers of anti-Communist speakers and literature to campuses, and warned that the "many Communists in America" were "everywhere—in factories, offices, butcher stores, on street corners." With such tactics, the President and the Attorney-General played into the hands of the spreading McCarthyism.

Soon few were free of suspicion. A McCarthyite line properly applied could end any controversy. "It seems that the only argument some persons can present is to holler about Alger Hiss and then refer to Yalta," Senator Tom Connally complained. "Every time something comes up, they get out a Communist and chase

---

[13] Rovere, *McCarthy*, pp. 110, 167–170. The book on Marshall is *America's Retreat From Victory; The Story of George Catlett Marshall* [n.p.] 1952.

him around."[14] In too many cases this sufficed. Even the Americans for Democratic Action, that staunch defender against the Progressives in 1948, fell under suspicion because its 1950 convention urged the abolition of the House Un-American Activities Committee and suggested ties, "sooner or later" with "the Chinese people." As soon as the Korean War erupted, the Americans for Democratic Action dropped any reference to the House Committee and continued to do so until 1959; it also modified its enthusiasm for the Chinese.[15]

Congress demonstrated its patriotism in September by passing the McCarran Internal Security Bill. A measure so confused that its supporters could not explain parts of it, the act required Communist organizations and their members to register with the Attorney-General. It did not call such membership a crime, but this was covered by the Smith Act of 1940 which prohibited membership in any group advocating violent overthrow of the government; if the Supreme Court declared the Communist party to be such a group, those registering under the McCarran Act would automatically incriminate themselves. With such conditions, skeptics doubted that registrars would be overwhelmed by people insisting on labelling themselves criminals. The bill also allowed the deportation of aliens who had been Communists, no matter when, and in time of war allowed detention of persons whether they were Communist or not. This legislation passed the House 354-20 and the Senate 70-7. Many Congressmen who hated it in private voted for it in public. Their political lives were at stake. Truman gave the bill a ringing veto on September 20, arguing that the act could not work properly and so would result in an even more repressive act in the future. The House took one hour to pass the act over the President's veto. The Senate did so after a handful of liberals led by Hubert Humphrey and Paul Douglas attempted a twenty-two hour filibuster. The political facts were plain for all to see, and the doubters were soon convinced by the results of the November Congressional election. The Republicans picked up twenty-eight seats in the House. In the Senate they won five more seats, and in three of

---

[14] Connally, *My Name is Tom Connally*, pp. 351–352.
[15] Brock, *Americans for Democratic Action*, pp. 143–144.

those contests (John Marshall Butler's victory over McCarthy-nemesis Millard Tydings in Maryland, Everett Dirksen's defeat of Majority Leader Scott Lucas in Illinois, and Richard Nixon's triumph over Helen Gahagan Douglas in California), McCarthy played a starring role in helping the winners.

The election occurred when American forces were advancing to greater victories in Korea. What magnifying effects a series of battle losses would have on Republican power and McCarthyism, Democrats did not wish to contemplate. General MacArthur had apparently removed this possibility on September 15 with a brilliant landing at Inchon, back of the North Korean lines, while simultaneously launching a counterattack from the shallow perimeter at Pusan. Within two weeks the United Nations forces joined to cut off large sections of North Korean troops. The Administration's political goals developed accordingly. In late June, Truman reported that the main objective was the restoration of the 38th parallel; on September 1, he told the nation that the Koreans "have a right to be free, independent, and united"; ten days later he approved a National Security Council recommendation that MacArthur should drive the North Koreans north of the 38th and, if encountering no Chinese or Russian troops, to move north of the parallel and prepare for occupation; on September 27, Truman ordered MacArthur north of the parallel; and on October 7, the General Assembly cooperated by endorsing Truman's order 47-5. That day the lead troops of the United States First Cavalry Division crossed into North Korea.

All eyes now turned to China. Throughout July and August, the new Communist government had made little response to the conflict. Recovering from famine, a quarter century of war, and having as her top diplomatic objective the conquest of Formosa, China did not pose an immediate threat to the United Nations forces. In late August, Foreign Minister Chou En-lai made his first important move. At the United Nations, American delegate Warren Austin asked for the open door "within all parts of Korea," and later in the month, Secretary of Navy Francis Matthews applauded "a war to compel co-operation for peace." At this point, Chou reminded the world that "Korea is China's neighbor" and urged that the neighbor's problems be settled "peacefully." Mass anti-American rallies began to appear in Chinese cities. Ten days after the Inchon landing Peking warned India, which had become China's main link with the Western world, that it would not "sit back with folded hands and let the Americans come to the border." After the first remnants of the North Korean troops retreated behind the 38th, Chou formally told India in a dramatic midnight meeting on October 2 that China would attack if United Nations troops moved into North Korea. The United States discounted this threat, believing that it was aimed at influencing upcoming votes on the conflict in the United Nations. MacArthur responded by issuing an ultimatum for the complete surrender of North Korea. On October 7, as the first American troops crossed the border, Chinese troop concentrations on the Manchurian border just across the Yalu River from Korea increased from 180,000 to 320,000. On October 16, a few Chinese "volunteers" crossed the Yalu.[16]

The Truman Administration remained convinced that China would not intervene. Emphasizing, as he had in earlier speeches, that China's immediate concern was with Russian penetration in the north, Acheson commented on national television on September 10, 1950, "I should think it would be sheer madness" for the Chinese to intervene, "and I see no advantage to them in doing it."[17] Acheson later admitted that until late September, American intelligence considered Chinese intervention improbable. On October 9, the danger reached the boiling point when two American F-80 jets strafed a Soviet airfield only a few miles from Vladivostok, a major Russian city close to the Korean border. After the Soviets strongly protested, the United States apologized. Vexed that such a crisis could arise, and angered that he had to back down before Soviet protests just a month before national elections, Truman cancelled a trip to Independence, where he was to watch his sister installed as Worthy Matron in the Order of Eastern Star, and flew to Wake Island to check on MacArthur's policies. In the heavily-censored text of that meeting, little was implied about Russia, but the General

---

[16] This account follows in most respects that of Allen Whiting, *China Crosses the Yalu* (New York, 1960).

[17] Acheson, *Pattern of Responsibility*, p. 265.

assured the President, "We are no longer fearful of [Chinese] intervention. We no longer stand hat in hand." The Chinese, he informed Truman, possessed no air force. They might move 50,000 or 60,000 men across the Yalu, but if these troops attempted to move farther south without air cover, "there would be the greatest slaughter."[18]

Eleven days later, on October 26, the first Chinese prisoner was captured, "so that you began to know, at that point," Acheson later commented, "that something was happening." This realization, however, made little apparent impact on American policies during the next four weeks. On November 21, advanced elements of American troops peered at Chinese sentries stationed several hundred yards across the Yalu. Three days later, MacArthur grandly announced the launching of the end-the-war offensive. At this point the United States government was still not certain whether, in Acheson's words, the Chinese "were committed to a full-scale offensive effort." Two days later, on November 26, the Chinese moved across the river in mass, trapping and destroying large numbers of United Nations troops, including 20,000 Americans and Koreans at the Chosin Reservoir; this outfit finally escaped with 4400 battle casualties and 7000 noncombat casualties, mostly severe cases of frostbite. Three weeks later the retreating United Nations forces once again fought below the 38th parallel, and now it was Chou En-lai who proclaimed his nation's intention of reunifying Korea. "They really fooled us when it comes right down to it; didn't they?" Senator Leverett Saltonstall once asked Acheson. "Yes, sir," the Secretary of State replied.[19]

Throughout September and October the United States had continually assured Peking that Americans never wanted to fight Chinese or threaten in any way China's vital interests. All the Administration wanted, the Secretary of State remarked on November 29, was to "repel the aggressors and restore to the

---

[18] U.S. Congress, Senate, Committee on Armed Services and Committee on Foreign Relations, *Substance of Statements Made at Wake Island Conference on October 15, 1950*, Compiled by General of the Army Omar N. Bradley (Washington, 1951), p. 5.

[19] *Military Situation in the Far East*, pp. 1832–1835.

people of Korea their independence." The Chinese retaliated precisely because they interpreted "independence" and Austin's request for "full access" to all Korea to mean the stationing of American power on China's doorstep. From there the United States could exert pressure on both Mao's internal and external policies.[20] China's intense hatred for the West, a hate nurtured by the just-concluded century of western exploitation of China, and Mao's determination to restore Chinese supremacy in Asia made impossible the acceptance of such an American presence. Although historically accustomed to hairsplitting on points of diplomacy, the Chinese failed to see the difference between American presence on the Yalu and American danger to Chinese industries and politics just across the Yalu.

Soviet thinking during November and December was more inscrutable than usual, but Stalin seems to have agreed with the Chinese that the United States could not be allowed to conquer all of Korea. Chinese intervention was a preferred preventive because it would not involve Russian men or large Soviet resources. Stalin meanwhile attempted to use the Chinese successes to pressure the West into reversing German rearmament policies.

In Washington, Administration officials were thoroughly frightened, and Truman's response to the intervention was considerably more explicit than Stalin's. The President reiterated that the United States had no "aggressive intentions toward China," and believed that the Chinese people opposed this sending of troops by their leaders. (This remark was in line with Truman's general theory that Communism anywhere never had popular support.) Because these people could not be heard, the President continued, the aggression must be crushed or "we can expect it to spread throughout Asia and Europe to this hemisphere."[21] As in late June, however, Truman's response was measured. He countermanded MacArthur's order to bomb Chinese troops and supplies in Manchuria. The President finally allowed only the Korean halves of the bridges crossing the Yalu to be bombed, a compromise that infuriated MacArthur and

---

[20] Whiting, *China Crosses the Yalu*, pp. 155–159.

[21] *Public Papers of the Presidents . . . Truman, 1950*, pp. 724–727.

told the Chinese exactly how restrained American retaliation to their intervention would be. In a news conference of November 30, Truman showed signs of losing this restraint. He intimated that the United States would use all the power it possessed to contain the Chinese, and he explicitly did not exclude using atomic bombs. This remark brought Prime Minister Attlee flying to the United States on December 4.

Attlee was not without responsibility for the crises; his government had participated in the decision to send United Nations troops to the Yalu. He now worried that in the newly expanded war Truman would not be able to control the military, and particularly wondered at the spectacle of Truman flying 5000 miles to Wake Island to meet MacArthur who had flown 1900. ("I thought it a curious relationship between a Government and a general," Attlee commented later.) The Prime Minister received Truman's assurances that the United States was not planning to use the bomb. The two men then undertook a full, candid, and most revealing evaluation of the Asian tinderbox.

Both agreed that a general war must be averted and that the United Nations forces should not evacuate Korea unless forced out militarily. Then basic differences emerged. Attlee argued that China's admission to the United Nations could bring her into regular consultations leading to a cease-fire. Acheson doubted that in their present advantageous military position the Chinese would want a cease-fire; if they did and negotiations resulted, Mao would next demand a United Nations seat and concessions on Formosa. The United States had refused to discuss these two items before the intervention and Acheson now was in no mood to reward aggressors. Attlee countered that a cease-fire would make explicit the divisions between China and Russia: "I want them [the Chinese] to become a counterpoise to Russia in the Far East," Attlee argued. If "we just treat the Chinese as Soviet satellites, we are playing the Russian game."

Truman now hardened his earlier view of the Chinese. They were "Russian satellites," and if they succeeded in Korea "it would be Indo-China, then Hong Kong, then Malaya." Acheson interposed that he did not think it mattered whether China was a satellite or not, for she would act like Russia anyway. He believed the invasion into Korea "had design," and, like Truman, adopted the domino theory to warn that any compromise with the Chinese would have a "serious" effect on the Japanese and Philippine islands. Acheson recalled a "saying among State Department officials that with communistic regimes you could not bank good will; they balanced their books every night." Therefore, he argued, the West must develop great military power to stop "this sort of thing from happening in the future." Acheson and Truman also reminded Attlee that the United States could not be "internationalist" in Europe and "isolationist" in Asia; domestic political pressures made that impossible.

At that point Attlee questioned the basic American premise, the fundamental belief that underlay United States policy in Europe as well as Asia. He emphasized that the United Nations must be kept together even if this meant alienating important segments of American public opinion. Whatever the United States and Great Britain did would have to be done through the United Nations, Attlee argued, and this could not be accomplished by the efforts and votes of only the United States and the United Kingdom, "important as we are."[22] Truman and Acheson disagreed; they believed the two nations were "important" enough. By controlling the United Nations forces and now, apparently, the United Nations itself through the "Uniting for Peace" resolution, American officials believed they could keep the American people united, prevent a bigger war in Asia, follow an "internationalist" policy in both Europe and Asia, punish China for moving into Korea by excluding her from the United Nations and Formosa, build up great military power throughout the world, and through it all keep the other United Nations members in agreement with American policies. It was a tall order, so demanding and inflexible that it fixed the American position on China for the next fifteen years.

American intelligence estimates reinforced Truman's and Acheson's views. A December 13 report stated that the Soviet Union hoped to use the war to move American power away from Korea and Formosa, establish China as the dominant power in the Far East and seat her in the United Nations, eliminate Ameri-

---

[22] Truman, *Memoirs*, II, pp. 396–411.

can power in Japan, and prevent German rearmament.[23] The Administration expected little help from the United Nations in thwarting these Soviet drives. The most the United Nations could do was brand the Chinese as aggressors, which it did on February 1, 1951 by a vote of 44-7 with 9 abstentions. As the United Nations debated, its forces retreated from the South Korean capital of Seoul.

Although the military situation steadily eroded, not even the other nations in the Western Hemisphere would offer much assistance. The Latin Americans dutifully voted with the United States on resolutions in the United Nations and the Organization of American States, but in the early spring of 1951, when Truman personally appealed to Latin American Foreign Ministers to "establish the principle of sharing our burdens fairly," only Colombia responded with troops. Several other nations sent materiel, but Latin America as a whole failed to see the relevance of Korea to their own economic deprivation and political instability. Later in 1951 a shocked Administration attempted to woo its southern neighbors by extending to them the Mutual Security Program of military aid. Eight nations took the money in 1952 to protect themselves against Communist aggression; this both giver and receiver interpreted to mean preservation of the *status quo*. No other Latin American nation, however, sent men to Korea.

The United States would have to depend primarily upon its own resources in defending what Niebuhr had called "our far-flung lines." In December and January, the President requested emergency powers to expedite war mobilization. Closely following the guidelines suggested in NSC-68, he submitted a $50 billion defense budget; this contrasted with the $13.5 billion budget of six months before. The Administration doubled the number of air groups to ninety-five and obtained new bases in Morocco, Libya, and Saudi Arabia. Army personnel increased 50 percent to 3.5 million men. Truman thereby placed the nation on the Cold War footing on which it would remain, with few exceptions, during the 1950s and 1960s.

---

[23] *Ibid.*, pp. 420–421.

The President also embarked the United States upon another costly and momentous journey by committing it to developing and protecting the Western Pacific and Southeast Asia. The riches of the area made it a formidable prize: Burma, Thailand, and Indochina provided rice for much of Asia; Southeast Asia produced nearly 90 percent of the world's natural rubber, 60 percent of the world's tin, and the bulk of Asia's oil. Movements toward independence threw the area into turmoil immediately after the war, but with several exceptions (particularly Vietnam and the Philippines where an Un-Filipino Activities Committee tried to aid the Army in ferreting out the "Huk" rebels), a semblance of order appeared by 1950. Attempted Communist uprisings had been contained in most countries by nationalist elements.

Throughout Asia these anticolonial, nationalist movements had triumphed either peacefully or after short struggles. Vietnam was a tragic exception. There Ho Chi Minh had conducted anti-Japanese underground operations during the war and emerged in 1946 as the leading Communist and nationalist leader. Roosevelt had pressured the French to evacuate Indochina in early 1945. De Gaulle resisted that pressure until the Truman Administration reversed the American policy in order to obtain French cooperation in Europe. After a year of uneasy truce with the French, who were determined to reclaim their control over Indochina, full-scale war broke out in December 1946. The French army moved back into Vietnam carrying large numbers of American lend-lease weapons to eradicate Ho's forces. The Soviets, like the United States, refused to recognize Ho's Republic of Vietnam. Typically distrusting such revolutionaries, Stalin, like Truman, concentrated on European problems in 1946 and early 1947. By 1948 Ho was turning to the Communist Chinese for aid. He had not easily reached this decision, for the Indochinese had historically feared and distrusted their giant neighbor. On January 18, 1950, China recognized Ho's government. The Soviets followed thirteen days later.

After an intensive policy review, the United States fully committed itself to the French cause. On February 6, four and one-half months before the Korean War began, the United States recognized the Bao Dai government which had been established by the French. On June 12, an American military advisory mission prepared to aid the French forces. As early as May, Truman discussed large-scale aid for Bao Dai, and after the Korean conflict, began to pump in aid at the rate of half a billion dollars per year. When French General de Lattre de Tassigny visited Washington in September 1951, the State Department endorsed French war aims and methods.

Although involving itself in the French struggle long before June 1950, the Korean war provided a convenient background as the United States began explaining its commitments in Vietnam. A State Department pamphlet of 1951 defined United States interests as the "much-needed rice, rubber, and tin," but added, "perhaps even more important would be the psychological effect of the fall of Indochina. It would be taken by many as a sign that the force of communism is irresistible and would lead to an attitude of defeatism." The statement concluded that "Communist forces there must be decisively conquered down to the last pocket of resistance"; to accomplish this, large amounts of American aid had been given. "Without this aid," the analysis concluded, ". . . it is doubtful whether [Bao Dai and the French] could hold their ground against the Communists."[24]

After mid-1950 Congress began its first systematic aid program to Southeast Asia. The Administration coupled with this economic approach a program for overall military security. The linchpin would necessarily be Japan, the most highly industrialized Asian nation and the only one capable of providing a counterpoise to the Chinese. For three years Truman had failed to write the peace treaty which would cement an independent Japan to the West. The Soviets naturally opposed the pact Truman had in mind, but another intra-Administration dispute between the Defense and State Departments also retarded progress. Defense feared a pact would weaken its hold on Japanese military bases, but State argued that healthy political relations demanded a new agreement.

In March 1950, John Foster Dulles assumed control of the

---

[24] U.S. Department of State, *Indochina: The War in Southeast Asia* (Washington, 1951), pp. 1–7; Dean Rusk, *The Underlying Principles of Far Eastern Policy* (Washington, 1951), p. 8222.

negotiations and almost single-handedly drove the treaty through to a successful conclusion in September 1951. It was a bravura performance. He silenced Defense Department critics by giving them a separate security pact assuring American bases in Japan. Russia was simply excluded from the early, decisive negotiations while Dulles talked only with Japan. When the Soviets finally were asked to participate, Dulles interpreted their proposal as an attempt to dominate the area around Japan; he read out the Russian resolution, one participant later recalled, demonstrated its effect on a map, "took this map dramatically and held it up like this . . . and then threw it on the floor with the utmost contempt. And that made a tremendous impression." [25]

After shrewd parliamentary maneuvering by Dulles, who led the American delegation, and Acheson, who chaired the conference, the treaty was signed by fifty-one nations at a San Francisco conference on September 8, 1951. Russia was not one of the signatories. The treaty restored Japanese sovereignty over the home islands, but not over the Ryukyus (which included the large American base at Okinawa) or the Bonin Islands; these remained in American hands. The agreement allowed Japanese rearmament and "the stationing or retention of foreign armed forces on Japanese territory." In the security pact signed the same day, Japan allowed the stationing of American troops and planes on her soil, but not those of any third power.

The Administration hoped that the treaty would serve as the basis for a long-lasting anti-Communist alliance. For this reason Dulles rode roughshod over demands from American allies and neutrals in Asia who demanded reparations from Japan for her occupation of those countries during World War II. Dulles retained vivid memories of how the Versailles Peace Conference in 1919, in which he had participated as a young economic adviser, had blundered by fastening unreasonably high reparations on Germany. Now, he warned, he would brook no "Carthaginian peace" which would "lead to bitter animosity and in the end drive Japan into the orbit of Russia." Many allies in the Pacific area also urged reparations in order to weaken Japanese war

---

[25] Interview with C. Stanton Babcock, in Dulles Oral History Project, Papers of Dulles, Princeton.

potential; their memories of 1941-1945 matched the vividness of Dulles' recollection of 1919. Dulles solved this problem by negotiating a series of mutual defense treaties to insure the Philippines, Australia, and New Zealand against both reemerging Asian giants, Japan and China. Thirty months before, Acheson had assured Senator Lodge that other than NATO, the Administration contemplated no further regional arrangements. On September 1, 1951 the United States signed with Australia and New Zealand the so-called ANZUS treaty, pledging the security of these two nations and establishing a foreign ministers council for regular consultation.

Because Australia and New Zealand belonged to the British Commonwealth, Great Britain was conspicuous by its absence from ANZUS. As early as March 1914, Winston Churchill, then First Lord of the Admiralty, predicted that with British resources increasingly devoted to Europe, the "white men" in the Pacific would soon have to seek American protection. Thirty-seven years later the British were not as understanding. Angered because Dulles had informed it neither of prior arrangements on the Japanese treaty nor of the discussions of ANZUS, the London government argued that ANZUS derogated British prestige and left the vital British areas of Hong Kong, Malaya, and Burma outside its defensive perimeter. Dulles granted these arguments, but countered that if Britain came in, the French and Dutch would also and thereby transform ANZUS in the eyes of suspicious Asians into a colonial alliance.[26] This argument effectively reduced British influence in the Pacific. "All roads in the Commonwealth lead to Washington," a Canadian official observed.[27]

These negotiations in late 1950 and 1951 determined the geographical extent of the American commitment in the Pacific. During the spring of 1951, with drama and flourishes seldom seen in American history, the military extent of that commitment was decided. In late January, United Nations forces opened a successful drive back to the 38th parallel. As the battle stale-

---

[26] Interview with General Matthew Ridgway, in Dulles Oral History Project, Papers of Dulles, Princeton.

[27] Quoted in Geoffrey Barraclough, *An Introduction to Contemporary History* (New York, 1964), p. 67.

mated along the former boundary line, State Department and Pentagon officials cautiously explored the possibility of negotiations with the Chinese on March 20. Three days later General MacArthur issued a personal statement urging that the Red military commanders "confer in the field" with him on surrender; if he could attack her "coastal areas and interior bases," the General insisted, China would be "doomed" to military collapse. MacArthur had again undercut his superiors in Washington.

As early as July 1950, he had shown reluctance to accept Truman's decision that Chiang Kai-shek should be contained on Formosa rather than unleashed on the mainland or allowed to ship troops to Korea. A month later, MacArthur sent a message to the annual convention of the Veterans of Foreign Wars, which the President viewed as an attack upon his policy toward Chiang. Truman angrily demanded that this message be recalled, and MacArthur complied although it had already been published. The Wake Island conference muted these differences, but the published minutes are embarrassing in their revelation of MacArthur's incredible condescension and Truman's tittering insecurity. Once the President was back in Washington, this insecurity disappeared. After MacArthur again recommended a naval blockade of China, air attacks to level Chinese military and industrial installations, and the use of 30,000 Formosan troops in Korea, Truman patiently explained on January 13 "the political factors" involved in the "world-wide threat" of the Soviet Union which made containment of the Korean war necessary.[28] When MacArthur issued his March 23rd ultimatum, Truman's patience, never inexhaustible, evaporated.

Only the method and timing of relieving the General remained to be decided. On April 5, Representative Joe Martin, the leading Republican in the House, read a letter from MacArthur which charged that "here we fight Europe's war with arms while the diplomats there still fight it with words." "We must win," the letter emphasized. "There is no substitute for victory." The Joint Chiefs of Staff agreed with Truman that MacArthur would have to be relieved immediately; reports from the field indicated that the General was losing the confidence of his men and had already

---

[28] *Military Situation in the Far East*, pp. 503–504.

lost confidence in himself.[29] On April 11, the President recalled MacArthur.

Truman knew the political dynamite in the decision. Less than two weeks earlier he had agreed with top advisors that an all-out speaking campaign would have to be undertaken by Cabinet-level officers because the Administration's " 'story' was not reaching the American public."[30] The American people preferred quick victory to containment. This preference was dramatically demonstrated when the General returned to the greatest popular reception in American history. Senator McCarthy expressed the feelings toward Truman of not a few Americans when with characteristic restraint he told a press conference, "The son of a bitch ought to be impeached." Congress warmly received MacArthur's speech before a joint session, then in April and May settled down to investigate the case of the President versus the General.

In a battle of MacArthur versus Truman, the long-range issues tended to be overshadowed by the personalities involved. In MacArthur's case this was not an advantage. Having last set foot in the United States fourteen years before, the General seemed unable or unwilling to grasp the political and social as well as the diplomatic views of his country. He revealed much describing the power he wielded in Japan between 1945 and 1950: "I had not only the normal executive authorities such as our own President has in this country, but I had legislative authority. I could by fiat issue directives." Although he had repeatedly advocated policies which contained the most somber worldwide ramifications, he now admitted having only a "superficial knowledge" of NATO and European affairs.

His basic message was curiously close to Truman's and Niebuhr's in 1948: because Communism posed a threat to all civilization, "you have got to hold every place." Or again, "What I advocate is that we defend every place, and I say that we have the capacity to do it. If you say that we haven't you admit defeat." Like Acheson, he insisted on not putting military power

---

[29] Philipps, *The Truman Presidency*, pp. 337–347.
[30] "Memorandum for the President," from Joseph Short, Secretary to the President, April 2, 1951, Office file 386, Truman Mss., Truman Library.

and politics into the intellectual equivalent of a cream separator; in time of war, however, MacArthur demanded the reversal of Acheson's priority: once involved in war, the General argued, the military commander must be supreme over all military and political affairs in his theater, "or otherwise you will have the system that the Soviet once employed of the political commissar, who would run the military as well as the politics of the country." Such a remark cut across the grain of traditional American policies of subordinating military to civilian officials unless the nation was involved in total war. This MacArthur assumed to be the case. When he heard the suggestion of Assistant Secretary of State Dean Rusk that war in Korea must not become a "general conflagration," MacArthur branded it "the concept of appeasement, the concept that when you use force, you can limit the force."

The General believed that by controlling the sea and air no one could "successfully launch an effort against us," but the United States could "largely neutralize China's capability to wage aggressive war and thus save Asia from the engulfment otherwise facing it." He expressed contempt for the Chinese Communists. "Never, in our day, will atomic weapons be turned out of China. They cannot turn out the ordinary weapons." Nor was there threat of Soviet intervention. Time, however, was short. If, as MacArthur once told Forrestal, Europe was a "dying system," and the Pacific would "determine the course of history in the next ten thousand years," victory must be won immediately. The "dreadful slaughter" had to end, MacArthur pleaded; American blood as well as dust is settling in Korea, and the "blood, to some extent" rests "on me." But now, he concluded emotionally, "There is no policy—there is nothing, I tell you, no plan, or anything."[31]

The Administration had a plan, and Acheson outlined it in his testimony after MacArthur finished. Korea must be viewed as part of a "collective security system," Acheson argued. When so viewed two things readily became apparent. First, all-out war in Korea would suck in Russian force to aid Stalin's "largest and most important satellite." "I cannot accept the assumption

---

[31] *Military Situation in the Far East*, pp. 39, 45, 54, 66–68, 78, 81, 83, 86–87.

that the Soviet Union will go its way regardless of what we do," the Secretary of State declared. If Russia did intervene, there could be "explosive possibilities not only for the Far East, but for the rest of the world as well." Unlike MacArthur, Acheson insisted on keeping the European picture uppermost in dealing with Korea. (Truman once added a variant on this: expansion of the war could "destroy the unity of the free nations," the President declared. "We cannot go it alone in Asia and go it with company in Europe.") Second, if Europe and the prevention of Russian entry in force did comprise the main objectives, American forces were not engaged in a "dreadful slaughter," or as Acheson remarked, "a pointless and inconclusive struggle," but had "scored a powerful victory" by dealing "Communist imperialist aims in Asia a severe setback" in preventing the armed conquest of all Korea.[32]

MacArthur lost the argument. He lost it so decisively, moreover, that while negotiations to conclude a stalemated war fitfully began in Korea during the summer of 1951, Acheson accelerated the military buildup of Europe.

---

[32] *Ibid.*, pp. 924–926.

CHAPTER VI

New Issues, New Faces (1951-1953)

THE MacArthur hearings epitomized a wide-ranging debate over American foreign policies during the twenty-four months before the 1952 presidential election. Viewed from the vantage point of fifteen years later, the importance of this debate is not limited to those particular months, but has grown with time until historians of the mid-1960s can discover at that early point the turn of American thinking that led the nation into the involvements, particularly in Asia, of the next decade. One can also observe the beginnings of the dissent which would later divide American liberals and split intellectuals from policy-makers. If the period is extended to 1953, it is equally important for Soviet policy, but with one difference: the internal debates arising out of the Party Congress of late 1952 and Stalin's death five months later marked an end to an epoch in Russian history. In the United States the debates signaled the beginning of new directions in American policy.

By the time the *de facto* armistice was agreed upon in July 1953, the Korean War had made as much impact upon American aid to Europe as to Asia. The agreement in principle upon German rearmament and the sending of additional American troops to Europe were major steps in this direction. American strategy in NATO during 1951 and 1952 rested first upon the "tripwire" theory that any Soviet attack upon a NATO command containing American troops would automatically trip a nuclear attack from the United States. One European official stated this theory in elementary terms; when asked how many American soldiers must be stationed in Europe to protect the West, he replied one would be enough if that one was shot during the first wave of an

123

attack. To further its nuclear capability, the United States conducted its first successful thermonuclear test at Eniwetok Island
in the Pacific during March 1951. A year later the American
army began infantry practice with atomic cannon and other
nuclear field pieces at Yucca Flats, Nevada. In mid-June 1952,
the keel went down for the USS *Nautilus*, the first submarine to
be powered by atomic energy. Truman proposed a $60 billion
defense budget for 1952, 20 percent above that of 1951. If the
wire was tripped, the United States was preparing to respond
massively.

NATO strategy also rested upon the hope that the war could
be contained east of the Elbe. For this, a large conventional force
would be needed; Eisenhower wanted thirty-five to forty ready
divisions and ninety-six more which could be brought up within
a month. The present three hundred aircraft would have to multiply ten times. These grandiose plans, Truman observed,
"tripped over one hard, tough fact. This fact was the poverty
of western Europe."[1] Three years after the launching of the
Marshall Plan, the recipient nations were sinking back into an
economic morass. Industrial production and favorable dollar balances had risen in Europe until mid-1950, although they did not
rise as rapidly or with the stability that economic officials wished.
With the outbreak of the Korean War and the quickening American demands for European armament, the defense expenditures
of European NATO countries shot up 50 percent between 1950
and 1951 to $8 billion. In terms of the gross national production
of these far-from-recovered economies, this meant an increase
in military expenditures from 5.3 percent in 1950 to 7.6 percent
in 1951. At the same time the price of raw materials upon which
European industries depended rose 40 percent between June and
November 1950, and 20 percent more in 1951 and 1952.[2] Only
Germany gained ground; it used the new concern over military
power to rearm and end the Allied occupation of its territory.
The other Europeans discovered that jamming their meager resources into defense spending produced scanty results. They

---

[1] Truman, *Memoirs*, II, p. 258.
[2] Charles Wolf Jr., *Foreign Aid: Theory and Practice in Southern Asia*
(Princeton, 1960), pp. 115–116.

owned more conventional arms in a nuclear era and lost resources that they had hoped to invest in their own overseas empires.

Some nations attempted to bolster their economies with increased exports to the Communist bloc. These shipments included goods that, many Americans feared, would greatly aid the Sino-Russian war machines. Congress retaliated by passing the Kem Amendment and the Battle Act which in certain circumstances cut American aid going to those nations that exported strategic goods to Communists. Another response was more positive. In 1951, Congress passed the Mutual Security Act which coalesced the economic, military, and technical assistance programs. This allowed an injection of a stronger military emphasis than ever before. As Acheson remarked, the "whole impact" of MSA would be "to carry out the rearmament program," for, he somehow concluded, the Marshall Plan's "original task has been accomplished."[3]

NATO strategy, as well as Cold War politics, rested also on a third approach: that the basis of the alliance be expanded as far as possible. In May 1951, the United States proposed adding Greece and Turkey to the military pact in order to prevent those two nations from entertaining ideas of becoming neutral politically. Yugoslavia, although not wishing to enter NATO, began requesting military assistance in addition to the economic aid that it had already obtained from the West. In September 1951, the Western Foreign Ministers agreed to release Italy from restrictions imposed in 1945 upon her military. Most notable was the rapidly evolving American attitude toward Franco's Spain.

Kennan had observed in 1947 that the Truman Doctrine implied a new view of Franco. By 1949, a Congressional-Defense Department axis had formed to force the issue. Senators Pat McCarran, Owen Brewster, and Robert Taft urged the Administration, in Taft's words, to "shake loose from its communist-front philosophy" by working with Franco. One Congressman, among the many who junketed to Madrid in 1949 and 1950, publicly called the Spanish dictator a "very, very lovely and loveable, character." Lower-echelon naval and air force officers heartily cooperated; they wanted bases as widely dispersed, as

---

[3] *Ibid.*, pp. 114–116.

close to the Soviet bloc, and as independent of British bases as possible. In several secret meetings in McCarran's Senate office, these Pentagon officers and Congressmen charted political strategy. In March 1950, McCarran succeeded in securing a $62.5 million loan for Franco. For ideological reasons, Truman despised this and every other pro-Spanish move, but after June 1950, the logic of his own military policy forced him to recognize the Franco government late that year. The following summer the Administration began negotiations to obtain Spanish military bases. On August 25, 1953, the Spanish Ambassador to the United States pinned the special medal of the Grand Cross on McCarran for the Senator's exceptional devotion to Spain. A month and one day later the base treaty was completed. Franco had driven a hard bargain. The United States granted economic assistance and a quarter-billion dollars of military aid in return for the right to construct and use military bases which would remain under Spanish sovereignty.[4]

The Spanish base treaty augmented American military power in Europe but contributed less to Acheson's political objectives; most of Western Europe too vividly remembered Franco's co-operation with Hitler. The political aims rested instead on the success of the Pleven Plan and German rearmament. To the accompaniment of shrill Soviet protests, the Western Foreign Ministers worked on these issues throughout 1951, then gathered at Lisbon in February 1952 to hammer out final ground rules for the new Western alliance. Agreement did not come easily. The big four split down the middle on the form of German rearmament as well as on other problems. "More often than not, I found myself agreeing with . . . Adenauer," Acheson recalled, "and Eden [agreed] with Schuman."[5]

The French and British split, however, on the critical issue. The Pleven Plan had been transformed in earlier negotiations into a European Defense Community (EDC) comprised of France, Germany, and the Benelux. EDC would operate under

---

[4] Theodore J. Lowi, "Bases in Spain," in *American Civil-Military Decisions: A Book of Case Studies,* edited by Harold Stein (Birmingham, Alabama, 1963), pp. 667–697.

[5] Acheson, *Sketches From Life,* p. 47.

separate European control, but be linked with NATO so Germany could directly participate in NATO defenses. Schuman and the Netherlands officials now insisted that Great Britain formally join EDC. They did not want to be in the EDC virtually alone with German power, and refused to consider American and British presence in NATO sufficient to control the possibility of German domination of the new grouping. The newly elected government of Winston Churchill refused to commit itself so solidly to European affairs. Too many Anglo-American ties would be severed. Any British integration into European affairs would have to come "in doses rather than at a gulp," Eden later remarked.[6] Acheson could not settle this dispute by quieting the French fear. Several months after the Lisbon conference, President Auriol of France told the Secretary of State "with considerable passion," as Acheson later recalled, "that our policy toward Germany was a great mistake. He knew Germany; he reviewed German history since Bismarck. We were wrong in thinking that the greater danger came from Russia. It came from Germany."[7]

Acheson finally obtained Schuman's consent to allow 500,000 Germans in twelve divisions to enter the EDC, but the French exacted a price. Adenauer agreed to allow Western forces to remain in Germany for internal security as well as military purposes, swore to deal with Russia only through the Allies, and allowed the West to continue governing Berlin. Acheson opened wide the American and German pocketbooks, promising to aid France meet her defense expenditures in Vietnam and Europe. For this, Acheson even won an agreement to double NATO manpower to fifty divisions (including twelve French) by the end of 1952.

There would never be fifty NATO divisions, there would never be an EDC. In the long run, the Lisbon Conference produced much ill will. Acheson's troubles began immediately after the conference adjourned. On March 10, the Soviets proposed to the three Western powers that discussions be held on a peace treaty which would declare Germany united and independent.

---

[6] Anthony Eden, *Full Circle: The Memoirs of Anthony Eden* (New York, 1960), p. 34.
[7] Acheson, *Sketches From Life*, p. 53.

Russia further suggested allowing Germany to have a national army with ties neither to the East nor West, withdrawing all foreign troops, and admitting Germany to the United Nations. This breathtaking proposal came out of cold Russian fear of a rearmed, Western-oriented Germany. It might have been a propaganda ploy, a mere delaying tactic. Or it might have been an opportunity to neutralize Germany and drastically reduce the Cold War tensions infecting the Central European cockpit which had germinated so many hot wars in the past.

No one will ever know what the Soviets meant. Acheson refused to follow up the proposal. At this point, his diplomacy stood revealed not as the building of "positions of strength" to facilitate negotiations for the easing of East-West conflict, but the building of strength so that such negotiations might be avoided. The West had to be kept together. This meant Germany had to be rearmed under Western guidance. The "peace offensive" out of Moscow was a " 'golden apple' tactic," Acheson announced in April. The Soviets resembled the Goddess of Discord who, angered that she had not been invited to a wedding party, threw a golden apple over the fence "hoping to cause a ruckus among the guests and break up the party."[8] The wall would be built higher to make such apple-throwing more difficult, and so on May 26 and 27 Acheson, Eden, and Schuman signed the agreement ending the occupation of Germany. They then initialed the EDC treaty. Now the EDC had only to pass the various parliaments before coming into effect. In France, however, its chances did not appear rosy, nor were they helped when the United States Congress cut Acheson's promise of $750 million in aid to France back to $525 million.

When a transfigured defense arrangement finally appeared in 1954, it resembled the Marshall Plan in marking the end, not the beginning, of a central phase of American foreign policy. Even as Acheson threaded his way through the EDC negotiations of 1951 and 1952, Americans vigorously debated new policies which by the middle-1950s would set their foreign policies on new paths. In short, the debates of 1951-1952 thrashed out the

---

[8] Dean Acheson, "Progress Toward International Peace and Unity," *Department of State Bulletin*, XXVI (April 28, 1952), p. 648.

premises which would govern American foreign policy for at least the next decade and a half. At the simplest level, the arguments pivoted on the question of whether Asia should enjoy equal priority with Europe in American policy. Overall, the debate was far more complex. It became a prime example of how over-simplified (often unquestioned) premises of one historical era could, almost inevitably, develop into apparently unrelated but far-reaching policies affecting life and death in a later era. Chiang's defeat on mainland China, American involvement in Korea, and the sending of additional United States soldiers to Europe initiated the debate. The MacArthur Hearings greatly intensified it. Then the arguments were systematically reformulated and can now be found in Senator Robert Taft's *A Foreign Policy for Americans*, Hans Morgenthau's *In Defense of the National Interest*, Reinhold Niebuhr's *The Irony of American History* and, finally, the 1952 election campaign.[9]

Taft's and Morgenthau's books chalked in the boundaries of the debate. Like the vast majority of Americans, both men agreed on the need to contain Russia. They substantially differed on the means to accomplish this, and it was on the issue of these means that the argument was waged. Morgenthau was a distinguished professor of international relations at the University of Chicago and Taft was running for the 1952 Republican presidential nomination, but despite their different vantage points, the two men surprisingly agreed on a number of issues. Both considered the United Nations, particularly after the passage of the "Uniting for Peace" resolution, to be a fifth wheel in world diplomacy; both badly oversimplified their argument by tracing the origins of the Cold War back only to the 1945 Yalta and Potsdam conferences. More fundamentally, both feared that Truman and Acheson used insufficient restraint in employing American power. Morgenthau attacked Acheson for harping about "positions of strength" when "the supreme test of statesmanship," to Morgenthau's mind, was not building power blocs but discovering areas in which tensions could be reduced through

[9] Robert A. Taft, *A Foreign Policy for Americans* (New York, 1951); Hans J. Morgenthau, *In Defense of the National Interest* . . . (New York, 1951); Reinhold Niebuhr, *The Irony of American History* (New York, 1952).

negotiations. Morgenthau did not believe Acheson could stand up to that test.

On four basic points, however, the Senator and the Professor profoundly differed. Taft tended to see the Cold War as a crusade against the Anti-Christ, and he bolstered this view by emphasizing the purity of American intentions. Morgenthau realized the unique virtues of American democracy, but he held no brief for the spotlessness of American morality or ideology. After all, he was not running for office. Nor in this particular did he share Taft's view of history, for Morgenthau believed that the new technological and political problems, which appeared in 1945, marked "the definite and radical end of the . . . conditions under which the Western world lived for centuries." The professor drily observed that Russia's use of the "religious order" of Communism to remake the world in its image was not unlike those Americans who "heed the noble words of Jefferson, Wilson, and Franklin D. Roosevelt, and . . . set out on a crusade to make the world safe for true democracy." A moral commitment to save the world from Communism, particularly if that commitment was grounded in a past that was increasingly irrelevant, destroyed the clarity of view needed by the United States for survival.

Taft would not entirely discard military power. He advocated the development of air and naval units but not the infantry. He believed that this policy would save manpower, cut military expenditures and, in all, be politically attractive. Taft could also in this way slash the Executive power to involve the United States in European problems through the commitment of American troops. Morgenthau would have none of this. He deplored the common tendency of both Taft and the Truman Doctrine to lay out "a world-embracing moral principle" that committed American power, of whatever nature, to such broad, undefined, and dangerous limits. The United States must realize, Morgenthau admonished, that military threats to American interests in Europe call for different solutions than the dangers posed by "genuine revolutions" in Asia. American policy-makers must follow not the dictates of "moral principle," but the classic formula of spheres-of-interest. The United States could no longer wish for an open world. It would have to accommodate itself to the realities of power, and anyone who refused to believe in balances of power, Morgenthau added, resembled "a scientist not believing in the law of gravity."

The professor considered the spheres-of-interest approach feasible because the Soviet threat was powered not by Communist ideology but by traditional Russian national power. Unlike the religious passion of Communism, Russian national power could effect compromises because it was subject to the same restraints and limitations as American power. Taft, on the other hand, viewed Communist ideology as the principal threat. He cared little whether it was attached to Soviet national power, except that by being so attached, its power became immeasurably increased. The Senator, therefore, refused to settle for the spheres-of-interest approach, for this would not neutralize Communist ideology; instead, he advocated fighting Communism everywhere, including inside the labyrinthine bureaucracy of the State Department. Here Morgenthau sharply scored Taft. Many "anti-communists," the professor observed, talk about protecting American security when they really mean protecting the "security of the status quo" at home and abroad.

These differences on the roles of morality, the place of power, and the nature of the Soviet threat inevitably led Taft and Morgenthau to opposite conclusions on the climactic question of Asia. The Senator deplored past American policy which treated Western Europe like one big happy family while allowing Asia to go Communist almost by default. Running close to the MacArthur line, Taft sought "only . . . the same policy in the Far East as in Europe." That is, he wanted the use of air and naval power as a deterrent in both Europe and Asia. In case of a conflict, his policy lessened the chances for limiting the war short of nuclear exchange, but he could reply that by making no further commitments in Europe and by allowing European nationalisms to solve their own problems, that area would remain stable while in Asia no power would be able to challenge American naval and air power. He left unanswered the question of how this naval and air power could deflect the considerably more subtle threat of Communist ideology.

Morgenthau necessarily reversed Taft's priorities. Europe, particularly Germany, he argued, comprised such a technological, industrial, and cultural powerhouse that "he who controls all of Europe is well on his way toward controlling the whole world." Europe could not be left to chance, possibly to Communism. A further point necessarily shaped American policy: the United States could understand and cooperate with Europe because of common backgrounds and values. Asia, however, was immeasurably different. Unlike the "phoney" revolutions in Eastern Europe, those in Asia were "genuine." This meant that Russian imperialism and "genuine" revolution were by no means the same thing. To confuse the two could lead to an American involvement in Asia which would be calamitous. Asian revolutions, Morgenthau observed, were generated not by Communism but, ironically, by the West's political, technological, and moral revolutions which the West transferred to the Orient. Once Asia mastered this technology, a "shift in the distribution of power" would result which, "in its importance for the history of the world, transcends all other factors. It might well mean the end of the bipolarity centered in Washington and Moscow." Given their different race and culture, Americans could not hope to control this momentous change, but only adjust to it. The United States had no real means of dealing with "genuine revolutions" in non-Western lands.

In 1951 and 1952, Niebuhr neatly combined Taft's emphasis on ideology with Morgenthau's conclusions. Partly because of such feats, one observer called Niebuhr's views "part of the canon of a new generation of American liberals and the spiritual guide of those who are now revisiting conservatism."[10] More significant than his appeal to various shades of the political spectrum was Niebuhr's change of tone. Something had happened to the earlier advocate of a quickly revitalized Germany; now he acknowledged that the rearming of Germany "was too precipitate and too indifferent" to European feelings. The battle cry of 1948 to guard the far-flung battle lines became a quiet listing of the reasons why American policy-makers must not become overly committed to battle lines in the underdeveloped world, especially Asia. Niebuhr now lectured the wielders of the titanic American power that they too were subject to the sins of all mankind.

---

[10] Morton White in *New Republic*, May 5, 1952, pp. 18–19.

The Irony of American History argued that because of pride, presumed innocence, and lack of restraint, American power was walking the rim of the abyss. American idealism, which had been instrumental in developing immense national power, now ironically blinded the United States to the dangers of overusing that power. "American power in the service of American idealism," Niebuhr approvingly quoted a European official as saying, "could create a situation in which we would be too impotent to correct you when you are wrong and you would be too idealistic to correct yourself." In addition, not even extensive use of this power could solve fundamental American dilemmas. This provided a second irony: a century or two before, when their power was much less, Americans could solve their problems more easily than now.

To Niebuhr, Communism remained as evil as it had been in 1947 and 1948, but the United States had become the victim of many of the same inconsistencies and delusions about human nature and the so-called virtues of science that had corrupted Communism. In the past, Americans had been protected from themselves by the Constitution, whose authors knew more about human nature and the limitations of science than their twentieth-century descendants. They had been protected also by the good fortune that in having blown hot and cold in their dedication to remake the world, Americans had been saved by their own historical inconsistencies. Niebuhr cited John Adams: "Power always thinks it has a great soul and vast views beyond the comprehension of the weak; and that it is doing God's service when it is violating all his Laws." Niebuhr extended Adams's observation by adding that Americans believed they could solve problems simply "by the expansion of our economy." The frontier, Niebuhr intimated, had closed; expanding production "has created moral illusions about the ease with which the adjustment of interest to interest can be made in human society."

In the penultimate section of *Irony*, Niebuhr applied his views to the Asian situation. The United States, he echoed Morgenthau, had little in common with the Orient. Any attempt to use the present American Cold War weaponry to save Asia from Communism would be, as he had mentioned earlier in the book, like the "spears of the knights when gunpowder challenged their reign." In phrases not untinged with condescension, Niebuhr warned that Asia wanted Western technology, but refused to accept the West's view of man, society, or history. He advised working with Japan and the Philippines to contain Asian Communism by means of a militarized Pacific "island littoral." So contained, Communism would repeat the history of Islam during the Middle Ages and be destroyed "not so much by its foes as by its own inner corruptions." But if it hoped to witness that collapse, the United States would have to remedy its own "inner corruptions" first.

Niebuhr's fear of extending the Cold War to the mainland of Asia partly explained the changed tone in his writings. No doubt the explosion of the Russian atomic bomb, the growth of McCarthyism, and the Truman Administration's fervent dedication to remolding Europe also gave the theologian pause. Above all, Niebuhr feared that the new Republican Administration of Dwight D. Eisenhower could commit the ultimate transgressions in foreign policy. A year earlier, in 1951, Niebuhr had looked with much concern on the rising influence of businessmen and Republicans on foreign policy formulation. Eisenhower's victory transformed this influence into domination: "His victory was significantly engineered by eminent proconsuls of the budding American imperium, partly drawn from the Army and partly from business." Niebuhr feared the effect of this victory upon Washington's Asian policies, for "American conservatives" viewed Communist gains in that area as resulting from State Department perfidy

and as capable of rectification by rigorous military action on our part. This "illusion of American omnipotence," . . . is a natural mistake of a commercial community which knows that American hegemony is based upon our technical-economic power but does not understand the vast complexities of ethnic loyalties, of social forces in a decaying agrarian world, of the resentments which a mere display of military power creates among those who are not committed to us.[11]

Niebuhr's abhorrence of "the budding American imperium" did not noticeably brake the Eisenhower steamroller in 1952.

---

[11] Reinhold Niebuhr, "The Foreign Policy of American Conservatism and Liberalism" in *Christian Realism and Political Problems* (New York, 1953), pp. 58, 64.

The General won on a platform that committed the Party to save Asia and with a campaign in which he refused to repudiate McCarthyism. Adlai Stevenson ran a more literate and less successful campaign for the Democrats, but significantly patterned his appeal after that of Eisenhower's in two respects: Stevenson refused to embrace the record of the Truman Administration with any enthusiasm (at one point asking privately that Acheson publicly announce his intention to resign after the election); and once went farther than Eisenhower in a specific commitment to save Asia.

On October 24, the Democratic nominee warned that to withdraw American troops from Korea and allow "Asians to fight Asians," as the General wanted, "we would risk a Munich in the Far East, with the probability of a third world war not far behind." Unlike Eisenhower, Stevenson did see indigenous nationalism, not international Communism, at the root of the Asian upheavals but, as the campaign progressed, Stevenson's dedication to Asia and his determination to apply military strength in the area seemed to increase as Eisenhower's declined. On September 4, the Republican candidate explained how the United States must protect "the far corners of the earth" which provided the nation with "materials essential to our industry and our defense." Yet on October 24, when he dramatically pledged, "I shall go to Korea" he advocated as a military backstop only the building up of the South Korean forces and shaping "our psychological warfare program into a weapon capable of cracking the Communist front." This was a less militant course than Stevenson was advocating in a speech that same day.[12]

Beneath the Eisenhower moderation, however, was the less-restrained Republican platform. It contrasted "Russia's 'Asia first' policy" with "the 'Asia last' policy" of the Truman Administration. "We have no intention to sacrifice the East to gain time for the West," the platform echoed MacArthur. It went further. "Containment is defensive," one plank read, "negative, futile and immoral [in abandoning] countless human beings to a despotism and Godless terrorism." John Foster Dulles, who was largely responsible for these sections of the platform, later

---

[12] *New York Times*, October 25, pp. 1, 8.

announced in a campaign speech at Buffalo, New York, that the new Republican Administration would, if elected, use "all means to secure the liberation of Eastern Europe." When Eisenhower heard this, he immediately phoned Dulles to inform him that the phrase should have read "all peaceful means." "Yes," Dulles promptly replied, "It's just a complete oversight."[13] It was a strange oversight for a renowned international lawyer who had spent forty years honing words to great precision.

Behind Eisenhower also loomed the figure of Joseph McCarthy. We will "eliminate" from the Federal government, the platform pledged, those "who share responsibility for the needless predicaments and perils in which we find ourselves." This was a rather loose definition of malfeasance, but the Republicans were not to be denied the profit of hammering the point at the voters. "There are no Communists in the Republican Party," began one long party plank.[14]

Eisenhower's speeches were not that blunt. He also refused to invite General Douglas MacArthur to participate in the campaign, although this would have appeased a large number of conservative Republicans. Eisenhower, however, never publicly repudiated McCarthy's activities. That would not have been sound politics. Sitting on the same stage with McCarthy in Milwaukee, Eisenhower held a speech paying loving tribute to General George Marshall, who had been a sponsor of Eisenhower's rise in the military but termed a traitor by McCarthy. At the last minute, Eisenhower bowed to McCarthy's brand of Americanism and deleted the tribute.

Stevenson and many other Democrats seemed particularly open to the charge that, as one McCarthyite journal phrased it, "Chinese coolies and Harvard professors are the people . . . most susceptible to Red propaganda." At Wheeling, West Virginia, in 1950, McCarthy had declared that it was "not the less fortunate" Americans who "have been selling this nation out, but rather those who have had all the benefits." Those "bright

---

[13] Interview with Dwight Eisenhower, Dulles Oral History Project, Papers of John Foster Dulles, Princeton.

[14] *Documents of American Foreign Relations*, 1952, edited by Clarence W. Baier and Richard P. Stebbins (New York, 1953), pp. 80–85.

young men" in the State Department who were "born with silver spoons in their mouths are the ones who have been worse." Such attacks on the "Eastern intellectual establishment" paid dividends, especially when voters were reminded that Acheson and Stevenson had rushed to the defense of Alger Hiss. Many of "the less fortunate" supported McCarthy and the Republicans, and thus one more group left the New Deal coalition. Polls revealed that the most earnest supporters of the Wisconsin Senator were the small businessmen, who felt squeezed between the big unions and big corporations, and manual laborers. Other support came from the new wealth groups (such as oil wildcatters and real estate manipulators), ethnic groups such as Irish and Germans determined to prove their "Americanism" and, paradoxically, some Eastern intellectuals who had prayed to the Communist "God Who Failed" in the 1930s and now attempted to gain redemption by embracing either McCarthy's causes, effects, or both.[15] These groups endorsed the Senator's definition of McCarthyism as "Americanism with its sleeves rolled." No Republican politician without quixotic tendencies tried to buck that slogan in 1952.

Having won on issues that Republican Senator Karl Mundt neatly formulated as K_1C_2—Korea, Communism, and Corruption—the Eisenhower Administration's foreign policy could not be impervious to McCarthy or the Cold War mentality which had spawned McCarthyism. Unlike 1948, foreign policy played a central role in the 1952 campaign,[16] and the campaign in turn left its mark on the foreign policy of the following months. In early 1953, the new Chief Counsel for McCarthy's committee, Roy M. Cohn, and a friend, David Schine, junketed throughout Europe upbraiding American diplomats supposedly soft on Communism, attacking United States Information Service libraries for exhibiting the work of such "radicals" as Mark Twain and Theodore Dreiser, and provoking the wrath of the European

---

[15] Seymour Lipset, *Political Man: The Social Bases of Politics* (New York, 1960, pp. 171–172; Daniel Bell, *The End of Ideology; On the Exhaustion of Political Ideas in the Fifties* (Glencoe, Illinois, 1960), pp. 110–112; Rovere, *McCarthy*, p. 13.

[16] Angus Campbell, Gerald Gurin, and Warren E. Miller, *The Voter Decides* (Evanston, Illinois, 1954), pp. 46, 67, 119.

press. Secretary of State Dulles did nothing to stop Cohn and Schine. On the contrary, Dulles accepted the appointment of a McCarthy adherent, Scott McLeod, as the State Department's Personnel and Security Officer. McLeod now supposedly held the power of passing upon all appointments in the Department. Dulles helped by circulating a memorandum demanding "positive loyalty" from all personnel. One veteran diplomat recalled that this "did not go down very well" with the Foreign Service officers who had served faithfully through many administrations.

The test came when Dulles, without consulting either McCarthy or McLeod, suggested Soviet expert Charles Bohlen as Ambassador to Russia. The Senator immediately unleashed an attack that centered on Bohlen's role as Roosevelt's interpreter at Yalta. Bohlen correctly assured Dulles that there was nothing injurious in his past record. The Secretary of State was glad to hear this, since, as he sighed, "I couldn't stand another Alger Hiss." Dulles, however, did little to aid Bohlen, refusing even to have pictures taken of them together. The appointment finally went through the Senate only after Eisenhower and Taft worked out a deal whereby Taft and Senator John Sparkman, Democrat of Alabama, closely examined Bohlen's record in confidential State Department files, and the President promised not to make any more major appointments to which McCarthy might object.

Within four months after taking office, the Administration bragged that it had fired 1,456 federal employees under its "security program." The program had not, however, uncovered one proven Communist. So challenged, the Democrats replied that they had effectively fired even more "risks" under Truman's loyalty program.[17] In the midst of this frenzy, one distinguished American Foreign Service officer who had never been tainted by any McCarthyite accusation commented, "If I had a son, I would do everything in my power to suppress any desire he might have to enter the Foreign Service of the United States."[18] One doubts that this is what Dulles meant when he remarked, in early 1953, before a Senate Committee that the "most change that is needed"

---

[17] Rovere, *McCarthy*, pp. 17–18, 32–33.
[18] Emmet John Hughes, *The Ordeal of Power; A Political Memoir of the Eisenhower Years* (New York, 1963), p. 91.

in American foreign policy "is a change of heart. . . . It is the spirit and not the letter, as you know, which, according to the Bible, is a very important thing."[19]

The Secretary of State frequently quoted his favorite Biblical quotation: "All things work together for good to them that love God, to them who are called according to His purpose." He once remarked that people often forgot about the last part of that phrase: "The promise comes true only to those who love God and who are in harmony with his purpose."[20] Like Truman, Dulles had few doubts about the allegiances of the Creator. The Secretary nevertheless left little to chance. He built his power base within the Administration with great care. No Cabinet officer in American history ever had a closer working relationship with a President than did Dulles. Remembering the difficulties that his uncle Robert Lansing had as Secretary of State under Woodrow Wilson when Lansing tried to operate independently of the President, Dulles took pains to maintain contact with Eisenhower. When competing power centers began to appear in the White House under the aegis of Harold Stassen or Nelson Rockefeller, Dulles moved ruthlessly to maintain sole control of foreign policy. "He cut off Nelson at the ankles," was the way one official described the encounter. "With my understanding of the intricate relationship between the peoples of the world and your sensitiveness to the political considerations involved," Dulles supposedly told Eisenhower, "we will make the most successful team in history."[21]

Few could challenge Dulles's grasp of world events. He had learned much about Europe as a young law student at the Sorbonne, although that particular training in French and Latin law evidently gave his mind a caste which diplomats trained in Anglo-Saxon law, such as Anthony Eden, had difficulty in fathoming. As a senior partner in the distinguished law firm of Sullivan and Cromwell of New York City, Dulles operated regu-

---

[19] U.S. Congress, Senate, Committee on Foreign Relations, 83rd Congress, 1st Session, *Nomination of John Foster Dulles, Secretary of State-Designate*, January 15, 1953 (Washington, 1953), p. 4.

[20] Dulles to John Nagel, January 21, 1952, Correspondence, Papers of John Foster Dulles, Princeton.

[21] Sherman Adams, *First-Hand Report* (New York, 1961), p. 89.

larly during the 1920s and 1930s out of the firm's Paris and Berlin offices. He had undertaken his first important diplomatic mission in 1919-1921 under Wilson, and had served with the Truman State Department on important assignments. The press widely reported that he was Dewey's pick for the Secretaryship in 1944 and 1948, although, as Dulles later remarked, "We suddenly woke up that that was a little bit premature."[22]

In Cabinet meetings few took issue with him. "After all," Sherman Adams remarked, "how are you going to argue with a man who has lived with a problem—for instance, in respect to Iran—for longer than most of us knew there was such a country?"[23] John Quincy Adams had been the most recent Secretary of State whose training for the post rivaled Dulles's, and Adams had departed from the Department in 1825. Dulles usually carried the Cabinet along with him on his choice of diplomatic moves, but his inability and unwillingness to make the Pentagon and Secretary of Treasury George Humphrey subordinate to his own policies drastically cut his options in foreign affairs. He could override Secretary of Defense Charles Wilson's retort to the proposal that East-West trade be eased ("Well," Wilson had commented, "I'm a little old-fashioned—I don't like selling firearms to the Indians,"[24]), but Dulles seldom attempted to adjust the Pentagon to his overall policies. He deferred to the military. This meant he also deferred to Humphrey who admired Air Force General Curtis LeMay's idea of maintaining peace with relatively cheap nuclear bombs carried by the Strategic Air Command. Humphrey, on the other hand, abhorred "some of the Army generals" who wanted larger budgets to develop armies for conventional ground warfare; they were "just Army-minded morning, noon, and night," Humphrey complained. "If you gave a nickel to anybody, the Army had to have a lot more."[25] He demanded, and got, "a completely new military posture" by cutting the defense budget and giving LeMay much of what the

---

[22] Interview with Eisenhower, Dulles Oral History Project, Princeton.
[23] Interview with Sherman Adams, Dulles Oral History Project, Princeton.
[24] Hughes, *Ordeal of Power*, p. 76.
[25] Interview with George Humphrey and Herbert Hoover, Jr., Dulles Oral History Project, Princeton.

Air Force wanted. This approach might have worked better if the Defense, Treasury, and State Departments had broken as well with the Truman Administration's views of Communist strategy.

Dulles instead stiffened those views at the same moment he sliced his possible policy alternatives by cooperating with Humphrey and refusing to fight McCarthy. This rigidity proved singularly unfortunate, since the Soviet Union, during those early days of the Eisenhower Administration, was also undergoing dramatic changes which suddenly opened new possibilities in East-West relations. In August 1952, Stalin surprised the world by calling the 19th Party Congress to convene on October 5. Although such Congresses are to convene every three years, thirteen years had elapsed since the 18th session of 1939; and although the conclave theoretically constituted the Party's highest authority, in reality there had been no dissent in a Congress since Trotsky was thrown out in 1927. The Soviet dictator obviously had a task for the Congress to perform.

Western officials doubted that the Congress would ease tension. Throughout 1951 and 1952, Stalin had enforced a tough foreign policy line by nearly doubling the Soviet Army to 4.9 million men and increasing defense expenditures by fifty percent. At the Kremlin he was carefully watching a growing intra-Party struggle for power between Georgi Malenkov and Nikita Khrushchev. That fight could turn Soviet policies into new, unknown, and perhaps highly dangerous directions. Malenkov was to make the keynote speech of the Congress. Since 1949 he had become identified with the relatively peaceful, consumer-oriented faction of the Party. Three days before the Congress opened, however, Malenkov's keynote speech suddenly became much less important.

On October 2, Stalin published his *Economic Problems of Socialism*, a text enunciating the main line of Soviet domestic and foreign policies. This set the tone for the Congress. The Soviet dictator announced not only that primary emphasis would continue to be placed on heavy industry, but that state ownership must be extended over portions of the agricultural economy that had long remained in the hands of agricultural collectives. He attacked "some comrades" and "voluntarists" who believed that the Soviets could "do anything," warning that the regime must adhere to "objective economic laws" that had been followed under his rule. This sharply disappointed any who had hoped for an easing of internal repression.

Stalin then assaulted those who challenged his foreign policies. The West, he predicted, would soon be overwhelmed by economic catastrophe. Communist successes since 1945 had contracted the capitalists' market. This contraction had so aggravated the Western economic system that the capitalists would soon begin a death struggle among themselves. Because the United States had placed Western Europe, Germany, and Japan on a "dole," Stalin observed sarcastically, "some comrades" see only "the external appearances which glitter on the surface." "To think that these countries will not attempt to rise to their feet again, smash the U.S. 'regime' and break away on a path of independent development is to believe in miracles." (Malenkov dutifully repeated this section in his keynote address.) This development, Stalin concluded in a brief speech at the Congress, indicated two courses for Communists: the tightening of Party control to prepare fully for the protection of the bloc against capitalist warfare, and cooperative efforts with nationalists everywhere, but especially those in Germany, Japan, and France, in order to accelerate the revolt against American control.[26]

In his keynote message, Malenkov slightly hedged his parroting of Stalin's remarks by observing that a capitalist war could severely test the Soviet system. This speech, however, was anticlimactic. The theme of the Congress was a renewed emphasis on the inevitability of war. This was only partly tempered by Stalin's and Malenkov's remarks upon the desirability of international peace movements, united fronts, and a German treaty. The strategy toughened while the means softened. A second, more implicit theme also became apparent. The Congress emphasized through omission the Soviet domination of the Com-

---

[26] J. V. Stalin, "Economic Problems of Socialism in the U.S.S.R." in *Current Soviet Policies; The Documentary Record of the 19th Communist Party Congress and the Reorganization After Stalin's Death*, edited and with an introduction by Leo Gruliow (New York, 1953), pp. 1–10, 235–236. This is an exceptionally useful compendium of primary documents which emerged from those events between October 1952 and April 1953.

munist world. Although Chinese officials attended and spoke, only insignificant references to China occurred in the hundreds of thousands of published words uttered by Russians at the Congress.

A third result of the Congress became the most significant. In an apparent attempt to cement his control over both the Malenkov and Khrushchev factions, Stalin announced at the Congress the creation of a new Politburo, to be named the Party Presidium, consisting of twenty-five instead of eleven members. The new additions would be fervent young Stalinists. This stroke cut the present and potential power of both Malenkov and Khrushchev while giving Stalin even greater authority. In January 1953, Stalin's power received further impetus from an important article which appeared in the Party's leading theoretical journal, *Kommunist*. After elaborately developing the "capitalist encirclement" doctrine, the analysis concluded that because of the growth of the Western economic crisis and the success of the international Communist movement, not détente but "a fierce struggle against the enemy" must now be pursued. Here was perhaps the most extreme and explosive culmination of the Stalinist line that had been resurrected in the speech of February 9, 1946.[27]

On January 13, 1953 concrete evidence dramatically appeared to support the "capitalist encirclement" thesis. A group of Kremlin doctors was suddenly arrested by Soviet security police for the killing of Zhdanov in 1948 and were accused of being in the hire of American and British espionage agents. *Pravda* warned that the conspiracy provided clear proof of the capitalist danger. Some observers believed the episode indicated Stalin's firm belief that an East-West détente of any kind, including possible armistice in Korea, was impossible. Closer to the ruling circles of the Kremlin the "Doctors Plot" had another meaning, for it uncomfortably resembled the circumstances which surrounded the murder of Sergei Kirov in 1934. Stalin had used the death of that high party official as an excuse to launch a bloody four-year party purge. As the "Doctors Plot" unfolded,

---

[27] *Ibid.*, p. 105, has Malenkov's speech; the *Kommunist* article is analyzed in Tucker, *Soviet Political Mind*, pp. 30–31.

Stalin evidently made indirect threats to lives of Central Committee members, including some as close to him as Molotov and Mikoyan. These threats, apparently, were the breaking-point. On February 17, the Chief of Security in the Kremlin who had protected Stalin for thirty years suddenly was announced by the Soviet press to be dead. Within three weeks Stalin fell victim to what was officially termed "hemorrhage of the brain."

Georgi Malenkov quickly assumed Stalin's old roles as both Chairman of the Council of Ministers, the foremost policy-making post, and Secretary of the Communist Central Committee, the key Party job. Malenkov immediately cut back the Politburo membership to eliminate the new Stalin appointments. (Leonid Brezhnev and Aleksei Kosygin were among the first to go.) [28] The new policies rested domestically on the power of the "collective" rather than on the whims of one man, or so the new Kremlin leadership announced. Malenkov issued amnesties for a number of political prisoners and also announced that those accused and prosecuted by the late dictator in the "Doctors Plot" had now been found not guilty. The confessions, announced the Soviet press, had been obtained "through the use of impermissible means of investigation which are strictly forbidden under Soviet law."

This final twist to the "Doctors Plot" indicated changes in Soviet foreign policies, changes which Malenkov confirmed in a speech before the Supreme Soviet: "At the present time there is no disputed or unresolved question that cannot be settled peacefully by mutual agreement of the interested countries," he announced. "This applies to our relations with all states, including the United States of America." [29] The new leadership soon gave evidence of this change by allowing Russians married to foreigners to leave the country, re-establishing diplomatic relations with Greece, Israel and later Yugoslavia, withdrawing former objections to the appointment of a new Secretary-General of the United Nations, renouncing Soviet claims to Turkish territory, and, most important, agreeing to an end to the Korean War. These words and acts assumed new importance when con-

---

[28] Edward Crankshaw, *Khrushchev, A Career* (New York, 1966), pp. 185–187.
[29] Gruliow (ed.), *Current Soviet Policies*, pp. 249–251, 256–260.

trasted with Mao Tse-tung's eulogy of Stalin. The Chinese leader reiterated the two-camp policy in prophesying that Stalin's "force" would even in death bring "all who still groan under the oppression of the old, vice-stained capitalist world . . . to a bold assault against the enemies of the people."[30]

Neither the contrast between Mao and Malenkov nor the significance of the change from Stalin to Malenkov brought any immediate overall change in the policies of John Foster Dulles. In part this was due to an ensuing two-year struggle for power between Malenkov and Khrushchev, a power struggle which distorted the importance of the Soviet policy changes. To a much greater degree, however, the lack of change was due to the after-effects of Korea and McCarthyism. The economic impact of these forces could be measured by the more than quadrupling of defense expenditures between 1950 and 1953. At this point the nation assumed the Cold War economic and military posture in which Americans would remain long after the end of the Korean fighting; this change was particularly noticeable when compared with the military budgets of 1946-1949. The psychological and political effects, however, were immeasurable. Militarily the Korean War was "limited." It did not move beyond the Korean peninsula, neither side employed atomic weapons or the full extent of their conventional forces, and both sides finally settled for the restoration of the 38th parallel. Its nonmilitary effects were less limited and, when combined with McCarthyism, fixed Americans in a rigid position from which they found difficulty in moving to explore the newly opened possibilities of easing the Cold War.

---

[30] *Ibid.*, pp. 253–255.

CHAPTER VII

A Different Cold War (1953-1955)

FORMER SECRETARY OF THE TREASURY George Humphrey recalled his impressions of Washington when the Eisenhower Administration moved into power. "We were under war controls," Humphrey remembered, "and we were in war."[1] Entering office as the struggle continued in Korea, the President pledged that he would more efficiently and successfully wage the Cold War against Stalinist Russia. "Let's face it," one Republican adviser had remarked in early 1952. "The only excuse for Ike's candidacy is that he's the man best qualified to deal with Stalin."[2]

In early March 1953, Stalin died. The Cold War that began to confront Eisenhower and Dulles during their first months in power assumed new and puzzling traits. Georgi Malenkov assumed Stalin's place in the Soviet government, but he did not appropriate the departed leader's foreign policies. Malenkov instead began urging friendly negotiation in Europe and peace in Korea. Rapid changes in other parts of the world also began to confuse Americans. The Republicans had won with a platform promising more military firepower and a firming up of the containment policy, but new international crises increasingly revolved around rampaging nationalisms in the Middle East, Latin America, and Southeast Asia rather than around military problems in Europe or Korea. As Morgenthau and Niebuhr had foreseen, the Eisenhower Administration was soon engaged in a new kind of Cold War.

---

[1] Interview with George Humphrey and Herbert Hoover Jr., Dulles Oral History Project, Princeton.

[2] Norman A. Graebner, *The New Isolationism* (New York, 1956), p. 98.

Immediately after Stalin's death, American intelligence informed the President that the new Soviet Premier would have to consolidate his internal control and consequently would not undertake new departures in foreign affairs.[3] Many Americans believed that Stalin's death would create a chaos which might permanently damage Soviet power, or at least force a long, painful, and unproductive transition period upon new leadership. This did not happen. The possibility of one-man rule by Malenkov apparently disappeared after a severe intra-Party struggle. He maintained his Premiership, but surrendered the key post of First Party Secretary to Nikita Khrushchev.

A precarious collective leadership emerged as Malenkov, with his power based on the technicians and government bureaucracy, and Khrushchev, with his strong support from the Party, began a struggle for supreme power. The first important casualty in the battle was Lavrenti Beria. When Beria moved too fast and overtly in making the secret police his own political tool, the new rulers arrested and executed him in July. In stark contrast to Stalin's methods, however, Beria was probably the only victim of execution within the high Party hierarchy. While conveniently blaming Beria for many of the excesses of previous years, Malenkov cautiously moved to liberalize the functioning of the Party and demanded a reduction of investment in heavy industry so that Russians could enjoy more consumer goods.

This policy of relaxation was soon extended to foreign affairs. If the Western alliance was unable to agree upon such ventures as the European Defense Community in the present "tense international situation," Malenkov observed to the Supreme Soviet on August 8, 1953, "a lessening of this tension might lead to [the] disintegration" of that alliance. The Premier, however, hedged his bet. In the same speech he announced that the Soviets had successfully tested a thermonuclear, or hydrogen, bomb. With the American thermonuclear monopoly broken, the Soviets stood ready to negotiate on European problems. To strengthen their position further, they dropped their emphasis on revolution by an international proletariat and attempted to influence West-

---

[3] Dwight D. Eisenhower, *The White House Years: Mandate For Change, 1953–1956* (Garden City, New York, 1963), pp. 148–149.

ern policies by playing upon the peace hopes of the European middle classes.[4] Malenkov could effectively make such an appeal, for he was able to parade his internal reforms as proof of his desire for more liberal and peaceful policies, while at the same time pointing to his new thermonuclear weapon as a hint of what might occur if tensions continued to mount.

The American response to these Soviet changes was slow and unsure. The Washington bureaucracy was fearful and confused, partly because of its terror of the ubiquitous McCarthyism, partly because of the usual problems found in changing governments. Underneath this confusion lay a deeper problem. Soviet Communism, Dulles told the Senate Foreign Relations Committee in January, "believes that human beings are nothing more than somewhat superior animals . . . and that the best kind of a world is that world which is organized as a well-managed farm is organized, where certain animals are taken out to pasture, and they are fed and brought back and milked, and they are given a barn as shelter over their heads." Apparently the Secretary of State had read George Orwell literally. "I do not see how, as long as Soviet communism holds those views," Dulles concluded, ". . . there can be any permanent reconciliation. . . . This is an irreconcilable conflict."[5] By defining the conflict as so intensely ideological, Dulles severely limited the possibility of easing tensions through a flexible diplomacy.

On April 16, 1953, Eisenhower made the first formal response to Malenkov's new tactics. If the Soviets sincerely desired a détente, the President remarked, there must be "free elections in a united Korea," the end of Communist revolts in Malaya and Indochina, "United Nations control and inspection" of disarmament, "a free and united Germany, with a government based upon free and secret elections," the "free choice" of governments in Eastern Europe, and a treaty restoring Austria's independence.[6] The day following this address, Dulles appeared before the Senate Foreign Relations Committee; his testimony was head-

---

[4] *Current Digest of the Soviet Press,* V (September 5, 1953), pp. 3–12, 26.
[5] U.S. Congress, *Nomination of Dulles,* pp. 10–11.
[6] Department of State, *American Foreign Policy, 1950–1955, Basic Documents.* 2 vols. (Washington, 1957), I, pp. 65–71.

lined by *The New York Times* as "Dulles Bids Soviet Cooperate or Face Vast West Arming." The Secretary emphasized that the Soviet peace moves would not endanger French ratification of EDC; the chances for passage, he added, were better than they had been four months before. Dulles would not allow the threat of a thaw to endanger the Western alliance.

Within a month, however, the American approach was questioned by the most eminent statesman within that alliance. Without previously informing either Eisenhower or his own Foreign Office, Winston Churchill announced on May 11 that the time had arrived for world leaders to confer "on the highest level" to see which problems might be solved. The Prime Minister indirectly attacked Eisenhower's demand that a multitude of questions would have to be settled at once. This was obviously impossible and, moreover, might unfortunately "impede any spontaneous and healthy evolution which may be taking place inside Russia." Churchill instead recommended a piecemeal approach, tackling solvable problems but assuming all the while that Russian security must be assured. Another theme also appeared in the speech. Great Britain would defend its own interests, Churchill warned, particularly in the Middle East where nationalism threatened Suez; this would be accomplished without help from "the United States or anyone else." The Prime Minister was trying to bring the United States into an East-West détente while, at the same time, cutting back his ties with Americans as he dealt with the whirling problems of nationalism in the newly emerging nations.[7]

Senate Majority Leader William Knowland responded by accusing Churchill of "urging a Far Eastern Munich." The official Washington response was characterized as "cool." Eisenhower explained why to a news conference: "The world happened to be round and it had no end and he didn't see how you could discuss the problem, the great basic problems of today, which were so largely philosophical in character, without thinking in global terms," or so reported the official text of the conference.[8]

---

[7] *New York Times*, May 12, 1953, pp. 8–9.
[8] *New York Times*, May 15, 1953, p. 6.

The President was arguing that because the Soviet menace was basically ideological, or "philosophical," it was also indivisible and thus posed a threat everywhere in the world. One implication followed: problems in Europe and those in Asia were linked and could be approached with similar strategies. A second implication was that the ideology posed a worldwide threat regardless of whether the Soviets possessed the military, economic, and political power to support that ideology globally. In a sense, this seemed an accurate appraisal, for Communism could become disruptive in areas closed to Soviet arms. But Eisenhower's approach led to confusion, for it blurred over the fact that the ties between Communist ideology and other types of Communist power varied greatly in different parts of the world.

The Administration later discovered the dissimilarities between underdeveloped areas and Europe when it tried a NATO-like approach to stabilize Southeast Asia. The lesson on the relationship between ideology and other forms of power occurred immediately. In May 1952 and again in January 1953, Dulles condemned "containment" as a "policy which is bound to fail because a purely defensive policy never wins against an aggressive policy." He advocated instead "liberation of these captive peoples" in Eastern Europe through such "processes short of war" as "political warfare, psychological warfare and propaganda." In late May 1953, the Soviets loosened political controls in East Germany, but also demanded more production from workers for the same wages. Laborers protested with a march down East Berlin's Stalinallee on June 16. The next day began with a general strike and demonstrations which climaxed with the tearing down of Communist flags and demands for free elections. The American radio in West Berlin broadcast encouragement to the workers and lauded the spreading of the strikes throughout East Germany. Then suddenly Soviet tanks appeared in Berlin, Dresden, Leipzig, Magdeburg, and Jena. As the armor smashed the demonstrations, Dulles made no move. "Liberation" had failed its first test and had done so in Germany, the European prize of the East-West struggle.

Facing the problem of captive peoples in North Korea shortly after, the Administration came up with a more satisfactory, if not exactly happy, solution by recognizing the limits of its military and political power. Eisenhower's trip to Korea in December 1952 buttressed his belief that the United States should not be entrapped in a conventional war on the Asian mainland. For his own reasons, Secretary of Treasury Humphrey supported this view. One-third of the budget had to be cut to eliminate deficit spending, Humphrey told the President, and that means "you have to get Korea out of the way."

To get Korea "out of the way," the Administration first employed what would later be called "brinksmanship." Returning from Korea on December 14, Eisenhower warned that unless the war ended quickly, the United States might retaliate "under circumstances of our choosing." Six weeks later in his first State of the Union Message, the President announced that the American Seventh Fleet would "no longer be employed to shield Communist China." He hurriedly added that this meant no intended aggression "on our part," but this so-called "unleashing" of Chiang Kai-shek so frightened England and France that Dulles flew to Europe to reassure the Allies. As tension mounted, Stalin conveniently died. The new Soviet leaders hinted their willingness to sponsor negotiations. On the crucial question of prisoner exchange (the United Nations forces reported that many North Korean and Chinese prisoners did not want to return home and should not be compelled to do so), the Chinese suggested on March 30 that prisoner repatriation be placed in the hands of international authorities. On April 23, armistice talks recommenced, but Dulles soon concluded that the Chinese were raising unnecessary barriers to a peace. On May 22, he hinted to Peking through Indian diplomats that if peace was not forthcoming the United States would bring in atomic weapons. The next day the State Department issued more moderate instructions on the prisoner exchange problem.

Within eleven days the Communists accepted the plan with minor changes. They held to the agreement even after President Syngman Rhee of South Korea tried to sabotage the negotiations by releasing 27,000 Chinese and North Korean prisoners on June 18. The seventy-eight year old Rhee was outraged that the American acceptance of a division roughly along the 38th parallel would prevent him from ever ruling a unified Korea. The final armistice was signed on July 27. Talks in 1953 and 1954 on reunification failed, and the United States proceeded to pour six billion dollars of aid into South Korea between 1954 and 1966. Industrial production tripled, exports increased eight times to nearly $250 million, and the economy became increasingly self-sufficient. Rhee was not as fortunate politically. He fell from power after students rioted against his autocratic regime in April 1960, and was replaced by a military-controlled government. The North Korean government also endured political upheavals, although on lower levels, and rebuilt its air force with hundreds of modern Soviet fighter planes. The United States installed tactical guided missiles with atomic warheads pointing northward. Outside Panmunjom, where negotiators still gather to insult one another, grandstands and loudspeakers accommodate tourists who like to witness this spectacle of international diplomacy and peer out over the desolate, bare hills where thousands of men died in a "limited" war.[9]

Many lessons were to be learned from the Korean involvement. Dulles chose to apply most of them to both Europe and the rest of Asia. Far Eastern affairs are "closely related to our work here and to the defense of Europe," the Secretary told the NATO Council of Ministers on April 23, the day the Korean talks commenced. Military defenses in both areas must be bolstered, he continued, and Malenkov's peace overtures could not be allowed to prevent the completion of EDC. Dulles artfully pointed out, particularly to the doubting French, that although the Kremlin used new phrases, it had also just launched "the carefully planned and prepared offensive" in Laos, a French colony. In his European policies, Dulles made Germany the pivot. As a lawyer in Germany between the wars he admired the German people; as a bulwark against Soviet expansion he prized Germany's location, industrial power, and military potential; and through a steadily developing friendship with Konrad Adenauer, the Secretary enjoyed a similarity of views which he had with no other world leader.

In July 1953, Dulles made these views clear to everyone. Following the Churchill speech in May, Russia had proposed a coalition of East and West Germans to prepare a peace treaty which would neutralize Germany; then, and only then, Germany could have free elections. In July, Dulles rejected this procedure. He proposed instead that free elections first be held throughout Germany and then a peace treaty be drawn. The Russians would have none of this, particularly after Dulles also insisted that EDC could not be involved in the discussions; if a reunited Germany wanted to rearm and tie itself to the West through EDC, Dulles thought it should be able to do so. Dulles continued these strategies inherited from Acheson in the belief that any immediate détente was impossible, for, as he had told a distinguished assemblage of European statemen, "the Soviet leaders are to a very large extent the prisoners of their own doctrine which is intensively held by their followers, who are fanatics." The Russians "look upon anybody who is not for them as against them; and . . . as we know, the leaders of Soviet Russia are not subject to any moral inhibitions against the use of violence where it will serve their purpose."[10]

Accepting the *status quo* in Europe, or at least the *status quo* once the French formally endorsed EDC, Dulles turned to ponder the problems of the newly emerging areas. These now required more and more attention. He hoped to build into those areas many of the same military and political institutions which had established the *status quo* in Europe. This policy moved from the assumption that disturbances anywhere outside the Iron Curtain usually worked against American interests sooner or later. This view was not uncommon in American thinking, although it had made a relatively recent appearance in the nation's history.

From the Declaration of Independence until the Civil War, Americans generally sympathized with revolutions abroad. In several respects, however, they dispensed their sympathy with care. They disliked revolutions that went beyond the political, social, and economic boundaries of their own. Americans also believed their own revolution superior to revolutions on the "right" (as John Quincy Adams viewed the Latin American upheavals) or on the "left." They best liked revolts on the North American continent, such as those in Florida, Texas, California,

---

[10] "Statement of Secretary Dulles at April 23 Session of North Atlantic Council Ministers' meeting," Conference Dossiers, Dulles Papers, Princeton.

and Canada, which opened up possible areas for annexation to the expanding Union.

In the middle of the nineteenth century, two events began to reshape American views toward revolutions: the continental conquest was completed, and Americans began emphasizing the commercial aspects of their foreign policy instead of landed expansion. These overseas commercial interests became especially important, for stability, peace, and confidence in the sanctity of contract were essential to any great trading venture. By 1900, the United States had burgeoned into a power which combined the interesting characteristics of being conservative ideologically and expansive economically. Such a combination would not be encouraging to revolution. Interventions against a rebellion in Cuba and the Philippines were followed by Theodore Roosevelt's pronouncement that the United States would act as a policeman to prevent upheavals in the Caribbean area. A decade later Woodrow Wilson rationalized the use of economic and military force against Mexico with an ideological justification that employed the traditional American liberal rhetoric. The threat of revolution reached a crisis when, in 1917, Lenin joined the use of force to a doctrine worldwide in its ambitions and repugnant to most Americans.

Such was the historical inheritance of the Eisenhower Administration. Dulles became an heir at the time when European colonial rule was crumbling before nationalist uprisings in the Middle East, Africa, and Asia. As Secretary of State, he first faced the dangers posed by revolutions in the Iranian crisis of 1953. In 1951, an Iranian nationalist movement headed by Mohammed Mossadegh had undercut the power of the Shah and proceeded to nationalize the Anglo-Iranian Oil Company. The British government had received more taxes from the company than the Iranian government had received for its own natural resource, and the company consequently provided a very convenient target in an impoverished land where five hundred babies died out of every thousand births. The British demanded payment for the confiscated holdings, a demand that the Iranians could not meet without binding themselves to foreign lenders. With oil exports at a standstill, the Iranian economy began to sink, since income from oil provided thirty percent of its total income and sixty percent of its foreign exchange. When Eisenhower entered office, the United States, in spite of extensive efforts by Acheson, had not been successful in acting as a mediator.

After a three-week trip through the Middle East in May 1953, Dulles reached some disturbing conclusions. Western power had "deteriorated" in the area, he believed, and unless drastic action was taken, the Arab nations would become "outright" neutrals in "the East-West struggle." Israel and intra-Arab squabbles accounted for some of the problems, but Dulles also wondered about the British. "They interpret our policy as one which in fact hastens their loss of prestige in the area. To some extent," the Secretary admitted, ". . . this may be true," but Great Britain's loss of power was also due to "altered world power relationships." Dulles decided that he would have to convince the Middle East that the United States had little to do with British and French colonialism.[11] The opportunity came within the next two months when the State Department concluded that Mossadegh was moving into the Soviet orbit. Rumors of a Soviet-Iranian loan began to circulate, and in August, Mossadegh received 99.4 percent of the votes in a plebiscite, a percentage which Eisenhower later used as proof of 'increased Communist influence.[12] Having earlier refused to help Mossadegh rebuild the Iranian economy, the United States now cut off all aid.

In August the Shah staged a successful *coup* to regain power. The United States provided guns, trucks, armored cars, and radio communications for the Shah's forces.[13] The new government quickly undertook discussions with representatives of the oil company, but the representatives were not those of the year before. Since the turn of the century the United States had been trying to get into the Iranian oil fields only to be constantly repulsed by the British. Now the breakthrough occurred by the grace of the Shah and under the guidance of State Department official Herbert Hoover, Jr., who had gained wide experience in the complexities of the international oil problem as a private

---

[11] "Conclusions on Trip," May 9 to May 29, 1953, Conference Dossiers, Dulles Papers, Princeton.
[12] Eisenhower, *The White House Years: Mandate For Change*, pp. 160–166.
[13] Robert Engler, *The Politics of Oil* (New York, 1961), p. 206.

businessman. A new international consortium was established giving the British 40 percent, five American firms (Gulf, Socony-Vacuum, Standard Oil of California, Standard Oil of New Jersey, and Texaco) 40 percent, and Dutch Shell and French Petroleum the remaining 20 percent of Iranian oil production. Profits would be divided equally between the consortium and Iran.[14] Iranian oil once more freely flowed into international markets, the Shah's government was securely within the Western camp, and the British monopoly on the oil fields had been broken. For Dulles and Eisenhower, it was one revolution with a happy ending. More accurately, it was not a revolution at all.

Dulles, nevertheless, was not content. Similar eruptions threatened other areas of the Middle East. In Egypt, for example, a *coup* led by junior army officers under Mohammed Naguib and Colonel Gamal Abdel Nasser had overthrown the corrupt regime of King Farouk in 1952 and initiated a program of economic and land reform which included control of the Suez. Negotiations on the canal issue resulted in an Anglo-Egyptian agreement in 1954 that allowed British technicians to remain to operate the canal, but forced Her Majesty's troops to begin evacuation within eighteen months; the troops could return to defend the canal if Turkey, Egypt, or any Arab country was attacked by any nation other than Israel.

Recognizing the tenuous nature of the 1954 Suez agreement, and cognizant that the Middle East held two-thirds of the world's crude oil reserves and also bordered upon 3000 miles of the Soviet Union, Dulles determined to stabilize the situation with a Middle East version of NATO. In February 1955, Britain, Turkey, Iran, Iraq, and Pakistan joined the Middle East Treaty Organization (or the Baghdad Pact). Fearful of becoming involved in the Israeli-Arab conflict, and already allied to Pakistan, Iraq, Iran, and England through various military assistance treaties, the United States decided, in Dulles's words, to "cooperate with" but not become a member of the organization. The Secretary related the pact to the American views that had evolved since the middle of the nineteenth century: "Now, the purpose of the pact is not in any way to disrupt the Arab world,"

---

[14] *Ibid.*, p. 207.

and, he added, its other "basic purpose is to create a solid band of resistance against the Soviet Union." [15]

Seven years before, American diplomats had hoped that similar objectives would be achieved in Latin America through the Rio Pact and the OAS. Dulles found to his frustration that Latin American (and later Middle Eastern and Asian) governments too often moved outside the American interpretation of these agreements. Dulles had phrased the problem dramatically in February 1953. Latin American conditions, he stressed, "are somewhat comparable to conditions as they were in China in the mid-thirties when the Communist movement was getting started . . . . Well, if we don't look out, we will wake up some morning and read in the newspapers that there happened in South America the same kind of thing that happened in China in 1949." [16] Despite this awareness, Dulles never attempted to work out a comprehensive policy for encouraging Latin America to follow a path different from that which China trod in the 1930s. He instead approached the problem piecemeal. The first test for this approach came in Guatemala during the spring of 1954.

That country's population is mainly comprised of diverse tribes of Indians who are poor, illiterate, and isolated. In an area roughly the size of Tennessee, only 10 percent of the land is tillable, yet 74 percent of the population is agrarian. Two percent of the landowners own 60 percent of the usable land. Until 1944, a succession of strong men prevented any radical change in this society, but in that year student riots and unrest among professional classes brought in a new government, led by Juan José Arévalo, which supported land and labor reform. In 1951 Colonel Jacobo Arbenz Guzmán replaced Arévalo through proper constitutional procedures. Guatemalan politics bipolarized; the Communists, who supported Arbenz, insisted against strong conservative opposition that further reforms were requisite. Arbenz's main objective became the United Fruit Company. For more than a half century that company had employed upwards

---

[15] U.S. Congress, Senate, Committee on Foreign Relations, 84th Congress, 2nd Session, *Hearing on the Situation in the Middle East*, February 24, 1956 (Washington, 1956), p. 23.

[16] U.S. Congress, *Nomination of Dulles*, p. 31.

of 40,000 Guatemalans; monopolized shipping, communications, and railroads; and had helped shape the country's politics.

In 1953, Arbenz confiscated the company's property. The Department of State demanded proper payment, a demand Arbenz could not meet partly on nationalist grounds, and partly because it would require his country to tie itself economically to obligations which would prevent the financing of desperately needed internal reforms. When Arbenz refused to take the dispute to the Court of Arbitration at The Hague, Dulles moved to isolate Guatemala at the Tenth Inter-American Conference meeting at Caracas, Venezuela, in March 1954. He pushed through by a 17-1 vote a declaration that because "international communism . . . is incompatible with the concept of American freedom," the American states would "adopt within their respective territories the measures necessary to eradicate and prevent subversive activities." [17] Guatemala voted against, Mexico and Argentina refused to vote, and Costa Rica did not attend the meeting. Dulles interpreted the resolution as an application of the historic Monroe Doctrine. As Monroe's original message had been aimed at the political system of the Holy Alliance, now the Doctrine sent similar warning to international communism, a political threat "more dangerous than the open physical aggression." [18]

On May 15, Guatemala received 1900 tons of arms from Czechoslovakia. The United States stepped up its opposition by airlifting arms to Nicaragua and Honduras, sudden beneficiaries of mutual assistance pacts with Washington. On June 18, Colonel Carlos Castillo Armas, a former Guatemalan officer who was in exile, led a small army over the Honduras-Guatemalan border. With the aid of the Central Intelligence Agency and the American Embassy in Guatemala City, Castillo Armas overthrew the Arbenz regime. The American aid was decisive, but perhaps

---

[17] Dept. of State, *American Foreign Policy, 1950–1955, Basic Documents*, I, pp. 1300–1302.

[18] U.S. Congress, Senate, Committee on Foreign Relations, 83d Congress, 2nd Session, *Statements of Secretary of State John Foster Dulles and Admiral Arthur Radford . . . ,* March 9 and April 14, 1954 (Washington, 1954), p. 18.

equally significant was lack of support for Arbenz from the supposedly Communist-controlled labor unions and army. The
deposed President meanwhile begged the United Nations for
help. The ensuing United Nations debates are highly instruc-
tive to students of the Cold War, for Russia suddenly emerged
as a staunch supporter of the world organization, while the
United States refused to allow the Security Council to interfere
in matters which, Dulles argued, concerned only the OAS.
Vandenberg's work had not been in vain.

The Secretary of State pledged the "loyal citizens of Guatemala" that the United States would "alleviate conditions in
Guatemala and elsewhere which might afford communism an
opportunity to spread its tentacles throughout the hemisphere." [19] After working for three years with large amounts of
American aid to stabilize the chaotic situation, Castillo Armas
was assassinated by members of his own government. A conservative triumphed in the 1958 elections, but only at the price
of again bipolarizing the political alignment. Constantly harassed
by army, student, and peasant revolts, the regime fell in March,
1963 before a *coup* led by military leaders who feared, and with
good reason, that in general elections liberal and radical politicians would win power. Shortly after the *coup* a left-wing,
Communist-oriented guerilla movement appeared in the interior.

During those same hours that Dulles acted in Guatemala,
the Administration made even more fateful decisions on the
crisis in Southeast Asia. Between 1950 and 1954, the United
States provided $1.2 billion in aid to the French effort in Indo-
china, and by 1954 was paying for 70 percent of the French
military budget. Several hundred American mechanics and
military technicians also went in to aid the forces fighting Ho
Chi Minh. In early 1954, Eisenhower viewed the implications of
such aid with some concern. "I cannot conceive of a greater
tragedy for America," he told a press conference in February,
"than to get heavily involved now in an all-out war in any of

---

[19] Dept. of State, *American Foreign Policy, 1950–1955, Basic Documents*, I,
p. 1315.

those regions, particularly with large units." [20] Then came Dien Bien Phu.

Ground down by the guerilla tactics of Ho and the political instability in Paris, the dispirited French army decided to make its major stand at Dien Bien Phu. It was an odd choice. The town was located away from the coast, close to the Laotian and Chinese borders, and lay at the bottom of a valley easily commanded by the Viet-Minh forces controlling the mountain tops. Wheeling up large artillery pieces, a feat the French refused to believe Ho's forces could accomplish, the Viet-Minh lobbed a murderous bombardment upon the French garrison. On March 20, General Paul Ely, the French Chief of Staff, flew to Washington to request United States intervention. This set off a tumultuous six-week debate with the Administration and among the Western Allies. Dulles and Chairman of the Joint Chiefs, Admiral Arthur W. Radford, urged an American air strike to save the French. Air Force Chief of Staff Nathan Twining agreed and later outlined his thoughts on how the crisis might have been handled:

I still think it would have been a good idea [to have taken] three small tactical A-bombs—it's a fairly isolated area, Dien Bien Phu—no great town around there, only Communists and their supplies. You could take all day to drop a bomb, make sure you put it in the right place. No opposition. And clean those Commies out of there and the band could play the Marseillaise and the French would come marching out of Dien Bien Phu in fine shape. And those Commies would say, "Well, those guys might do this again to us. We'd better be careful." And we might not have had this problem we're facing in Vietnam now had we dropped those small "A" weapons. [21]

Dulles and Eisenhower disagreed with Twining on the use of atomic bombs, but the President began to waver on the question of American intervention in any form. On April 3, Dulles intimated to Congressional leaders that the Administration would appreciate a resolution allowing the commitment of United

[20] *Public Papers of the Presidents . . . , Eisenhower, 1954* (Washington, 1960), pp. 247–253.
[21] Interview with General Nathan Twining, Dulles Oral History Project, Princeton.

States forces. The Congressmen and Senators refused after questioning revealed that the Joint Chiefs were split on the problem (Army Chief Matthew Ridgway especially opposed any massive intervention), and that the Western Allies had not been consulted. The next day Eisenhower wrote Churchill that the threat in Vietnam compared with the dangers of "Hirohito, Mussolini and Hitler," and asked that the United States and Great Britain form a coalition to prevent a catastrophe.[22]

Three days later, the President outlined what was at stake by presenting his "domino theory" to a news conference. The struggle was crucial, Eisenhower observed, because the area contained tin, tungsten, and rubber; if, moreover, France lost, "many human beings [would] pass under a dictatorship. . . . Finally you have . . . what you would call the 'falling domino' principle. You have a row of dominoes set up, you knock over the first one, and what will happen to the last one is the certainty that it will go over very quickly. So you could have a beginning of a disintegration that would have the most profound influences." He especially worried about the economic and political effects upon Japan, the key to the containment of Russia and China in the Far East.[23]

The Administration next intensified the pressure on the British. At the height of the crisis, April 20 to 24, Dulles flew to London to ask for the go-ahead from Churchill so the President could send Congress the intervention resolution. The Prime Minister never flashed the green light. He refused to commit his government to the lost French effort, particularly during the forty-eight hours before the interested powers were to meet in Geneva on April 26 to negotiate the Indochinese problem. Churchill and Eden brushed aside Dulles' counterargument that the impending conference made the air strike imperative, since without the strike the Western position at the negotiating table would be embarrassingly weak. Without British cooperation, Senate and House leaders refused to support an intervention resolution. Within the White House, General Ridgway was persuading Eisenhower not to follow any line that might lead to

---

[22] Eisenhower, *The White House Years: Mandate For Change*, pp. 346–347.
[23] *Public Papers of the Presidents . . . , Eisenhower, 1954*, pp. 382–383.

the landing of American conventional forces. Logistics, politics, and the memories of Korea, Ridgway argued, worked against such a commitment. On May 7, the decimated French garrison surrendered.

Despite the debacle at Dien Bien Phu, the diplomats made little progress in their negotiations at Geneva. Then in mid-June the Laniel government fell in Paris and was replaced by a Gaullist-Radical coalition led by Pierre Mendès-France. The new Premier promised either a peace in Indochina or his resignation by July 20. When the Soviets intensified their pressure on the Chinese and Vietnamese to agree to a settlement, reports circulated that the Soviets exerted the pressure in exchange for an understanding that the French National Assembly would reject EDC. The Assembly did so within the summer, but that did not mean that such a deal had been struck. Ho Chi Minh, the Chinese, the British, and the French, as well as the Russians, had good reason to be satisfied with the Geneva agreements. In the two pacts concluded on July 20-21, the Geneva Accords (or Final Declaration), and the Geneva Armistice Agreement, the parties agreed: first, that a truce would occur between Ho's forces and the French (not, it is important to note, any Southern Vietnamese government); second, on a temporary partition at the 17th parallel with French troops withdrawing from north of that line; third, that North and South Vietnam would neither join military alliances nor allow foreign military bases on their territories; fourth, that national elections, supervised by a joint commission of India, Canada, and Poland, would be held within two years to unify the country and, the parties understood, France would remain in the south to carry out those elections; fifth, that regrouping of pro-Communist Pathet Lao forces would be allowed in Laos, and in that country and Cambodia general elections would be held.

Ho's armies controlled two thirds of Vietnam, but by accepting these agreements he pulled his troops into the northern half of the nation. He so compromised because he apparently preferred to deal with Mendès-France, rather than with another Premier who might come in after the July 20 deadline, and because Ho further believed that the French would hold to their promise of conducting elections in 1956. In such an election the North

Vietnamese leader would certainly win, for he was the best known and most powerful nationalist in all Vietnam. (Eisenhower later estimated that Ho would have received possibly 80 percent of the vote if the elections had been held at that time.) The triumphant Vietnamese also needed time to solve their political and economic chaos in the North; this they set about accomplishing with important aid from the Soviets. In his careful analysis of the situation, Ho had overlooked just one possibility: the United States might replace the French in South Vietnam. If this occurred, the Geneva agreements would become devalued.

The American delegation had not been a party to the negotiations on the armistice, and had refused to agree formally to the Accords. Affixing an American signature to an agreement with Communists that turned over half of Vietnam to Ho would not have enhanced the Administration's popularity at home. The United States only announced that it would support "free elections supervised by the United Nations," and look with "grave concern and as seriously threatening international peace and security" any renewal of "aggression in violation of the aforesaid agreements." [24]

Within a year the United States replaced France as the Western power in South Vietnam. The process began at least as early as September-October 1954, when Dulles announced that henceforth American aid would go directly to the South Vietnamese and not through the French. As the Secretary explained, this change would destroy the French "protected preferential market" and allow good friends like the Japanese to sell goods directly to the Vietnamese. Dulles denied any "desire" to "displace" French influence, but "a certain displacement is, I think, inevitable." [25] In November, American Army officers who had been pulled out the previous summer now moved back into the country. Military advisors under General J. Lawton Collins began training a South Vietnamese Army which hopefully could defend its homeland without the aid of American troops. The

[24] Dept. of State, *American Foreign Policy, 1950–1955, Basic Documents*, I, pp. 750–788.
[25] Press conference in Manila, March 2, 1955, Conference Dossiers, Dulles Papers, Princeton.

effect of Korea upon American thinking was immense. Collins had been Chief of Staff during the Korean War and was a charter member of the "Never-Again Club," a group of American Army officers, including Matthew Ridgway, who swore they would never again commit American troops to Asia without having an ironclad promise from Washington that the troops would be supported by the bombing of such enemy cities and supply lines as sanctuaries in Manchuria and China. The Vietnamese Army now learned from its American advisors how to move in large units with heavy weapons from fortified points. The Vietnamese were being prepared to fight the Korean War all over again.[26]

This American aid carried political implications. For example, the revitalized Vietnamese Army soon was plotting against the government. That government had been placed in the hands of Ngo Dinh Diem over strenuous French objections. The United States had brought in Diem from his self-imposed exile at Maryknoll Seminary in Ossining, New York. Eisenhower pledged in a letter of October 1954 that the United States would support the Vietnamese government in the south with economic aid in order to enable Diem to resist subversion or aggression. The President made no offer of open-ended military aid, further hedging the offer by asking for economic and social reforms so that the aid could be beneficially used.

By July 1955, most of the French had evacuated Vietnam. Diem announced that the elections agreed to in the Geneva Accords would not be held. Dulles fully supported the announcement with the argument that Diem's government had not signed the Accords which promised the elections. More to the point, Dulles and Diem knew that the latter would have grave difficulties defeating Ho in a fair election, and American officials did not believe that the northern government had any intention of running a fair election. The Secretary of State had set the stage for this announcement in May 1955 when he gave reporters a lesson in comparative history. The United States, he warned, would recognize an anti-Diem government in the south only if "it seems to be expressive of the real will of the people and if it is truly representative." The American Revolution, Dulles ob-

---

[26] Joseph Kraft, *Profiles in Power* (New York, 1966), pp. 139–143.

served, deferred to what "is called a decent respect for the opinions of mankind," and, he continued, all "changes" should be undertaken soberly and "with a decent respect for the opinions of mankind." [27]

Despite such remarks, Dulles no doubt realized that Asian revolutions bore a closer relationship to the ideas of Mao Tsetung than to those of Thomas Jefferson. At least he acted upon such an assumption shortly after the Geneva Conference when he led the drive to establish the Southeast Asia Treaty Organization. Such a military pact had long been discussed. In November 1951, Dean Rusk, Assistant Secretary of State for Far Eastern Affairs, had urged "the further organization of security in the Pacific area." Dulles brought Rusk's idea into reality in a treaty signed at Manila on September 8, 1954 by the United States, France, Great Britain, Australia, New Zealand, Thailand, Pakistan, and the Philippines. These nations agreed that any armed attack upon them "or against any State or territory which the Parties by unanimous agreement may hereafter designate" (this would include, through a separate protocol, Cambodia, Laos, and Vietnam), would endanger the "peace and safety" of each of the signatories. Another provision provided for immediate consultation if a signatory or a state included in the protocol was threatened by subversion or indirect aggression; in this case intervention could occur only with the approval of the government threatened.[28]

This agreement hid crucial differences among the signatories. Dulles realized that the treaty would have to run the gamut of the United States Senate, so he carefully provided for sending American forces only when "communist aggression" was evident, and only then after due "constitutional processes" were observed by Congress. He further assured the Senate that any immediate American response would be with bombs and not infantry. Pakistan, however, did not like the "communist ag-

---

[27] Off the Record News Conference, May 7, 1955, in Paris, Conference Dossiers, Dulles Papers, Princeton.

[28] U.S. Congress, Senate, Committee on Foreign Relations, 83d Congress, 2nd Session, *Hearing . . . on the Southeast Asia Collective Defense Treaty . . .* (Washington, 1954), Part 1, pp. 4–5, 28.

gression" clause because she wanted help against possible trouble with India. (India refused to join because Prime Minister Pandit Nehru feared association with the Western colonial powers.) After an intense debate, the defensive zone of SEATO was not extended to either Taiwan or Hong Kong, but did include Cambodia, Laos, and South Vietnam. This left the treaty open to the charge that it was violating the Geneva Accords by implicitly bringing the former French colonies into an alliance system. Despite such potentially explosive issues, the Treaty sailed through the Senate by a vote of 82-1.

The Senate ratification is of major significance in American diplomatic history. As Republican Senator Alexander Wiley of Wisconsin observed, SEATO differed from NATO because the United States was now committed not only "to resist armed attack, but also to prevent and counter subversive activities directed from without."[29] Dulles acknowledged this, and had earlier warned the Cabinet of the inherent dangers in such an agreement: "If we take a position against a Communist faction within a foreign country, we have to act alone," he lamented. "We are confronted by an unfortunate fact—most of the countries of the world do not share our view that Communist control of any government anywhere is in itself a danger and a threat."[30] Dulles was nevertheless willing to commit the United States to such a view.

This carried another historic implication. The traditional "open-door" policy would no longer be followed in Asia. Instead of a policy of "fair field and no favor" to anyone, as Secretary of State John Hay had asked for at the turn of the century, Dulles announced that the Monroe Doctrine was being extended to Asia. As the Doctrine had warned the Holy Alliance to keep "hands-off" Latin America in the 19th century, now the United States, in Dulles's words, "declared that an intrusion [in the Far East] would be dangerous to our peace and security."[31] Whether the United States could unilaterally enforce that Doctrine in Asia remained to be seen.

---

[29] *Ibid.*, Part 1, p. 10.
[30] Adams, *First-Hand Report*, p. 124.
[31] U.S. Congress, *Hearing . . . on Southeast Asia Collective Defense Treaty . . .*, Part 1, p. 21.

A first challenge was successfully blunted in 1954 and 1955 when the Chinese Communists threatened the offshore islands of Quemoy, Matsu, and the Tachens which lay between the mainland and Taiwan. As the Communists shelled the islands and then announced the imminent "liberation" of Taiwan, Eisenhower warned that such "liberation" forces would have to run over the American Seventh Fleet stationed in the Formosa Straits. State Department officials split on the question of whether the offshore islands were worth defending, but Dulles settled the issue by agreeing with Admiral Radford and the Joint Chiefs that force, if necessary, should be employed. Dulles flew to Taiwan in December and signed a mutual defense pact with Chiang Kai-shek, pledging the United States to defend Chiang in return for his promise not to try to invade the mainland without American approval. Nothing was said in the pact about the offshore islands. On January 18, 1955, the Communists took the small, northernmost island of the Tachen group. Eisenhower declared that because this island had no relationship to the defense of Taiwan, the attack required no counteraction. Within five days, however, he asked Congress for authority to "assure the security of Formosa and the Pescadores," and, if necessary, "closely related localities." Congress whipped through the resolution by a vote of 409 to 3 in the House and 85 to 3 in the Senate.

Some questioned the means involved. Perhaps the resolution was a dangerous precedent for less responsible Presidents who would demand open-ended authorizations from Congress to use force against Communism. Herman Phleger, the legal advisor of the Department of State who helped Dulles draft the resolution, called it a "monumental" step, for "never before in our history had anything been done like that." The method, Phleger later observed, solved for future Presidents the problem that had brought down severe criticism upon Truman when he did not obtain Congressional assent for the Korean intervention.[32] Anthony Eden, on the other hand, told Dulles of his concern about the objective of the resolution. Dulles vigorously defended protecting Chiang in this way, since, the Secretary of State warned, the Chinese Communists "have become more intem-

---

[32] Interview with Herman Phleger, Dulles Oral History Project, Princeton.

perate." Any surrender of Quemoy and Matsu would allow the Communists important military staging areas, weaken morale on Taiwan, and encourage Mao "to probe our resolution by putting it to the test of action." [33]

Eden's questioning was a symptom of the strains working upon the Western alliance between 1953 and 1956. Many of the disputed points became clear when Dulles struggled to obtain French ratification of EDC. The Secretary of State had tried to force the hand of the French government in mid-December 1953 when he warned that France must ratify or face an "agonizing reappraisal" by Washington of American commitments to Europe. This implied a retreat to a "Fortress America" concept which would leave Great Britain and France alone to face once again a revitalized Germany. Dulles was playing a risky game, but he was deadly serious. Realizing that any French government which forced the passage of EDC could well be committing political suicide, Dulles was willing to have one French coalition do this, for without EDC Adenauer might well lose interest in his links with the West. The French also seemed expendable because Dulles wondered if they could ever again become a great power. [34]

The Secretary's tactics varied during the next eight months, but his determination never wavered. In January 1954, he announced a military policy based on massive retaliation with nuclear weapons. This was dictated by George Humphrey's determination to cut the Army's budget and by General Curtis LeMay's notion that Communism could best be handled from a height of 50,000 feet. It also implied to West Europeans that Dulles was indeed willing to pull back American men from NATO unless Europe surrendered the *quid pro quo* of EDC. In the Indochinese crisis of April, Dulles was doubtless interested in helping the French not only because he wanted to contain Communism in Asia, but because he also hoped to prop up a government which might deliver the vote on EDC. In this sense both Dulles and Molotov played the same game with the French.

---

[33] "Copy of paper used in conversation with Eden," February 24, 1955, Conference Dossiers, Dulles Papers, Princeton.

[34] Eden, *Full Circle*, pp. 64, 108.

Both men saw the relationship between Indochina and EDC, and each determined to use the Vietnamese dilemma to accomplish his own European policies. Whichever victor obtained these objectives would have his hand immeasurably strengthened in Asia.

The French had become the pawns in a climactic power struggle. They tried to stall the fateful vote by following a policy best described as "de conserver le cadavre dans le placard" (keep the corpse in the closet). Three governments refused to bring the agreements to a vote. With the delay, French hostility grew. France, opponents argued, had an army that could lose its nationality in such a community; Germany, however, had nothing to lose for it had no army. Anyway, why create a German army? France would also have to divide her armies between Europe and overseas possessions; any German military force could concentrate on Europe. And why do such things when Malenkov was attempting to ease tensions? If France must take the step, why could not Eden also commit British troops so that France would not be the only major power locked in military embrace with the Germans? Eden answered the last question by announcing that neither Britain's ties with the Commonwealth nor her links with the United States would permit such a venture. Dulles answered the other points by declaring that German power was essential to the European alliance; that because Soviet ideology precluded any meaningful detente, the arming of Germany must receive priority; and that only through EDC could the revival of German militarism be adequately controlled.

In a dramatic last-minute meeting in August 1954, Mendès-France told Western diplomats he would finally take the corpse from the closet, but only after conditions were attached to EDC. These conditions have become historically important because they anticipated the later and better-known policies of Charles de Gaulle. Mendès-France demanded new emphasis in the agreement on the Russian desire for coexistence; the destruction of an integrated army concept except in "forward areas" (that is, there could be no integrated army on French soil without French permission, but there would be such an army in Germany); a thorough separation of EDC from the European Coal and Steel Community which the French prized; and, finally, the right of secession at any time. But not even these modifications were enough. After a bitter debate on August 30 in which Mendès-France significantly refused to stake his government's life upon the outcome, the Assembly defeated EDC 314-264 with 43 abstentions.

France had miscalculated. Not fully realizing how they were being acted upon rather than acting in the unfolding diplomacy, the French believed the defeat of EDC had scotched, perhaps killed, German rearmament. Instead they had simply exchanged EDC, which provided for controls upon that rearmament, for perhaps NATO, which had no such controls and would allow the development of a national German army. For Dulles was determined that Germany would be rearmed. United States policy rested upon that imperative. As Dulles defined the aftermath of the French vote as "a crisis of almost terrifying proportions," Anthony Eden worked out a solution.

The British Foreign Secretary advocated enlarging the Western European Union of 1948 (which originally had been an anti-German instrument) by including Germany. The WEU would not allow complete supranational control, but it would give France what it had begged for during the EDC struggle, the commitment of four British divisions to mainland Europe. The French were doubly assured when Dulles pledged that American troops would remain in Europe if France accepted the WEU idea. Adenauer cooperated by promising that Germany would not manufacture long-range missiles, or atomic, bacteriological, or chemical weapons without the approval of the NATO commander and a two-thirds majority of the WEU Council. The other signatories pledged that West Germany would not "have recourse to force to achieve the reunification of Germany or the modification of the present boundaries" of Germany. These promises were written into the Paris Agreements of October, 1954.[35] On Christmas Eve, Mendès-France drove the pact through the French Assembly, but only after overcoming strong opposition. German armies entered NATO in 1955.

---

[35] Dept. of State, *American Foreign Policy, 1950–1955, Basic Documents*, I, pp. 1476–1496.

In Indochina and Europe, Paris officials had learned lessons in Cold War power politics which would reorient their foreign policies and make them less amenable to American pressure. By no means coincidentally, Mendès-France secretly initiated the independent development of a French atomic and nuclear power project in the midst of these crises. Dulles, on the other hand, believed that the Paris Agreements created a situation which was in the best interests of both Europe and the United States. With that *status quo* apparently assured, the Eisenhower Administration returned its attention to the newly emerging nations.

CHAPTER VIII

East and West of Suez (1954-1957)

THE MASS OF THE NEWLY EMERGING PEOPLES had little interest in the ideological struggle between the Soviet Union and the United States. They wanted only political independence and release from grinding poverty. To obtain these, they were willing to borrow from both systems, and if Soviets and Americans would compete for their allegiance and resources, so much the better. That was indeed a compelling argument not to become too firmly aligned with each side but to remain in a "third world." Neither Russians nor Americans, however, appreciated such views. When in April 1953, Dulles accused the Russians of looking "upon anybody who is not for them as against them," he was unfortunately also characterizing American attitudes. The Secretary of State knew that, as he once phrased it, "to oppose nationalism is counter-productive," but as late as June 1956, his views of Communism and an apparent confusion over the meaning of nationalism enabled Dulles to say that neutrality had "increasingly become an obsolete conception and, except under very exceptional circumstances, it is an immoral and short-sighted conception."

By the mid-1950s each superpower believed that the future vitality of its ideological, economic, and strategic systems depended upon "winning" the third world, and each would have believed this even if the other superpower had not existed. The United States and Russia were expansive forces, and had been so in many areas (as, for example, in Asia) since at least the 19th century. The Cold War sharpened these drives, allowing each side to intensify its dynamic, historic expansion with the defensive terms "anti-Communism" or "anti-imperialism." As the nature of the Cold War changed between 1953 and 1956, pulling the attention of the United States and Russia away from Europe and toward long-time interests in the underdeveloped world, this different Cold War required important adjustments in the Soviet and American societies.

In the Soviet Union a bitter intra-Party struggle obscured the meaning and extent of the Russian adjustment. Throughout 1953 and 1954 Malenkov attempted to brace his position by weakening the Communist party apparatus controlled by Khrushchev, strengthening the governmental-bureaucratic powers which he ruled, and bringing into the decision-making process the industrial managers and technicians who agreed with his emphasis on investment in consumer goods instead of in military and heavy industry sectors. Khrushchev began undercutting Malenkov by appealing to the military and stressing the need for investment in heavy industry. Khrushchev was following many of Stalin's tactics of the 1920s as he mobilized his power within the Party. The question became whether the Party would control the bureaucracy, or vice versa.

On New Year's Day 1955, Malenkov announced that the Russian possession of hydrogen bombs made peaceful coexistence "necessary and possible." Khrushchev immediately accused the Premier of attempting to intimidate the proletariat revolution with atomic weapons.[1] This line of attack won the support of such military leaders as Defense Minister Nikolai Bulganin and World War II hero Georgi Zhukov, and brought old-time Stalinists like Molotov to Khrushchev's side. On February 8, Khrushchev demanded and obtained Malenkov's resignation. Bulganin became Premier, but Khrushchev held the real power as First Party Secretary. With the simultaneous fall from power of some of Malenkov's more liberal associates in Russia and throughout the bloc (such as Imre Nagy as Prime Minister in Hungary), Russia appeared to be sinking back into Stalinist political, economic, and foreign policies.

Such appearances deceived. By the middle of 1955, Khrush-

---

[1] Myron Rush, *Political Succession in the U.S.S.R.* (New York and London, 1965), pp. 48, 60; Arnold L. Horelick and Myron Rush, *Strategic Power and Soviet Foreign Policy* (Chicago, 1966), pp. 17–30.

chev turned against Molotov's policies and worked out a rap-
prochement with Yugoslavia and a peace treaty for Austria.
Having used the questions of economic investments and foreign
policy to oust Malenkov, Khrushchev now shrewdly adopted the
former Premier's policies. As early as 1949, Malenkov had realized that Stalin's two-camp policy paralyzed Soviet attempts to
influence the newly emerging nations. Khrushchev used this insight to work out a more subtle foreign policy which attempted
through the brandishing of military prowess, ideology, and economic aid to conciliate nationalist leaders with the Communist
nations.

Khrushchev structured this approach carefully. He safe-
guarded Soviet security both ideologically and militarily by developing the Warsaw Pact, a bloc military alliance patterned
after NATO which could allow Soviet military control of Eastern
Europe after the political controls were relaxed. On Aviation
Day 1955, the Soviets flexed awesome military muscles by flying
unit after unit of new jet planes over Moscow. (Only later did
American intelligence learn that Khrushchev simply had a relatively few planes fly around in circles.) He also tried to deal with
the challenges posed to Soviet authority by independently
minded Yugoslavia and China. Khrushchev first announced that
Russia was further along the road to Communism than any
other nation. This supposedly assured the Soviets of acting as
the chief ideologist within the Communist world. In late 1954,
he had magnanimously traveled to China and had personally
returned to Mao the former Chinese possessions of Port Arthur
and the Chinese Eastern Railway, long controlled by Russia. He
also sought to bring China within the Soviet economic orbit by
signing a new agreement to deliver large amounts of capital
goods. A similar line was followed in Yugloslavia, despite Molotov's warning that easing relations with Tito would weaken
Soviet control over the satellites. Khrushchev nevertheless went
to Belgrade, blamed past Soviet-Yugoslav troubles on Stalin, and
negotiated improved diplomatic and economic ties.

With the Communist world supposedly reconsolidated,
Khrushchev launched an aid program for the newly emerging
nations which, as he candidly told a group of junketing American Congressmen in 1955, he valued "least for economic reasons

and most for political purposes." By the end of 1956, fourteen economic and military assistance agreements had been signed with nations in Asia and the Middle East. Khrushchev was highly selective in compiling the list. North Vietnam and Indonesia were favored in Southeast Asia; between 1954 and 1959, Indonesia received a quarter-billion dollars in economic aid from Moscow, and by 1962, $1.5 billion. Cambodia, Laos, and Burma received aid as did India, where Nehru paraded neutralism to exploit both sides. During the eight years ending in 1962, Communist nations provided Southeast Asia with over $7.2 billion in grants and credits. The Soviets provided 78 percent of this, East European Communists 13 percent and China a little more than 6 percent.[2] In the Middle East, Iran, Afghanistan, Turkey, and Egypt were targets of the Soviet economic offensive.

The Chinese provided the proper ideological accompaniment for this drive by attending the Bandung Conference of nonaligned states in April 1955, and reaffirming the Five Principles of Peaceful Coexistence which had been agreed upon between India and China the year before. These promised mutual respect for sovereignty and territorial integrity, noninterference in one another's domestic affairs, and peaceful coexistence. Soviet ideologists supported the Chinese proclamation by emphasizing that Stalin's old two-camp approach had been replaced with a confidence that Communists and nationalists could work against Western imperialism and enter the promised land of socialism hand-in-hand. Never had the reputation of Communist China and Russia been higher among the newly emerging nations. Like the Eisenhower Administration, Khrushchev was also thinking in global terms. Only by breaking the rigid ideology and ending the blatant forms of police control within the bloc could he effectively appeal to the rising nationalisms in the Middle East and Asia.

Dulles fully appreciated what Communism was accomplishing. The Secretary of State analyzed in detail the new world situation for the NATO Foreign Ministers during the May meetings of 1955 and 1956. Communism was on the move in Asia, Dulles

---

[2] Russell H. Fifield, *Southeast Asia in United States Policy* (New York, 1963), pp. 252–253.

warned. The Chinese brand posed a greater threat than the Russian, since it controlled a greater population mass and possessed a cultural prestige in Asia not enjoyed by Russia in either Europe or Asia. The Secretary noted the major Chinese colonies which existed in many free Asian nations, and feared that Mao could follow a rule of divide and conquer because the non-Communist countries were scattered geographically and divided politically, culturally, and economically. The West, Dulles declared, must never surrender those nations: "the stakes are too high." Japanese industrial power could not be allowed to combine with China; Indonesia and Malaya contain vast amounts of oil, rubber, tin, iron ore, as well as hold strategic positions. The Philippines "represent a symbol of how the West can create independence in Asia." There were 1.6 billion people in the underdeveloped areas now exposed to Communist economic tactics. If those tactics prevailed, "the world ratio as between Communist dominated peoples and free peoples would change from a ratio of two-to-one in favor of freedom to a ratio of one-to-three against freedom. That," Dulles emphasized, "would be an almost intolerable ratio given the industrialized nature of the Atlantic Community and its dependence upon broad markets and access to raw materials." He recognized that SEATO would never be as strong as NATO, but stressed that the "U.S. in Asia is the same as the U.S. which you see in Europe. . . . Our attitude toward Communism is the same."[3]

In understanding the differences between the Chinese and Russian expansion, as well as defining the economic-strategic importance of the Far East, Dulles was ahead of most Americans, particularly those within the Eisenhower Cabinet. None of the President's advisors could contrive a coherent program which would appeal to the newly emerging nations while at the same time preserving American interests as Dulles defined them. Adjustments to the new directions of the Cold War would not come easily.

Militarily, for example, the Administration held fast to its determination to base security upon massive retaliation. Dulles

---

[3] "Far East Presentation," May 10, 1955, and "NATO Meeting, Etc." Paris, May 1–7, 1956, Conference Dossiers, Dulles Papers.

had defined this in May 1952 as "the will and . . . the means to retaliate instantly against open aggression by Red armies so that, if it occurred anywhere, we could and would strike back where it hurts, by means of our own choosing."[4] Neither the Soviet development of a hydrogen bomb nor the evidence in Iran, Egypt, Guatemala, and Indochina that the threats to American interests did not come in "open aggression by Red armies" significantly changed that policy after it was adopted officially in 1954. At each Cabinet meeting in which Dulles defended the free world against Communism, Secretary Humphrey defended the Treasury against the prodigals, especially those who wanted larger budgets for conventional military forces. Dulles acquiesced in these views. Having decided to stick with nuclear retaliation and small, mobile conventional forces, the President cut the armed forces from 3.2 million to 2.8 million in 1955.

During the Dien Bien Phu crisis one slight swing in American strategic thinking had begun to appear. Because NATO did not have manpower to match the Communists, the Secretary argued that the West should "use atomic weapons as conventional weapons against the military assets of the enemy whenever and wherever it would be of advantage to do so, taking account of all relevant factors. These include nonmilitary as well as military considerations." A conflict could therefore begin for nonmilitary as well as military reasons at a local level, and Dulles might approve the immediate use of atomic weapons.[5] When this tactic was employed in NATO war games in Europe, the results demonstrated that the type of limited war Dulles urged would incinerate most of Central Europe.

The only alternative seemed to be the development of American forces to fight wars which would stop short of nuclear exchanges. Scholars such as Bernard Brodie and Henry Kissinger began to advance this argument in late 1954. Within a year, Army Chief of Staff General Maxwell D. Taylor split the Joint Chiefs by unsuccessfully demanding, against Admiral Radford's opposition, that the military response become more flexible.

---

[4] John Foster Dulles, "A Policy of Boldness," *Life*, May 19, 1952, p. 151.
[5] "Proposed 'Talking Paper'", April 23, 1954, Conference Dossiers, Dulles Papers.

Taylor finally resigned in protest, as did Generals Matthew Ridgway and James M. Gavin. The new trend, which would become fully apparent in 1961, had set in and had done so as experts realized that massive retaliation was too inflexible for the demands of the changing Cold War. Whether, on the other hand, limited conventional war protected American interests in the underdeveloped areas remained to be seen. Limited wars did not automatically exclude massive retaliation; what could not be limited might have to be destroyed. The problem would always be less a proper choice of military means than a wise understanding of the objectives. In postwar American foreign policy, the debate over the nature of the Communist threat usually lagged behind the debate over which weapons to use against that threat.

Similar problems confronted the Administration in the economic realm. Here Dulles recognized the importance of aid for the newly emerging nations, but was powerless to do much about it, in part because of his own intellectual and political inhibitions. With the end of the demand generated by the Korean War, raw material prices slumped; economic depression struck underdeveloped areas relying upon the export of such materials. No one in the Administration had a solution. Eisenhower placed strong faith in productivity, "because it relieves pressures in the world that are favorable to Communism." He defined China as one huge claw reaching out for anyone who had five cents. Dulles's comment was dry and to the point: "In India today, the great peril of Communism comes from intellectual centers."[6] In his concern with productivity, Eisenhower had overlooked the demand of the newly emerging peoples for a rapidly developing productivity regardless of the social and political costs. He had also, like the previous Republican president, neglected the problems of distribution which so concerned the "intellectual centers." Eisenhower could only push through Congress Public Law 480 and an extension of Cordell Hull's reciprocal trade program. The former exchanged overflowing American agricultural surpluses for local currencies from the recipient countries.

---

[6] Robert J. Donovan, *Eisenhower: The Inside Story* (New York, 1956), pp. 3, 9.

Because such local currencies were not convertible on the world exchanges, they would then be respent on projects within the recipient country itself.

Innovation was also wanting in the field of foreign aid. Eisenhower responded to the Soviet economic offensive by reorganizing the foreign aid administration, but this did not touch the real problem. In the newly emerging areas, development had to occur literally from the ground up. This required internal stability and huge amounts of outside capital and technical aid. The Marshall Plan had worked because the Europeans had the technical know-how and capital resources to turn every dollar of American aid into six dollars of capital formation. This would obviously not be the case in Asia, Africa, or Latin America. George Humphrey warmly endorsed placing the burden on private capital, while allowing the World Bank (which depended upon the private money market) to make necessary long-term capital loans; the Export-Import Bank (operated by the government on money appropriated by Congress) would make only short-term loans to move American exports. Dulles attempted to show Humphrey that this approach would be insufficient, arguing that because of the growing importance of the newly emerging nations, an agency must be formed "to make political loans and 'soft' loans [that is, loans with low interest rates and payable in terms of local currencies] on a long term basis."

Dulles then proceeded to give Humphrey a lesson in political economy. In former days, private capital could provide soft, long-term loans because private persons ran the banks of issue and the governmental policies. "This," Dulles observed, "is all now changed." Governments everywhere make rules "for reasons quite unrelated to their effect upon investment." Private lenders consequently were no longer willing to make investments in unstable areas. Only governmental funds could promote such development in a meaningful way. Unless something was done quickly, Dulles warned, South America, for example, "might be lost" under Humphrey's policy: "It might be good banking to put South America through the wringer, but it will come out red." When Mutual Aid Director Harold Stassen attempted to mediate the Humphrey-Dulles debate by suggesting an institution comparable to Britain's East India Company (which had gone out of business in the 19th century), the Secretary of State did not even deign to comment.[7] Dulles knew his history, but Humphrey essentially won the argument. Primary reliance was placed upon private capital. Humphrey then reduced the lending powers of the Export-Import Bank until outraged American exporters and Congressmen forced him to issue more credit for American businessmen to use in their overseas trade. Despite such protests, Humphrey cut back so drastically that from fiscal 1955 to fiscal 1957 total loans repaid to the Bank actually exceeded disbursements by $58 million. Only after Humphrey's departure from the Cabinet was the Bank allowed to become a "soft loan" agency in 1958.[8] Meanwhile private capital did not assume the task, for it favored more stable areas; between 1953 and 1956, for example, United States investments in Latin America increased $1.4 billion or 19.2 percent, while they climbed in Western Europe and Canada $3.4 billion, or over 30 percent.[9] When two top Presidential assistants, C. D. Jackson and Nelson Rockefeller, attempted to circumvent Humphrey's policy with massive aid programs of their own, both men finally resigned in frustration.

Over all of these debates hung the pall of McCarthyism. Wisconsin's junior Senator, according to a public opinion poll, was regarded favorably by over half of those polled in early 1954. His popularity had jumped 16 points in six months, the same months he was encouraging the burning of supposedly "left-wing" books, and accusing the President of the United States of allowing the American allies to carry on a "blood trade" with China. Unfortunately, McCarthyism found sustenance not from just one man, but from a society. One ramification of this feeling occurred early in 1954 when Senator John Bricker of Ohio proposed an amendment to the Constitution which aimed to eliminate the possibility of any more one-man

---

[7] "Memorandum Re NAC Meeting," September 30, 1953, in file on NATO Meeting, December 8–15, 1956, Conference Dossiers, Dulles Papers.

[8] Robert Reuben Dince, Jr. "The Lending Policy of the Export-Import Bank: A Study in Public Policy," unpublished Ph.D thesis, Cornell University, 1960.

[9] U.S. Bureau of the Census, *Historical Statistics of the U.S., Colonial Times to 1957* (Washington, 1960), p. 566.

"sell-outs" similar, as some claimed, to that which Roosevelt accomplished at Yalta through Executive agreements. During and after the Roosevelt years, the Chief Executives tended more and more to circumvent the Senate's constitutional power to approve or disapprove treaties by using presidential control over foreign relations and military affairs to make personal agreements with foreign powers.

Under Bricker's proposal, Executive agreements would be effective only after Congressional action; no treaty of any kind, moreover, would become law until accepted by both houses of Congress and all forty-eight states. This latter provision was the stickler, since it could effectively preclude agreements even on the protection of migratory birds, and also make impossible United Nations-sponsored or international treaties on human rights, a test ban, or the abolishing of chemical warfare weapons. Because such treaties could give international organizations authority within the United States to enforce the agreements, Bricker received support from the American Bar Association, such "patriotic" organizations as the Daughters of the American Revolution, and many veterans groups. Realizing the impending danger to their own powers, Eisenhower and Dulles finally determined to fight the amendment. In February 1954, the Constitution was saved from radical overhauling when a rephrased Bricker Amendment lost 42 to 50 in the Senate, and then a resolution requiring acts of Congress to put all international pacts into effect lost by a single vote.

McCarthyism, of course, did not stop at the boundaries of politics. Although American scientists were increasingly relied upon by political and military decision-makers for judgments and weapons in fighting the Cold War, the scientific community was not immune to attack. The antiintellectualism which imbued McCarthyism, and the lack of ardor for the Cold War shown by some scientists, climaxed in the case of J. Robert Oppenheimer in 1954. Oppenheimer was perhaps the most distinguished physicist in the United States. He had directed the laboratory at Los Alamos which produced the first atomic bomb in 1945. His downfall began when he seriously questioned the building of the hydrogen bomb in 1949-1950. He was not alone in raising such questions. Many scientists, their political awareness made acute by their participation in the A-bomb project, had moved into Washington after 1946 to lobby long and earnestly for the imposition of strong controls upon the development and use of atomic energy. Probably a majority of American physicists opposed the decision to make the hydrogen bomb because they believed it strategically unsound and politically dangerous.[10]

Oppenheimer shared such sentiments, but unlike most of the other scientists, he had had close relations with Communist party members in the United States, and had made personal enemies on the Atomic Energy Commission. A four-feet, six-inch-high FBI folder on Oppenheimer detailed his past, but concluded that no evidence indicated that Oppenheimer had worked against the national interest. Eisenhower (who once defined an intellectual as "a man who takes more words than is necessary to say more than he knows") refused to take a public position. A special three-man board unanimously declared Oppenheimer to be "a loyal citizen," but nevertheless voted 2 to 1 against giving him continued access to classified information. This effectively removed Oppenheimer's voice from top governmental councils. The Atomic Energy Commission upheld this judgment 4 to 1 not on the basis of disloyalty, but because of "fundamental defects in his 'character.' " No one ever proved that Oppenheimer was disloyal; the one AEC member who thought so in 1954, Thomas E. Murray, several years later admitted that his vote had been cast "within the exigencies of the moment." This was a euphemism for the McCarthyite influence which angered and discriminated against important members of the American scientific and intellectual community.

With the Cabinet, the military, Congress, and intellectuals increasingly immobile, Dulles found himself torn between these political restraints and his own view of Communism on the one hand and, on the other, his recognition of the critical changes in international affairs. He had, for example, stalled off a Summit meeting by arguing that the Soviets would have to show their sincerity in wanting negotiations by signing an Austrian peace treaty. As a part of their reorientation of policy, the Russians suddenly signed the treaty in mid-May 1955. As Eisenhower

---

[10] Urs Schwarz, *American Strategy: A New Perspective* (New York, 1966), pp. 77–79.

later related, "Well, suddenly the thing was signed one day and [Dulles] came in and he grinned rather ruefully and he said, 'Well, I think we've had it.' "[11] Dulles's interpretation of the breakthrough on the treaty revealed the American dilemma. He initially claimed that "liberation" had borne rich fruit: "an area of Europe is, in a very literal sense, liberated." At the same time, however, Dulles felt compelled to warn Americans that "the new set of dangers comes from the fact that the wolf has put on a new set of sheep's clothing, and while it is better to have a sheep's clothing on than a bear's clothing on, because sheep don't have claws, I think the policy remains the same."[12]

Dulles adopted the latter approach in preparing for the Summit. He was primarily concerned that the Soviets would use the conference to gain "moral and social equality" with the United States in order to encourage neutralism. The Secretary consequently warned Eisenhower to maintain "an austere countenance on occasions where photographing together [with Russians] is inevitable," and to push hard publicly for "satellite liberation." The Secretary then set up American demands that would be quite difficult to realize. His first goal was the unification of Germany "under conditions which will neither 'neutralize' nor 'demilitarize' united Germany, nor subtract it from NATO."[13] To this the Russians would never agree. Dulles effectively sealed this policy when West Germany formally regained her sovereignty, commenced rearming, and entered NATO in May, just weeks before the Summit conference was to begin. On the eve of the meeting, Republican leader Senator William Knowland proposed the "Captive Nations" resolution; this expressed the Senate's hope that Soviet satellites "subjected to the captivity of alien despotisms shall again enjoy the right of self-determination."

Given this background, the Summit would produce little more than a "spirit of Geneva." Eisenhower, Eden (who had succeeded

---

[11] Interview with Dwight D. Eisenhower, Dulles Oral History Project, Dulles Papers, Princeton.

[12] "Press and Radio News Conference . . . , May 15, 1955," Conference Dossiers, Dulles Papers.

[13] "Estimate of Prospect of Soviet Union Achieving Its Goals," July 1, 1955, Conference Dossiers, Dulles Papers.

Churchill as Prime Minister), Bulganin (who fronted for Khrushchev), and Edgar Faure of France opened the meetings on July
18 and immediately ran into a deadlock over Germany. Following Dulles's suggestions, Eisenhower demanded free elections
and asked that a reunited Germany be allowed to join NATO if
it so desired. Bulganin responded by requesting a general European security pact which would include withdrawal of all foreign
troops from Germany; that is, he wanted NATO dismantled.
Eisenhower replied that Bulganin misunderstood NATO; it was
actually an instrument for curbing German ambition. Bulganin
said that if this were so, then NATO and the Warsaw Pact nations could guarantee in tandem the general security treaty. This
the President refused to discuss. A dead end was reached when
Khrushchev overruled a wavering Bulganin by announcing that
the Soviets would allow no elections in East Germany until West
Germany was disarmed. The United States had successfully
armed and tied West Germany to the Western alliance, while at
the same time pushing on the Soviets the blame for blocking
reunification through free elections.

The only major American initiative at Geneva was Eisenhower's "open-skies" plan proposing the exchange of plans of
each nation's military facilities, and allowing planes to photo-
graph each nation's territory to insure against surprise attacks.
This plan emanated from a panel, headed by Nelson Rockefeller,
which was concerned with quieting European fears over the stationing of American nuclear bombs in Europe.[14] The "open-skies"
proposal would quiet such fears while allowing the bombs to
remain. Khrushchev predictably rejected the plan on the grounds
that it would infringe Soviet territorial sovereignty. (This proposal was Eisenhower's second move in the controlled-arma-
ments field. In December 1953, he had proposed before the
United Nations a plan to establish an international agency that
would control the use of atomic materials for peaceful purposes. Although meeting initial resistance from the Russians and
from the American Congress, the speech bore fruit three years
later with the creation of the International Atomic Energy Agency.)

---

[14] Donovan, *Inside Story*, pp. 345–346.

Geneva, and the profitless Foreign Ministers meeting which followed in October, reaffirmed the new Cold War themes. Having failed to gain their coveted European security pact, the Soviets made the best of a disadvantageous situation. They worked out formal diplomatic relations with the Adenauer government in mid-September 1955, and a week later gave East Germany full powers in foreign affairs; the latter move would force Adenauer theoretically to deal with affairs in East Germany directly through the East German Communist regime instead of through the Russians. That was most repugnant to the West Germans and consequently reinsured the division of Germany. The split was widened in January 1956, when the East German People's Army entered the Warsaw Pact. Dulles's earlier hopes for reunification on Western terms now lost all foundation. At the NATO Foreign Ministers meeting in December 1955, Dulles announced that because the Soviets had been frustrated in achieving their Central European objectives, and since thermonuclear weapons made a profitable war impossible for the Communists, they would employ "indirect" threats "primarily developed in relation to the Near and Middle East and South Asia," and particularly aimed toward the Middle Eastern oil so "essential to the industrial life of Western Europe."[15]

Dulles had again charted the new directions of Soviet policy, but he failed to imagine the extent to which Khrushchev would reorient the Kremlin. At the 20th Party Congress in February 1956, Khrushchev surprised his listeners, shocked the satellites, and astonished the West by detailing Stalin's crimes against the Communist Party and (the same thing) Russian national interest.[16] But he exorcised the dictator's ghost with a scalpel, not a meat-ax. Nothing was said about the particular purges in which Khrushchev himself had controlled the cattle cars slowly moving out of the Ukraine toward Siberia during the late 1930s; instead, he discussed the bloodlettings in which his present enemies on the Presidium had been more closely involved. Khrushchev

---

[15] Statement at opening of NATO Ministerial Meeting, Paris, December 15, 1955, Conference Dossiers, Dulles Mss.

[16] Nikita S. Khrushchev, *The Crimes of the Stalin Era* . . . , Annotated by Boris I. Nicolaevsky (New York, 1956, 1962).

further emphasized that Stalin and the "cult of the individual" had been at fault, not the Communist system. He also carefully defended the Party and the Army against the Stalinist crimes, but not the masses or the intellectuals whom he himself would soon restrict and attack. Domestically, Khrushchev was trying to increase his own personal power, loosen Stalinist restrictions so that the Soviet economy could boom, and yet keep the society under absolute control without resorting to terrorist methods.

Foreign policy could not be walled off from this internal reorientation. The East European satellites were stunned. Khrushchev destroyed their supposedly unquestioning belief in Stalin and all acts of the Soviet Union. He thereby obliterated the frame of reference by which the satellites had been told since 1945 to measure their own policies. For this, Khrushchev substituted the idea that several roads led to Communism, emphasizing, nevertheless, that Communism was the destiny toward which all were heading. The point was made most clearly in the apology for Stalin's tactics towards Tito. Khrushchev recalled Stalin saying that he would shake his little finger and Tito would fall; "we have," Khrushchev concluded, "dearly paid for this shaking of the little finger." In this and other speeches at the Congress, the Soviet leadership announced that the two-camp approach, the belief that war was inevitable, and the fear of "capitalist encirclement," were all now unsound doctrine. The new policies were perhaps best illustrated in the destruction of Stalin's "capitalist encirclement" theme, for by questioning this, the "capitalist" and "neutralist" areas surrounding the Communist bloc became not objects generating fear in the Soviet peoples, but objects to be exploited by Soviet foreign policy. This turn in Russian thinking somewhat resembled the change in American thinking when the United States began to view the surrounding oceans not as barriers insuring isolation, but as highways for internationalism. Within a general policy of détente with the Western world, the Soviets would tear down Stalinist-imposed barriers and move down adjoining highways into the third, uncommitted world. In keeping with this policy, Mikoyan announced the dissolution of the Cominform on April 17, 1956.

After the Geneva conference of 1955, Dulles wondered whether the Soviet "maneuver" of easing tension "may in fact assume the force of an irreversible trend." Such seemed to be the case within weeks after Khrushchev's speech. In March 1956, riots erupted in Soviet Georgia, the home of the now degraded Stalin. In June, mobs rioted against Communist party leaders in Poland and Hungary, demanding that more liberal officials assume authority. Khrushchev also came under attack from the other side when such old-line Stalinists as Kaganovich and Molotov demanded that he forcefully quiet the East Europeans before things got completely out of hand. In September 1956, Khrushchev called on Tito to help keep the Hungarian and Polish ferment under control. Tito did what he could, but by the end of September neither he nor Khrushchev could rebottle the genii which had been uncorked in February.

In a sense, the moment of "liberation" seemed to be approaching. At the crucial point where the prophecy needed a nudge, however, the prophet was looking the other way. Throughout the summer and autumn, Dulles became caught in the maelstrom of Middle Eastern politics. A year and a half before, Israel had dramatically revealed the weakness of the Egyptian army with a quick, overpowering raid into the disputed Gaza strip. Nasser soon opened negotiations with Western and Communist powers for more modern military weapons. Declaring that American prices were not competitive, he discovered the Communists' anxious to do anything that would weaken the Baghdad Pact. In late September 1955, just after Dulles had interpreted the Summit conference as indicating Soviet attempts to exploit the newly emerging nations, Nasser signed an agreement to buy arms from the Czechs.

Dulles suddenly became interested in helping Egypt finance the planned Aswan Dam, a huge project which Nasser hoped would harness the vast power of the lower Nile, and serve as a symbol of how his regime was triumphantly taking Egypt into the twentieth century. In December 1955, the United States and Great Britain offered to help Nasser. As the United States realized, Egypt would have difficulty in paying for both the arms deal and the dam. To doublecheck this point, World Bank President Eugene Black traveled to Cairo to work out a deal whereby the World Bank, Great Britain, and the United States would supply the immediate funding for the $1.3 billion project while Egypt would provide the majority of the money over the long term. In February 1956, Black and Nasser reached agreement. The Egyptian leader then wrote Washington regarding discussions on the proposal. Five months later he was still waiting for a reply.

Dulles had become trapped in Washington. Testifying before the Senate Foreign Relations Committee in February, the Secretary argued that although Egypt and Syria might receive Communist arms, he should not have to bow before domestic political pressure and send arms to Israel. This could only lead to an all-out arms race in which Arabs would triumph because "thirty-odd million Arabs [have] far greater . . . absorptive capacity" than 1.7 million Israelis. Dulles was forced to admit, however, that the United States was sending tanks to another of Israel's enemies, Saudi Arabia, under terms of a mid-1951 agreement in which the latter country had allowed the United States to occupy Dhahran Airfield. Asked whether the arms build-up might cause Israel to launch a preventive war, Dulles admitted "there is some danger," but he emphatically added that because of the 1950 Declaration in which Britain, France, and the United States declared their opposition to the use of force in the Middle East, any such war "would not involve the United States on the side of Israel."[17] Having to take a stand on such questions in an election year was bad enough, but Dulles soon found his position worsening.

In April, Egypt, Saudi Arabia, Syria, and Yemen formed a joint military alliance obviously aimed at Israel. These nations, along with Iraq, Lebanon, and Jordan had refused to recognize the Israeli government. The Czech arms deal now assumed a more ominous aspect. In May, Nasser withdrew recognition from Chiang Kai-shek and recognized Communist China. This quickly mobilized the many American champions of Chiang to inform Dulles that they staunchly opposed any kind of deal with Nasser. On Capitol Hill, this China "lobby" found an easy alliance with Southern Congressmen who demanded to know why

---

[17] U.S. Congress, Senate, Committee on Foreign Relations, 84th Congress, 2nd Session, *Hearing . . . On the Situation in the Middle East*, February 24, 1956 (Washington, 1956), pp. 43–46, 68.

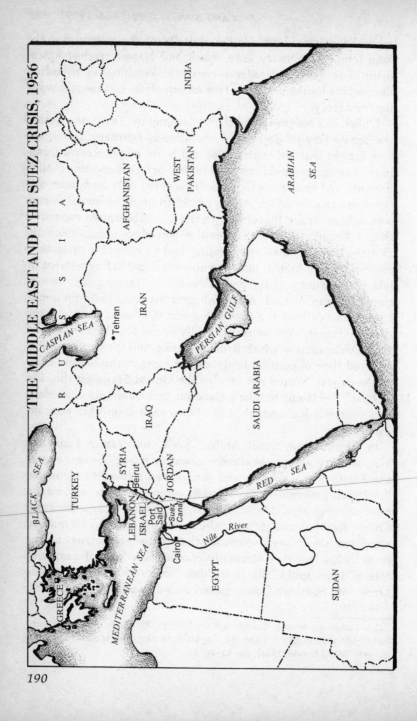

THE MIDDLE EAST AND THE SUEZ CRISIS, 1956

the United States was offering to build a dam which would allow huge crops of Egyptian cotton to compete with American cotton. Within the Cabinet, George Humphrey intensified his argument that Nasser had neither the technicians nor the industry to use the dam and, anyway, the financing would strain the cherished concept of a balanced budget. Above all, Egypt had not repudiated the arms deal. Dulles concluded that if he suddenly withdrew the offer, Nasser would suffer a disastrous political blow. The Secretary also assumed that Khrushchev would not, in fact could not, replace American aid, an assumption with which Eugene Black concurred because of his belief that Nasser could not afford to become further involved with the Communist bloc. Black nevertheless warned Dulles to go through with the deal or "hell might break loose."[18] Both of Dulles's assumptions were tragically wrong. He compounded the mistake by announcing the American decision in a formal, direct announcement on July 19, 1956 at the moment the Egyptian Foreign Minister was arriving to discuss the project, and as Nasser himself sat in a widely publicized meeting with Tito and Nehru.

One week later, Nasser seized the Suez Canal by nationalizing the British-controlled Universal Suez Canal Company. With a single stroke he recovered his lost prestige and gained the $25 million annual profit of the company for use in building the dam. The Egyptian leader also had his thumb on the jugular of the European economy; sixty-seven million tons of oil had moved to Europe through Suez in 1955. As long as he compensated the shareholders of the company, Nasser was legally justified in seizing the canal. He promised, moreover, to keep the waterway open to all former users of the canal. This was not enough for Great Britain and France. Acutely aware of Western shipping interests and the possible disintegration of the Baghdad Pact, perhaps even of NATO, Dulles tried to ameliorate the crisis by establishing a user's association to manage the canal. This proved unacceptable; the British and French had no inclination to put their vital petroleum imports in the hands of Nasser, and the Egyptians refused to share control of the canal. As early as the

---

[18] Interview with Eugene Black, Dulles Oral History Project, Dulles Papers, Princeton.

end of July, British Foreign Secretary Harold MacMillan revealed to Dulles Britain's plans for military action if the problem was not quickly settled.[19] Dulles, however, refused to put excessive pressure on Nasser, did not take the British and French threats seriously, and of course was reluctant to be too closely associated with the former colonial powers. The Administration announced that the United States would abide by the 1950 agreement which condemned the use of force in the area.

These policy differences were compounded by the growing personal animosity between Eden and Dulles. Before the 1952 election, Eden had dropped an unsubtle hint to Eisenhower that he preferred a Secretary of State other than Dulles. The Eden-Dulles relationship never improved much beyond this point. Yet Anglo-American relations depended upon these two men in the autumn of 1956, for their ambassadors in Washington and London were relatively uninformed; the British ambassador actually left the United States on October 11 just as the crisis began to worsen. During the last two weeks of October, communications between London and Washington almost completely broke down.

This was doubly tragic, for as the Middle Eastern situation deteriorated, rebellion erupted in Eastern Europe. The two events became closely related. Having unleashed unknown forces with his denunciation of Stalin, Khrushchev lost control of Poland's rapid de-Stalinization program headed by Wladyslaw Gomulka. Khrushchev flew to Warsaw, moved Soviet military forces into striking position, and delivered a blistering speech against the Polish changes. Gomulka responded by threatening to call out the Polish people. Khrushchev backed down. The news of Gomulka's success spread to Hungary. On October 23, students moved into the streets to demand that long-time Stalinist Ernö Gerö be replaced with Imre Nagy. When the secret police attempted to put down the protests, workers joined the students. One huge demonstration destroyed a gigantic statue of Stalin in central Budapest. The Soviets agreed to replace Gerö with Nagy, but that was no longer enough. The crowds demanded removal of Russian troops stationed in Hungary and the creation of a

---

[19] Interview with Robert Murphy, *ibid.*

political party in opposition to the Communists. On October 28, the Soviets began withdrawing the tanks that had moved to the outskirts of Budapest.

The next day the Israeli Army made a lightning attack which in hours nearly destroyed Nasser's Army and conquered much of the Sinai peninsula. In close cooperation with Israel, England and France delivered ultimatums to Israel and Egypt on October 30, warning both nations to keep their forces away from the canal. When Nasser rejected the note, British and French planes began bombing Egyptian military targets. The next day, October 31, the Presidium reversed its policy toward Hungary. Nagy had announced the withdrawal of Hungary from the Warsaw Pact. This was going too far, much farther, for example, than Gomulka was going in Poland. The confrontation in the Middle East provided Khrushchev with the perfect opportunity for counteraction. As Anglo-French columns moved into the Canal area on November 4 and 5, Russian tanks crushed the Hungarian uprising. The Soviets captured Nagy under false pretenses, shipped him off to Russia, and executed him sometime in 1957. The State Department watched all this helplessly. As one high official later remarked, Dulles, "like everybody else in the Department was terribly distressed," but "none of us had whatever imagination it took to discover another solution. We just were boxed." [20] At the height of the crisis on November 3, Dulles underwent emergency surgery on the cancer which would later kill him.

Having smashed the Hungarian rebellion, Khrushchev entered the Middle Eastern scene. He suggested to the State Department that a Russo-American settlement be imposed upon the area, and warned Anglo-French forces that unless they quickly withdrew, the Soviets would use force, perhaps long-range rockets, to squash their armies. On November 6, as Americans went to the polls in a presidential election, Eisenhower responded to Khrushchev's demands by placing American military forces on an emergency alert. He was not, however, primarily afraid of Soviet military action in the Middle East. The greater danger was that Khrushchev might inveigle his way into negotiating a settlement and thereby interject Soviet power in an area which

---

[20] *Ibid.*

for centuries Western Europe had fought to keep free of Russian influence.

Attempting to short-circuit the Soviet move, the State Department put tremendous pressure on London and Paris by passing a resolution through the General Assembly urging a truce, and then cutting off oil supplies from Latin America which England and France needed to replace their oil which could not get through the clogged canal. Hours before they would have seized the canal area, the British and French agreed to a cease-fire and pullback. Throughout November, Washington carefully rationed the oil flow to Europe. Not until the United Nations resolution was obeyed and the troops withdrawn did the oil flow freely. American officials argued that they could not afford to turn on the oil too quickly, for this would infuriate the Arab nations which held huge reservoirs of oil leased to Americans.[21] By December 22, the armies had left and a United Nations emergency force restored the canal area to Egyptian control. The Suez crisis was a graphic study of how the newly emerging peoples were reordering the power balance at the expense of the older and more powerful nations. These lessons were immediately taken to heart in Washington and Moscow.

In the United States the events in Poland and Suez occurred at the climax of the presidential campaign. Beginning at a time of relative quiet in foreign affairs, the early weeks of the campaign were marked by a discussion of farm issues and the possible effects of the heart attack suffered by Eisenhower a year before. Democratic nominee Adlai Stevenson tried to overcome this apathy, but he did so in a curiously paradoxical manner. At times he argued that disarmament must be placed at the heart of American policy, urged a restudy and possible discontinuance of the military draft, suggested the suspension of nuclear weapons tests, and accurately pinpointed "events in Eastern Europe and the Middle East" as "symptoms of a vast new upheaval in the balance of world power." At other times, however, Stevenson reaffirmed the Cold War clichés: half of Indochina had "become a new Communist satellite and . . . America emerged from that debacle looking like a 'paper tiger';" NATO's decline threatened

---

[21] Engler, *Politics of Oil*, pp. 261–263.

the entire Western world; the draft was to be restudied to create "stronger, not weaker" military forces; and in his last speech, Stevenson detailed how Harry Truman had stood up to the Russians while Eisenhower rejected the "great opportunities to exploit weaknesses in the Communist ranks and advance the cause of peace."[22]

In playing such a political game with Eisenhower, Stevenson was overmatched. Republican spokesmen could detail the times Dulles had gotten "tough" with the Russians (or had "gone to the brink" of war, to use Dulles's phrase), while Eisenhower could pose as the military man who made peace in Korea and knew just when to step back from the brink. When the United States and Russia again approached the brink in the last hours before the election, most Americans had no doubt whom they would entrust with their lives and their Middle Eastern interests.

Eisenhower overwhelmed Stevenson partly because of the President's personal popularity; he received 57 percent of the vote, but the Democrats captured both Houses of Congress, the first time that such a split had occurred since 1848. Yet in judging the rhetoric of the campaign and the post-election analyses, the election clearly demonstrated something more than personal popularity. It marked a consensus of ideology. Voting analyses later revealed that a small majority of Americans preferred Democratic domestic policy, but a larger majority supported Republican foreign policy.[23] Since 1952, Eisenhower had brought nearly all sectors of the Republican party into the internationalist camp, adding numerous Democrats and independents by combining appeals for peace with the history of brinksmanship. Henry Wallace, for example, would vote in essence to have John Foster Dulles as Secretary of State because Wallace believed that "Eisenhower . . . is the man most likely to preserve world peace." Reinhold Niebuhr, however, supported Stevenson because Eisenhower's foreign policies were "catastrophic" as a result of being based too much upon the peaceful "Geneva spirit." The United States, Niebuhr warned, had lost ground among the neutrals

---

[22] Adlai E. Stevenson, *The New America* (New York, 1957), pp. 27–34, 40–41.
[23] Angus Campbell, *et al.*, *The American Voter* (New York, 1960), pp. 198–200, 526–528.

and (a fascinating if illogical conclusion on Niebuhr's part) had therefore made "former neutralist nations into virtual allies of Communism." "We are in greater peril than at any time since our victory over the Nazis," the theologian gravely concluded.[24]

Niebuhr's explanation revealed a basic agreement with Dulles' views. Accurately pinpointing the growing dilemma of American policy in Vietnam a year earlier, Niebuhr had warned against using military power when "it lacks a moral and political base;" but he then applauded the "disinterested" Americans who were replacing the French as the Western power in South Vietnam.[25] Dulles, of course, had initiated this displacement, and was trying to build the moral and political base which Niebuhr wanted. In these circumstances, Niebuhr's dislike and mistrust of Dulles became less significant, for both men agreed on a fundamental point: the United States could not keep its hands off politically unstable nations because such instability could turn "former neutralist nations into virtual allies of Communism," to use Niebuhr's phrase.

From that point the argument between the mass of American "liberals" and "conservatives" was reduced to one over means. Niebuhr could logically place few restraints upon military means, for example, if a neutral nation (as Vietnam was supposed to be under the Geneva agreements) continued to wallow in internal upheavals. The "realists," as many of those who agreed with Niebuhr liked to call themselves, criticized Dulles for not keeping means and ends in balance. This criticism was beside the point, for both sides agreed that, first, the underdeveloped world was becoming the focal point of the Cold War, and second, the neutrals, unless tied closely to the United States, could become "virtual allies" of Communism. In the 1956 elections, Eisenhower best exploited this consensus, and that was even a greater irony, for most of the "realists" were Democrats.

Eisenhower wove this consensus into policy just a few months after his reelection. The Suez crisis had seriously weakened the Baghdad Pact and had stimulated Nasser to attempt to increase his power in the Middle East. On January 5, 1957, Eisenhower

---

[24] *Life*, May 14, 1956, p. 184; *New Republic*, October 29, 1956, p. 11.
[25] Reinhold Niebuhr, "The Limits of Military Power," in *The World Crisis* (New York, 1958), pp. 114–121.

tried to reverse those trends by replaying his performance of the Formosa Straits crisis. He asked Congress for authorization to extend economic and military cooperation and, if necessary, to employ American military forces in the Middle East if any nation in that area requested help against Communist-instigated armed aggression. The Middle East Resolution, or the "Eisenhower Doctrine" as it came to be known, sailed through the House. The Senate, however, balked.

Senators attacked the Resolution as being anti-Israeli, too vague, and injurious to the Western alliance. Dulles did not lessen this last criticism when he remarked that Anglo-French forces should remain in Europe, for "If I were an American boy . . . I'd rather not have a French and British soldier beside me, one on my right and one on my left." Such a remark was hardly tactful, but in a single sentence Dulles had given his view of how collective the security decision-making should be in the Middle East.[26] With the help of Majority Leader Lyndon Johnson, the Administration finally passed the resolution in March, 72-19. It did so despite little public support. Heavy Congressional mail, in fact, ran eight to one against the proposal in February.

The passage of the Eisenhower Doctrine had interesting political overtones. A Democratic Congress formally surrendered some of its power, especially that of controlling the outbreak of war, to a Republican President. Democratic Senators James Eastland of Mississippi, John Kennedy of Massachusetts, Hubert Humphrey of Minnesota, Joseph Clark of Pennsylvania, and Strom Thurmond of South Carolina (among others) joined Republicans to defeat Wayne Morse's amendment which would have directed the President simply to notify Congress before using armed force, or to submit any such action for congressional approval.[27] Ideological agreements on the Cold War easily cut across political parties and both sides of the states-rights argument.

If anyone doubted that Eisenhower would use this gift of power, they learned otherwise within a month after the Senate

---

[26] U.S. Congress, Senate, Committee on Foreign Relations, 85th Congress, 1st Session, *Hearings . . . to Authorize the President to Undertake Economic and Military Cooperation with Nations in the General Area of the Middle East*, Parts 1 and 2 (Washington, 1957), especially pp. 4–41.

[27] *Congressional Quarterly Weekly Report*, XV (March 8, 1957), p. 299.

completed action. In April, young King Hussein of Jordan came under attack from pro-Nasser elements within his country. Hussein asked for help because he was under attack from "international Communism and its followers." The Eisenhower Doctrine specifically and the general American ideological view of revolutions now faced a test: would the United States help Hussein defend the *status quo* against the Nasserite elements by brandishing the argument that Hussein was being saved from "international Communism?" Eisenhower responded by sending $10 million to Hussein and dispatching the Sixth Fleet to the Mediterranean area near Jordan. The official State Department announcement on the sending of this aid did not directly blame "international Communism"; instead it explained the action as safeguarding "the preservation of the independence and integrity of the nations of the Middle East."[28] With such ease was a resolution giving the President military powers to war against international Communism transformed into presidential power to intervene in any Middle Eastern situation which, by American definition, threatened the independence and integrity of any nation in the area. Anti-Communism had become a rather strange phenomenon. It had also been integrated into a global Monroe Doctrine. The Eisenhower Doctrine was an extension of the dogmas of 1823 into the Middle East in the same sense that, as Dulles observed, SEATO extended the original Doctrine into Southeast Asia.

In the early spring of 1957 the Eisenhower Administration could believe that it had emerged from the winter crises with increased powers and prestige. Such was not the case with Nikita Khrushchev. Despite his triumphant proclamation that Dulles's failure to interfere in the Hungarian uprising had proven the hollowness of "liberation," the fiasco of Khrushchev's policies in Eastern Europe and his inability to take advantage of the power vacuum in the Middle East immersed him in deep political trouble in Moscow. He came under vigorous attack for having invited Chinese officials to fly to Warsaw at a critical moment to quiet the Poles. Having Chinese play the role of mediator in Eastern Europe because of Khrushchev's mistakes at

---

[28] Dept. of State, *American Foreign Policy; Current Documents, 1957* (Washington, 1961), p. 1024.

the 20th Congress gave Molotov, Malenkov, and Kagonovich their opening. By December 1956, Khrushchev's name was not being mentioned in connection with important party decisions. He soon counterattacked with his tactics of 1953-1955. "We are all Stalinists," he loudly announced at a New Year's Eve party, and then launched into a denunciation of "capitalist countries" who wanted "a feverish arms race." His talk became increasingly tough. For the first time since 1955 the Soviet press accused the United States of following, in the words of a joint Chinese-Soviet announcement, "a policy of aggression and preparation for war."[29] With these moves, Khrushchev tried to divide Malenkov from the old-line Stalinists, while at the same time consolidating his alliance with Marshall Zhukov and the military. He meanwhile quietly increased his power at the roots of the Party bureaucracy; one important maneuver was his announcement in February of a radical new economic plan that would decentralize economic controls and thus place them in the hands of his friends at the regional level.

In June, the Malenkov-Molotov faction struck what it thought was the fatal blow when the Presidium voted by an apparently large majority in effect to remove Khrushchev from his post of First Secretary. Khrushchev, however, demanded that the decision be appealed to the 309-member Central Committee, the first time such an appeal had been made since 1926. His political supporters in the hinterlands soon crowded into Moscow and combined their votes with those of army officials to reverse the Presidium's decision. Malenkov was soon operating a far-off Siberian power station, and Molotov disappeared to a diplomatic post in Outer Mongolia. Khrushchev removed six members of the obnoxious Presidium, replacing them with nine of his closest supporters.

During the summer of 1957, Khrushchev gained supreme power. His first target was the military. Having helped make him, Zhukov could perhaps help break him. Khrushchev's opportunity arose when the General began to issue pronouncements on sensitive political issues as well as on military strategy. Party leaders interpreted this as a direct and dangerous threat to the

---

[29] H. S. Dinerstein, *War and the Soviet Union*, Revised Edition (New York, 1959, 1962), pp. 154–163.

supremacy of the Party over the military. The danger was indeed even greater, for since Beria's execution four years before, the weakening of the secret police had allowed the military to gain a large measure of independence from Party control. In late October, Zhukov was stripped of his post as Defense Minister. When he apparently tried to fight back, he was also removed from the Presidium and the Central Committee.[30] Khrushchev's next move was to attempt to educate the Soviet intellectuals who had apparently misunderstood the de-Stalinization campaign to mean that more candid criticisms of Soviet society would be tolerated. At a garden party, Khrushchev made such a verbal assault upon the invited intellectuals that one woman fainted. That harangue climaxed with Khrushchev shouting that Hungary would have remained orderly if several writers had been shot at the proper time; if such a threat ever faced the Soviet Union, he added, "My hand would not tremble."[31] The following year when the distinguished Russian author, Boris Pasternak, expressed some doubts about the results of the 1917 Revolution in his novel *Dr. Zhivago*, the book was banned from mass circulation inside Russia, and Pasternak was prohibited from traveling to Stockholm to receive the Nobel Prize in Literature. De-Stalinization had its limits, particularly if it threatened the power of the Party and Khrushchev.

After a four-year struggle, Khrushchev was supreme. In the United States, Eisenhower began his second term in power. The world outside Moscow and Washington had greatly altered between 1953 and 1957. Having created an acceptable *status quo* in Europe, Washington shifted more and more of its energies to fighting the Cold War in the underdeveloped areas. In the Soviet Union, Khrushchev brought about changes which allowed his government to exploit opportunities within the newly emerging nations. Dwight Eisenhower provided the proper epitaph for the history of those years: "Somehow or other," he wrote Dulles in February 1955, "it seems not at all extraordinary that you should celebrate your birthday in Bangkok."[32]

---

[30] Garthoff, *Soviet Military Policy*, pp. 52–54.

[31] Crankshaw, *Khrushchev*, pp. 253–255.

[32] The President to Secretary of State, February 15, 1955, Correspondence, Dulles Papers, Princeton.

CHAPTER IX

New Frontiers and Old Dilemmas (1957-1962)

O N THE MORNING OF OCTOBER 4, 1957, the Soviet Union successfully launched the world's first man-made satellite
Named "Sputnik," Russian for "traveling companion," the 184-
pound satellite swirled above the earth at 18,000 miles per hour.
More significant than the satellite was the powerful booster
rocket that thrust Sputnik into orbit, since that indicated Soviet
capability of sending a powerful weapon at very high speeds to
targets within a 4,000-mile radius. The launching also demonstrated the skill of Soviet missile science. Niebuhr's argument
that scientists could be as efficiently exploited by a totalitarian
as by a democratic society seemed true—and ominous.

Americans were extremely disturbed. Strategic Air Force units
were dispersed and placed on alert, short-range Jupiter missiles
installed in Turkey and Italy to offset the long-range Soviet
weapons, money poured into missile and bomber programs, and
"gaps" were suddenly discovered in everything from missile
production to the teaching of arithmetic at the preschool level.
Dulles attempted to play down the Soviet feat because he understood the impact it would make upon world affairs. The newly
emerging nations could view Russia as a people which in 1917
had been generations behind other industrialized nations, but
which through harsh regimentation, had assumed first place in
the race for control of outer space. They could also interpret the
launching as a dramatic swing in the balance of military power
towards Moscow. In August 1957, the Soviets had fired the
world's first intercontinental ballistic missile (ICBM), and that
same month had announced, "Coexistence is not only the absence
of war between the two systems, but also peaceful economic

competition between them, and concrete cooperation in economic, political and cultural areas."[1] Khrushchev could welcome such competition with the knowledge that the Soviet gross national product (the total amount of goods and service in the economy) had increased on the average of 7.1 percent annually between 1950 and 1958, nearly 50 percent greater than the American rate.

This economic growth was real, but the Soviet lead in ICBMs was less so. The Soviets made a basic decision in 1957 not to build an elementary first-generation ICBM complex, but to wait for the second and third generation models. This meant that for the next few years Russian foreign policy would attempt to exploit an apparent and false lead. One interesting way Khrushchev did this was to have Russian radio and newspapers quote back to the West the West's own exaggerated views of Soviet missile capacity, thereby reinforcing the exaggerations.[2] (Four years later a surprised Senator Stuart Symington, Democrat of Missouri, revealed that Soviet ICBM strength amounted to only 3.5 percent of an estimation made in 1959. Symington had been one of the leading voices demanding a crash program after 1957 to catch up, supposedly, with the Russians. He had also been a former Secretary of the Air Force.)

This policy was a dangerous gamble for Khrushchev. Within five years it would lead to the Cuban missile crisis. In a matter of months it would result, in part, in a critical widening of the growing Sino-Soviet split. Given Khrushchev's hope of using Sputnik to increase Communist influence in the underdeveloped areas, this latter result was ironic. In terming the ICBM the "ultimate weapon," Khrushchev carefully began emphasizing at this time the terrible destruction that would result from a nuclear exchange. At the 40th anniversary celebration of the 1917 Revolution, however, Mao Tse-tung insisted that "the international situation has now reached a new turning point. There are two winds in the world today: the East wind and the West wind. . . . I think the characteristic of the situation today is the East wind prevailing over the West wind."[3] Mao assumed, as a Chinese

---

[1] "The Leninist Course of Peaceful Coexistence," *Kommunist*, No. 11, 1957, p. 5.

[2] Horelick and Rush, *Strategic Power*, pp. 36–38.

[3] William Zimmerman, "Russia and the International Order," *Survey*, No. 58 (January, 1966), pp. 209–213.

newspaper commented in February 1958, that the Soviet successes had created a "qualitative change in the distribution of world power [which] had . . . torn apart the paper tiger of American imperialism and shattered the tale of the 'position of strength.' "[4] The Chinese urged strong support for "wars of liberation" in the newly emerging nations, wars that could be safely fanned because the American strategic power had been neutralized. Khrushchev refused to cooperate in such recklessness, particularly since he knew that his ICBM program was considerably more of a "paper tiger" than the American long-range bombing force.

The break between China and Russia also became evident in other areas. The Soviets strongly disagreed with Mao's "Great Leap Forward" program in 1958 with its emphasis on forced collectivization. This disagreement pinpointed intra-Communist differences, for the Russians, as they had historically, insisted first upon industrial productivity and only secondarily upon infusing the masses with revolutionary ideology. Mao, however, was trying at best to balance the two and, in fact, actually reversing the Soviet priorities in order to mobilize his tremendous manpower through mass revolutionary indoctrination. The Chinese became increasingly critical of Khrushchev's emphasis on consumer goods instead of military hardware and of the Soviet insistence on aiding "bourgeois" regimes in the underdeveloped world instead of fomenting revolution.

Dulles precisely and colorfully described the new Soviet attitude in May 1958. He no longer feared that the Soviets would pose a greater threat with their disavowal of force and "this policy of the smile." Dulles found hope in the belief "that a nation tends to become what it pretends to be. . . . I have seen lots of tough guys who have made their pile, who come to New York, wanted to get into society, and who have to behave differently."[5] The Secretary of State attempted to readjust American military thinking by placing increased emphasis on small nuclear weapons which could be used in limited wars.

In these last months of his life Dulles also tried to influence

---

[4] Zagoria, *Sino-Soviet Conflict, 1956–1961*, pp. 160–162.
[5] "Remarks to U.S. Ambassadors to Europe," Paris, May 9, 1958, NATO Ministerial meeting, Conference dossiers, Dulles Papers.

the newly emerging areas by readjusting American economic aid. Nothing could be done through direct trade arrangements. The traditional reciprocal trade agreements program was in fact seriously injured when in March 1959 Eisenhower imposed quota restrictions on foreign crude oil imports after two large oil companies refused to join in voluntary restraints. The restrictions were a body blow to Venezuelan and Middle Eastern oil producers and affected American foreign policy in those areas. The Administration only slightly offset that misfortune by increasing foreign aid assistance. In fiscal 1957 Mutual Security Program funds were raised nearly 40 percent, and much of this went to Burma, Indonesia, and South Vietnam. Even then Asia received only $785 million and Latin America $24.2 million while Europe received $892 million. By fiscal 1959, however, American aid to Southeast Asia alone climbed to $547 million; whereas South Vietnam received about $50 million in 1957, it obtained $207 two years later. In 1958 the United States began pushing a United Nations-sponsored program for developing the 1500-mile Mekong River basin in Southeast Asia by giving more than half of the $9 million needed to carry out initial investigations.

This increased emphasis upon Southeast Asia indicated the Eisenhower Administration's growing concern over Mao's China. Dulles's attitude became clear in late summer and autumn 1958, when the Chinese began to shell the offshore islands. Mao probably did not plan to invade the islands, but hoped that with the United States immersed in another Middle Eastern crisis, one of two results would occur: either the Quemoy garrison would surrender without being invaded, or the United States would strike back by bombing mainland China and thus bring the Soviets into the affair back of the Chinese. Neither occurred. The American Seventh Fleet escorted Nationalist troops and supplies into the islands, Dulles announced that Quemoy was "increasingly related" to Taiwan's safety, and American Marines moved into Quemoy eight-inch howitzers capable of firing atomic shells. Dulles's tough stand on the Chinese problem and his emphasis on tactical atomic weapons had merged into a concrete policy position. Khrushchev did little except assure Mao that Russia would help if China was actually attacked.

The Chinese calculations on the probable American response

and the Soviet-American balance of power should have been more accurate, for Mao could have drawn the appropriate conclusions from the Middle Eastern crisis of July. In that episode, the United States landed Marines in Lebanon without any counterstroke from Moscow. Two months before the landings, Dulles had expressed the fear that the growing power of Nasser and the United Arab Republic (formed by Egypt, Syria, and Yemen in early 1958), would endanger Jordan, Iraq, and Lebanon. On July 14, General Abdel Karim Kassim led a nationalist revolt which overthrew the Iraqi government and established a regime friendly to the UAR. The Baghdad Pact suddenly had a gaping hole, and repercussions were felt in Lebanon where pro-Nasser Moslems had been fighting Christians.

The news of the Kassim *coup* and the turmoil in Lebanon arrived in Washington early on the morning of July 14. Lebanon President Camille Chamoun, a Maronite Christian, urgently requested help from the United States. At 9:45 A.M. Dulles began explaining to Congressional leaders "recent Soviet political activities" in the area, announcing that "it was time to bring a halt to the deterioration in our position in the Middle East." The Administration wanted to land troops in Lebanon. There would be no military problem. General Nathan Twining of the Joint Chiefs assured Dulles, as General Twining later recalled, that the "Russians aren't going to jump us," and "if they do jump us, if they do come in, they couldn't pick a better time, because we've got them over the whing whang and they know it."[6] The only problem was again the proper interpretation of the Eisenhower Doctrine. Some Congressmen argued that because any Communist threat was only dimly apparent, Dulles was asking them to condone intervention in a Lebanese civil war. Logically, they continued, troops should also be sent into Iraq. But they placed no obstacles before Eisenhower, and at 2:30 P.M. the President issued the order. While British paratroopers landed in Jordan to help King Hussein once again stabilize his government, 14,000 American troops waded ashore around public bathers on Lebanon's beaches to quiet the threat of civil war.

---

[6] Interview with General Nathan Twining, Dulles Oral History Project, Princeton.

The size of the force warned both the new Iraqi government and Nasser that any threat to Western oil resources in the area would not be tolerated.

Kassim assured the West that its Iraqi interests were safe, and his government soon moved away from Nasser's influence. The Egyptian leader, so one top American official believed, received "one of the greatest lessons in world power politics that he ever had."[7] When Nasser flew to Moscow during the crisis to request Soviet help, Khrushchev refused to make any significant response. As for the United States, Dulles informed the Cabinet that once again the free world had thwarted Stalin's and Lenin's prophecies that Communism would march through the newly emerging nations to conquer the West. In March 1959, Kassim destroyed the shell of the Baghdad Pact by formally withdrawing. The United States attempted to replace the Pact by immediately signing new bilateral military aid treaties with Pakistan, Turkey, and Iran, while the remaining members of the Pact formed the Central Treaty Organization (CENTO).

In the Formosa Straits and Lebanon, the United States had carried through its policies with conventional military forces. By mid-1958 another type of crisis was facing Washington policymakers, a crisis that was more subtle, immeasurably complex, and that in the long run posed a greater danger to the United States. Latin America is a continent fundamentally different from Asia or the Middle East. It is more highly developed and, in some areas, in an intermediate stage of economic growth which presents more sophisticated economic and social problems than do the more primitive economies of Africa or Asia. Between 1948 and 1958, Latin America's economy grew at an impressive annual rate of 4.3 percent, but its population explosion of 3 percent annually was greater than any area in the world and would by the year 2000 result in 600 million people where 200 million lived in 1960. The economic growth also greatly varied from country to country. Venezuela's oil and Mexico's healthy social system gave those countries strong advantages. Otherwise the picture was not happy, for outside of Costa Rica and Mexico, 2 percent of the population owned 75 percent of the agricultural

---

[7] Interview with Robert Murphy, Dulles Oral History Project, Princeton.

land on a continent that was primarily agrarian. Many of the poor moved out of the countryside to live in some of the world's worst slums on the outskirts of the major cities.

Large areas of Latin America were controlled by extremely conservative governments which could not be removed from power as Africans and Asians were removing European colonial rulers from their continents. The United States had done nothing to ameliorate this problem, nor had it made any major effort to correct the inequities in economies which were closely tied to American producers and consumers. Between 1945 and 1960, the United States gave three times more aid to the Benelux countries than to all twenty Latin American nations. Private American capital, meanwhile, had invested $1 billion in oil, $500 million in mining, and $750 million in manufacturing, thus increasing the imbalance of the Latin American economies. On the other hand, the 1958 recession in the United States cut the flow of private and public monies to 61 percent of that of 1957. Although Americans took about half of Latin America's exports, this trade shrank between 1946 and 1958 until Latin Americans accounted for 29 percent of the United States import market in 1958 as compared with 36 per cent of twelve years before.

After signing their first trade agreement with Argentina in 1953, the Soviets tried to take advantage of these conditions. By 1957 their trade with Latin America amounted to only $200 million annually. It increased to $250 million the next year, $300 million in 1959, and $450 million in 1960. This economic offensive was aimed at a few select countries as Argentina, Brazil, Uruguay, and later Cuba. By 1960, Soviet trade remained small in absolute terms, but had doubled within three years, while the United States proportion was slipping.[8] This coincided with an upsurge of anti-Yankeeism throughout the continent. The depth of that feeling was not appreciated in Washington until April 1958 when Vice-President Richard Nixon and his wife visited several Latin American countries and were spat upon, had eggs and stones hurled at them, and in Caracas had their limousine

---

[8] Ronald James Clark, "Latin-American Economic Relations with the Soviet Bloc, 1954–1961," unpublished doctoral dissertation, Indiana University, 1963.

attacked by mobs. Eisenhower rushed a thousand Marines to American bases in the Caribbean, but Nixon flew home before further outbreaks could occur.

President Juscelino Kubitschek of Brazil seized this opportunity to push for Washington's acceptance of his proposed "Operation Pan America" in which the United States and Latin America would cooperate on an extensive, long-term developmental program. A pivotal part of the plan was an Inter-American Development Bank which could channel low-interest American loans into the southern continent and also serve as a clearing house for Latin American developmental capital. The Eisenhower Administration had been cool towards this proposal in 1957, but interest picked up considerably after Nixon's experience. In December 1959, the Bank was established with one billion dollars in capital. The following year, after Fidel Castro's rise to power in Cuba had intensified concern in Washington, Eisenhower committed another half-billion dollars for social-welfare projects. Through the Act of Bogotá in September 1960, the hemispheric nations began working out details of overall economic development. These events marked the real beginnings of what John F. Kennedy would later popularize as the Alliance for Progress.

If the supposed Soviet long-range missile superiority provided a cover for increased Russian activity in the newly emerging nations, similar Soviet weapons posed a considerably more direct threat to the *status quo* in Europe. Khrushchev threatened to use his Medium Range Ballistic Missiles to knock NATO countries "out of commission," in any future crisis, and he particularly emphasized that West Germany would have "no chance for survival" if war erupted between Russia and America. This Soviet offensive compounded an already embarrassing situation for the Acheson-Dulles policy. Having bargained its military rearmament to regain its sovereignty, West Germany became derelict in building conventional forces. The Adenauer government cut service time for draftees, refused to spend its full authorization for arms, and reduced force goals from 500,000 to 325,000. Adenauer instead ominously began to request missiles, artillery capable of firing nuclear shells, and fighter-bombers which could haul thermonuclear bombs. The West soon delivered the artillery and bombers. This turn in German affairs set off speeches in 1956 by opposition West German parties and by British Prime Minister Anthony Eden which proposed the neutralization and reunification of Germany before Central Europe entered a full-fledged arms race.

In the United States the debate climaxed in an angry exchange between two architects of postwar policy, George Kennan and Dean Acheson. In a series of lectures strikingly similar to Lippmann's proposals of ten years before, Kennan proposed that before Germany received nuclear arms, the threat of that possibility could be used to negotiate with the Russians a neutralization of Central and Eastern Europe which would include withdrawal of both the Soviet and American armies.[9] This plan soon became known as "disengagement."

Acheson's response in January 1958 was acerbic. If the United States withdrew its troops from Germany and Western Europe, Acheson declared, the Soviets would sooner or later exterminate "independent national life in Western Europe." He particularly feared that Communist parties in Europe would gain the initiative. This indicated his view of how NATO shaped the internal political life of European countries as well as the overall military strategies. Withdrawal from and neutralization of Germany would be disastrous, Acheson warned, for as he had once remarked, without American troops "to monitor the continued integration of Germany into the West, we should be continually haunted by the spectre of a sort of new [Nazi-Soviet] Agreement." As for Kennan, Acheson sarcastically observed that "Mr. X" had tried but had failed to convince any "responsible leader" of these ideas as early as 1949. "Mr. Kennan has never, in my judgment," Acheson commented, "grasped the realities of power relationships, but takes a rather mystical attitude toward them. To Mr. Kennan there is no Soviet military threat in Europe."[10]

This last sentence indicated a fundamental assumption on the part of Acheson and Dulles. During the six months following Acheson's outburst, however, a strange phenomenon occurred in Washington. Dulles apparently began to move away from

---

[9] George F. Kennan, *Russia, the Atom and the West* (New York, 1957).
[10] *U.S. News and World Report*, January 17, 1958, p. 63.

Acheson and towards Kennan. The first indication of a change came in a little-noted speech by the director of the White House disarmament staff, Robert E. Matteson. He declared in February 1958 that "we may very well be at one of those great historical divides where a boldness in exploration of the relaxation-of-tension concept might pay greater dividends than we now suspect."[11] In May, Dulles remarked that "disengagement" was such a "naughty word" that it "couldn't even be translated into a good language like French." He even went so far as to comment that "If I had to choose between a neutralized Germany and Germany in the Soviet bloc, it might be almost better to have it in the bloc. That clearly is not acceptable but disengagement is absolutely not acceptable either."[12]

On June 30, 1958, however, Dulles wrote a "My dear friend" letter to Adenauer. At the outset the Secretary discounted any dismantling of existing military establishments, but he then observed that domestic and satellite demands were making the Soviets more open to negotiation. Dulles wondered if there could not be a "limitation of armament . . . through establishing significant zones of inspection which would greatly minimize the fear of massive surprise attack."[13] He disavowed any talk of paying a high political price, such as cutting the power of the West German government through a reunification of Germany. The implication, however, was clear: negotiations with the Soviets could lead to the first hesitant steps towards a military neutralization of Central Europe.

Within ten months Dulles would be dead. Where the Secretary's thoughts of mid-1958 would have led is only speculation, but clearly he was taking into account those new international events which were reorienting East-West relations. The European *status quo* was further shaken in June 1958 (the month Dulles wrote Adenauer) when Charles de Gaulle returned to power in France. Franco-American relations had not improved

---

[11] Richard Rovere, "Letter from Washington," *New Yorker*, March 22, 1958, pp. 136–141.
[12] "Remarks to U.S. Ambassadors to Europe," Paris, May 9, 1958, NATO Ministerial meeting, Conference Dossiers, Dulles Papers.
[13] Dulles to Adenauer, June 30, 1958, Correspondence, Dulles Papers.

since the Suez debacle, and as the new government promised to end the bloody colonial war in Algeria, it attacked the Middle East policy of the United States which, as one leading Gaullist claimed, was "willing to sacrifice its European allies in its ridiculous search for Arab friends, lest they fall under Communist influence."[14] Dulles watched de Gaulle's disengagement from the Algerian revolt with some concern, for he appreciated how the General hoped to regain the *grandeur* of France through the reorientation of French foreign policy.[15] The reorientation would require considerable freedom-of-action, and that, Dulles believed quite accurately, would result in "neutralist" policies advanced by de Gaulle within the NATO alliance.

The General made his first major move in July 1958 when he requested the establishment of a three-power directorate of the United States, Great Britain, and France within the Western alliance. Washington and London promptly rejected this. De Gaulle also asked to be included in the program worked out between Prime Minister Harold Macmillan and President Eisenhower at the Bermuda Conference of March 1957, which provided for the sharing of some nuclear weapons. Maintaining a position consistent with his letter of a few days before to Adenauer, Dulles refused the General's request in July. Washington and London compounded de Gaulle's anger at these rebuffs when they landed troops in Jordan and Lebanon without consulting France. At the same time that the Communist bloc was dividing into Russian, Chinese, and Yugoslav factions, the Western alliance was also splitting apart.

The postwar world, like most 13-year olds, was entering a new and uncertain stage. The widening split within NATO became more evident in late 1958 when France, West Germany, Italy, and the Benelux prepared for the formal initiation of the European Economic Community, or Common Market, on January 1, 1959. Following an accord first reached in March 1957, these nations agreed that within fifteen years they would form

---

[14] Alexander Werth, *De Gaulle, A Political Biography* (New York, 1965, 1966), pp. 11–15.

[15] Alfred Grosser, *La Politique extérieure de la Ve République* (Paris, 1965), p. 44.

an economic union by eliminating tariffs and equalizing taxes within the community while creating a common tariff for outside goods. The immediate impact was political as well as economic, for in a stroke "the six" had decreased their economic dependence upon the United States, tied West Germany firmly within Western Europe, taken their first step towards possible political federation, and created a middle bloc between the United States and the Soviet Union. The importance of this last factor became evident during the eighteen months following New Year's 1960 when much to American dismay, Western Europe and, particularly, West Germany, France, and Italy, shipped approximately a billion dollars worth of strategic goods and equipment to the Soviet Union.

In the last months of 1958, Great Britain attempted to enter the Common Market, but she failed after refusing to surrender her economic ties to the Commonwealth and to the United States. The British countered by forming in November 1959, the Free Trade Association (or "Outer Seven") comprised of themselves, Sweden, Switzerland, Portugal, Austria, Norway, and Denmark. The new grouping, however, failed to keep pace with the booming Common Market, and Washington watched as the British became increasingly isolated from Western Europe's economic upsurge.

Moscow feared these developments even more than did Washington. The success of the Common Market and, above all, West Germany's possession of artillery and aircraft which had nuclear capabilities raised once again before the Soviets the spectre of a militarized and economically aggressive Germany. After several days of publicizing his growing ICBM arsenal, Khrushchev began a series of moves on November 10, 1958, which climaxed in the demand that the United States, Great Britain, and France withdraw their 10,000 troops from West Berlin, make it a "free city," and negotiate with the East German government (which none of the Western powers recognized) for access into Berlin. If agreement was not reached within six months, Khrushchev threatened to turn the access routes over to East German control. With complete Western support, Dulles rejected Khrushchev's demands, refused to contemplate recognition of East Germany, and intimated that if the East Germans did gain control of the access routes and refused to allow Western vehicles through, NATO would retaliate "if need be by military force." Khrushchev replied that this would mean World War III.

In focusing upon West Berlin, the Soviet leader had pinpointed the fulcrum that could change the balance of power within Europe. For American policy-makers feared that if the United States did evacuate West Berlin, the Adenauer government's confidence in NATO and the Common Market would be shaken, and the basis laid for a West German-Russian deal. It soon became evident, nevertheless, that Khrushchev had concluded that the fulcrum was not worth a nuclear exchange. Denying that he had issued an ultimatum, he modified the six-month limit so discussions could be held. Over strong Chinese protests, the Soviet leader visited the United States in September 1959. Just before his arrival, a Soviet "Lunik" hit the moon. Khrushchev reminded the world of his nation's capabilities by presenting a replica of the Soviet pennant aboard the "Lunik" to the President. The visit produced few diplomatic results. Plans were made for a summit conference in Geneva the following spring, after which Eisenhower would visit Russia.

Events during the first four months of 1960 hardly encouraged hopes for a productive summit. In April, the Chinese climaxed a series of harsh attacks upon Khrushchev by accusing the Soviets of appeasing the West. The United States meanwhile signed in January an agreement in which Japan allowed the continuation of American military bases on her soil. Anti-American riots broke out in Tokyo and Eisenhower cancelled a trip to Japan. Coming at a time when Southeast Asian affairs were again boiling, the American move was understandable within its own policy context, but it placed Khrushchev in a most uncomfortable position with China and the Communist parties in Southeast Asia.

These outbursts, however, were of secondary importance when compared with the German problem. Through the winter of 1959-1960, signs appeared that at Camp David Khrushchev and Eisenhower had cleared away certain obstacles as a prelude for major negotiations at the summit on Berlin. By the end of April 1960, hopes for a settlement had shriveled before blistering announcements from Moscow and Washington. During trips to Indonesia and France in early spring, the Soviet Premier again warned that either the German settlement would run along Russian lines or Western occupation rights in Berlin would be cancelled through a Soviet peace treaty with East Germany. On April 20, 1960, Under-Secretary of State C. Douglas Dillon attacked Khrushchev's statements with the observation that "the so-called German Democratic Republic [East Germany] is one of the outstanding myths in a vast Communist web of prodigious mythology." Requesting Soviet concessions in Eastern Europe, Korea, and the United Nations as well as in Berlin, Dillon gravely announced that in making his recent threats, Khrushchev "is skating on very thin ice." The American official flatly announced that although the United States was willing to consider "interim arrangements" which would provide time for careful negotiations, "We will not accept any arrangement which might become a first step toward the abandonment of West Berlin or the extinguishing of freedom in that part of Germany." Six days later Khrushchev reiterated the Soviet policy on Berlin, interpreted Dillon's remarks as a change in the American position since the Camp David discussions, and warned "such hotheads that when they start invoking force and not right and justice, it is but natural that this force will be countered with the force of the other side."[16]

On May 5, the eve of the summit conference, Khrushchev suddenly announced that the Soviets had shot down a U-2 American reconnaissance plane which had been violating Russian territorial sovereignty. The United States first denied that the aircraft had been on a spying mission, but then became trapped when Khrushchev produced film from the plane and the pilot who had parachuted to safety. After some hesitation, Eisenhower accepted full responsibility for the incident. He also finally announced that there would be no future overflights; the damage, however, had been done. This episode at Geneva did not ruin the conference. That had been accomplished by the growing intransigence over Berlin, the Sino-Soviet rift, and the

---

[16] *Documents on American Foreign Relations, 1960*, edited by Richard P. Stebbins (New York, 1961), pp. 106–113.

decision (made by some high American officials) to send a U-2 plane over Russian territory during highly critical hours in Russian-American diplomacy.

Khrushchev's major concern was not his relationship with Eisenhower; the President would shortly leave office anyway. More important was the embarrassing position the U-2 flights, which has been occurring over the Soviet Union for at least four years, placed him in his struggle with Mao. There could be little doubt that on previous U-2 flights the United States had discovered the truth about Russian ICBM strength. This thought probably influenced Khrushchev to call off the Berlin crisis temporarily while intensifying his threats of how Russia would destroy any American ally allowing U-2 planes to leave from its territory. He particularly seized upon an issue in the summer of 1960, which would somewhat appease China and at the same time allow him to wave his strategic power against the United States. Khrushchev welcomed Fidel Castro as a new force in Latin America and threatened to destroy the United States, "figuratively speaking," if it tried to attack Castro. The Monroe Doctrine, Khrushchev announced, was dead.

This turn of events had begun when the young middle-class lawyer, a species which the unbalanced Cuban society turned out in overabundance, led on July 26, 1953 an armed assault on the Batista regime. For this Castro was jailed, but he escaped to Mexico, organized a small revolutionary band, and landed in Cuba in 1956. Batista's police were waiting, and Castro struggled into the mountains with only ten other survivors. American officials paid little attention, believing Batista's word that Castro was dead. In 1957, *The New York Times* correspondent Herbert Matthews found the rebel's hideaway and revealed to the world Castro's program and his astonishing success among the Cuban peasants. Matthews' reports had little positive effect on Washington, however.

The American failure to worry about or understand Castro was not the major mistake, for this was symptomatic of a Cuban policy that had left much to be desired ever since the United States had first taken *de facto* control in the summer of 1898. By 1956 Americans owned 80 percent of Cuba's utilities, 40 percent of its sugar, 90 percent of its mining wealth, and the island's key strategic location of Guantanamo Bay. The Cuban economy could be manipulated by changing the amount of Cuban sugar allowed into the American market. The United States had also landed Marines three times after 1902 in efforts to stabilize Cuban politics. Washington had not intervened when Batista overthrew a constitutionally-elected government in 1952 and began consolidating his power by following such diverse policies as allowing American advisors to train his military forces while inviting Cuban Communist party members to assume governmental positions. The Communists were close enough to Batista to have almost missed joining Castro's movement before Batista was driven from power. In 1960, the American Ambassador to Cuba during Batista's last years, Earl E. T. Smith, summarized past Cuban-American relations and implicitly explained how disastrous the American colonial policy had been in Cuba for 62 years: "Senator, let me explain to you that the United States, until the advent of Castro, was so overwhelmingly influential in Cuba that . . . the American Ambassador was the second most important man in Cuba; sometimes even more important than the President. . . . Now, today, his importance is not very great."[17]

His importance declined because upon grasping power on New Year's Day 1959, Castro determined to balance the Cuban economy and to rectify the social injustices within the society. To accomplish this, a thoroughgoing revolution would be required. In the new ruler's mind, this meant ending Cuba's dependence on Washington. Castro's trip to the United States in April almost inevitably produced no positive results. The following month he announced an agrarian reform program which met American resistance. By the summer, Castro's personal power was unquestioned, but in his need for organized political support to carry out the revolution, he moved closer to the Communists within his 26th of July movement. By the end of the year, the anti-Communists within the movement were isolated and leaving Cuba. Confiscations of American property intensified, signaling increased anti-Americanism, as well as Castro's

---

[17] Robert F. Smith, *What Happened in Cuba? A Documentary History* (New York, 1963), p. 273.

need for resources to finance socio-economic changes. That was a need, moreover, which prohibited him from paying for the confiscated property.

In February 1960, the Russians signed a trade agreement to exchange Cuban sugar for Soviet oil, machinery, and technicians. Ironically, as Cuban-Soviet bloc trade increased from 2 percent of the island's trade in 1960 to 80 percent by the end of 1961, Castro was forced to accept the position as a food and raw material producer which he had so strongly deprecated in past Cuban-American relations. In July 1960, the United States cut the Cuban sugar quota from the American market. In August, Washington began to mobilize hemispheric opposition to Cuba and, three months later, American naval forces moved to Central American waters to quell a rumored invasion from Cuba. At this time, Eisenhower accepted a Central Intelligence Agency-State Department plan to train an anti-Castro army. Preparations began for an invasion in early 1961. In the first days of January 1961, United States-Cuban diplomatic relations were formally severed.

Castroism and the problems of other newly emerging areas dominated the foreign policy issues of the 1960 presidential campaign. True to his Republican heritage, Richard M. Nixon emphasized the need to defend the islands off the Chinese mainland, while Democratic nominee John F. Kennedy doubted whether Quemoy and Matsu were essential to Taiwan's defense. Kennedy moved closer to Nixon's position on this issue as the campaign progressed. The Democratic candidate started a more significant debate when he suggested American support of "non-Batista democratic anti-Castro forces." Nixon appeared appalled at even the suggestion of American support for such intervention. He later explained that having access to the invasion plans already under way, he was forced to act surprised publicly at Kennedy's suggestion. Outside of these exchanges, the two nominees differed significantly on no other foreign policy issues. The Eisenhower consensus, forged in 1956, was making its mark, and each candidate simply tried to exploit, not destroy, it. In one of the closest presidential elections, Kennedy won by a margin of 114,000 votes out of 68.3 million cast. The electoral college vote went to the Democrats 303-219.

John F. Kennedy was a most sensitive and astute politician, and the narrow victory margin affected the development of his foreign policy. Presidential assistant Theodore Sorensen defined the problem: "President Kennedy is acutely aware of Jefferson's dictum: 'Great innovations should not be forced on slender majorities.' "[18] Kennedy tended to defer to military and intelligence experts and to men in Congress who preferred to fight the Cold War rather than take the risk of negotiating its problems. His experiences abroad while his father, Joseph P. Kennedy, was Ambassador to Great Britain in the late 1930s, convinced him that democracies moved too slowly in reacting to totalitarian aggression, a view that permeated his widely-read book written while a Harvard senior, *Why England Slept*. His sensitivity to the political climate was also demonstrated during 1950-1954 when he was extremely reluctant to oppose Senator McCarthy. As a young Senator from Massachusetts, Kennedy nevertheless realized that the growing importance of the newly emerging nations required changes in foreign policy. A 1957 speech was outspoken in support of Algeria's fight against France. In 1954, he warned against any American attempt to prop up the French regime in Indochina, but on this issue Kennedy equivocated, for in June 1956, he lauded Diem as an "offspring" of the American effort to keep Southeast Asia free. Aware of the challenge of the newly emerging peoples, and fearful that the United States would not respond quickly or properly, Kennedy emphasized in a special message to Congress on May 25, 1961, "The great battleground for the defense and expansion of freedom today is ... Asia, Latin America, Africa and the Middle East, the lands of the rising peoples."[19]

In his first Annual Message on January 30, 1961, the President listed the priorities for waging the conflict beween "Freedom and Communism," by noting that "First, we must strengthen our military tools."[20] Upon entering office, the Administration had

---

[18] Theodore C. Sorensen, *Decision-Making in the White House: The Olive Branch or the Arrows* (New York, 1963), pp. 44–48.

[19] U.S. Government Printing Office, *Public Papers of the Presidents, J. F. Kennedy, 1961* (Washington, 1962), p. 397.

[20] *Ibid.*, pp. 23–24.

discovered that the "missile gap," which Kennedy had heavily emphasized in the campaign, was only fictional. The Soviets and the Chinese also knew this and, consequently, Kennedy and his advisors feared that the Communists would place more emphasis on conventional, local wars. In 1961, the Administration increased the defense budget 15 percent, doubling the number of ready-combat divisions in the Army's strategic reserve, expanding the Marine Corps, adding 70 vessels to the active fleet, and giving a dozen more wings to the tactical air forces. General Maxwell Taylor returned to act as the President's military advisor. A special Office for Politico-Military Affairs appeared in the State Department to coordinate State and Defense Department policies throughout the world.

Varying little in principle from Eisenhower's approach, this policy was a different kind of attempt to contain Communism and revolutionary instability. The policy had been thought through and widely publicized by the reports of the Rockefeller brothers in the late 1950s, and was the result of a logical progression of thought on the part of intellectuals like Henry Kissinger and Klaus Knorr. In this sense particularly, the Kennedy Administration seized upon American intellectuals in a manner unmatched since 1933. The scholars responded.

Other parts of the society also responded. In his "Farewell Address" in January 1961, Eisenhower had warned the American people against the "conjunction of an immense military establishment and a large arms industry" which was "new in American experience," and whose "total influence . . . is felt in every city, every state house, every office of the federal government. . . . In the councils of government, we must guard against the acquisition of unwarranted influence, whether sought or unsought, by the military-industrial complex," the President declared. "The potential for the disastrous rise of misplaced power exists and will persist." For Eisenhower, this was strong language. The Kennedy Administration, however, took little heed of this speech. Determined to help non-Communist nations militarily, and worried over the outflow of American gold caused by an unfavorable balance in the nation's financial and trade exchanges wih the rest of the world, the new President established in 1961 a special post in the Defense Department to sell American arms through private corporations to foreign nations. By 1965, American companies exported $1.9 billion worth of arms to Europe, Japan, Iran, Venezuela, and Saudi Arabia, among others. General Dynamics Corporation alone sold more than a billion dollars worth of arms overseas between 1962 and 1965. Most of the goods were sophisticated and expensive electronic equipment. As one business periodical observed, in the 1930s such companies were known as " 'Merchants of Death'. . . . Times have changed."[21]

The drive for a unified but multimilitary response to foreign policy problems was typified by Secretary of Defense Robert McNamara's management of the Pentagon. No more would individual services have wholly independent programs. McNamara instead brought the various services together under "program elements" in which the military units were coordinated for efficient war-making on various levels. The professional soldiers lost some of their political power, but they gained greatly in military efficiency. By mobilizing resources in this way, the Administration could massively retaliate on many military levels. The change under way since the days of Dulles had matured. Particular emphasis was placed upon preparing the United States for guerilla wars. The Jungle Warfare School in the Canal Zone and another at Fort Bragg, North Carolina brought Army Special Forces troops together with Latin American units. More than 600 Latin American policemen sharpened their talents in counter-intelligence work and the handling of mobs by undergoing training in the Canal Zone school established by the Agency for International Development. At the end of 1966, anti-American guerillas operated in Venezuela, Bolivia, Colombia, Peru, and Guatemala.

Kennedy picked Latin America for special attention, for besides the training of anti-guerilla forces and the establishment of the Peace Corps (young men and women trained to perform teaching and technical services in newly emerging nations), the President announced on March 13, 1961 the Alliance for Progress. To the Eisenhower policies of 1959-1960, Kennedy added a ten-year commitment of $20 billion of American money and an

---

[21] *Forbes*, February 1, 1966, pp. 15–16.

appropriate image. The plan was worked out at the Punta del Este, Uruguay, conference in August. The United States aid, including $300 million annually from private capital, would quadruple the annual economic assistance given the area between 1946 and 1960. In return, Latin America pledged $80 billion of investment over the ten-year period and, most important, land, tax, and other socio-economic reforms. Hopefully the combined efforts would result in a 5.5 percent increase in Latin America's growth rate, or a very modest net increase of 2.5 percent over the population increase.

These ambitious plans encountered major difficulties during the next two years. The programs were undercut by bureaucratic infighting in Washington, the marked reluctance of such major Latin American nations as Brazil, Argentina, and Mexico to submit their developmental programs to hemispheric scrutiny; and particularly by the inability or unwillingness of many governments to undertake the promised reforms. In some nations the requisite political stability could not be established; 106 illegal and unscheduled changes occurred between 1930 and 1965 among Latin American heads of state. The Kennedy Administration, trapped between the alternatives of intervening in the affairs of sovereign nations or watching the Alliance grow increasingly weaker, could not work out an effective response. When the Argentine Army overthrew the government of Arturo Frondizi in the spring of 1962 because Frondizi was losing power to Peronistas, the State Department recognized the military-established regime of José Maria Guido. When, on the other hand, the Peruvian Army (led by a Fort Benning-trained soldier driving a General Sherman tank) seized control of that country in order to prevent elections which would have returned a liberal government, Washington refused to recognize the new regime. The pressure, however, was soon abandoned and recognition was granted. By 1963, Alliance officials could claim that 35 million Latin Americans had benefited from the program, but only at the end of the first five years would the 5.5 percent growth rate be in sight, and not even then would there be evidence of important political and social reforms which could insure fair distribution of the benefits.

The Alliance was designed to create a stable and orderly Latin

America without having the hemisphere endure a series of Castro-type revolutions. The Cuban ruler had become a primary concern of American officials, and they moved to eradicate him on April 17, 1961 when the Administration supported an invasion at the Bay of Pigs by a group of Cuban exiles. This force had been trained for months in Guatemala by the Central Intelligence Agency. Although supposedly a secret operation, news of the preparations was widespread in American newspapers by April. President Kennedy was assured by CIA, State, and military officials that the invasion could succeed if, under American-provided air cover, the anti-Castro units could establish a beachhead and then link up with other guerillas in the mountains. Taking the word of his experts, Kennedy acquiesced, demanding only that no American troops be committed. Fifteen hundred Cubans waded ashore on the morning of the 17th, only to find that one key air strike had been cancelled because of clouds, that other naval and air supporting units had been immobilized by Castro's small air force, that the beachhead was indefensible, and that they had no hope of reaching the mountains. In the aftermath, American Ambassador to the United Nations Adlai Stevenson was caught lying about United States support of the operation. Kennedy ordered an investigation of the CIA, and this supposedly stripped it of some of its ability to plan similar operations. In Cuba, Castro was esconced more securely in power than ever before.

"All my life I've known better than to depend on the experts," the President wondered aloud shortly afterward. "How could I have been so stupid, to let them go ahead?"[22] The problem went deeper than that, however. Certainly the Guatemala operation of 1954 colored the view of both the CIA and the White House when they analyzed the Cuban project. The political-military philosophy of the invasion, moreover, was quite compatible with the new emphasis placed by the Administration upon guerilla-type warfare. The more fundamental problems were revealed by a State Department White Paper, authored by White House aide and Harvard historian Arthur Schlesinger, Jr., which attempted to rationalize the invasion just days before the tragedy occurred. The paper condemned the Castro movement as

---

[22] Theodore C. Sorensen, *Kennedy* (New York, 1965), p. 309.

Communist and attempted to place the United States on the side of social and economic reform within the hemisphere. It was, however, an unfortunate example of how history was misconstrued to serve political ends. From the first, when the paper claimed that "The hemisphere rejoiced at the overthrow of the Batista tyranny" (a fact not overly obvious in Washington in January 1959), until the conclusion that the "inter-American system was incompatible with any form of totalitarianism" (which failed to show how Trujillo, Duvalier, Somoza, and even Batista, among others, had prospered within that system), the State Department paper was more propaganda than a sober recital of facts.[23] But the paper revealed the dilemma of American policy toward Latin America. The Bay of Pigs was a public confession by the United States that it had failed to understand or deal with the most significant political change in the hemisphere in fifty years. This conclusion would have been tenable whether the invasion had succeeded or failed.

The President publicly accepted complete responsibility for the Bay of Pigs, and it was in the weeks immediately following this debacle that he traveled to Europe to visit West European leaders and Premier Nikita Khrushchev. The meeting in Vienna on June 3 and 4 with the Soviet leader resulted in an agreement to stop the growing conflict in Laos, but otherwise only increased Kennedy's apprehension that the Soviets were determined to create dangerous tensions by supporting what Khrushchev called "wars of liberation," that is, support of nationalist and pro-Communist elements in the newly emerging countries which were fighting Western political and economic influence. Worst of all, Khrushchev was militant about the necessity of eliminating Western power in West Berlin. The six-month notice was reimposed by the Soviet ruler, who became deeply angry at Kennedy's repeated warnings not to miscalculate American intentions. "I will tell you now," the President reported to the American people upon his return, "that it was a very sober two days."

Worried about the effects of the Bay of Pigs upon American credibility, and disturbed at public reports that Khrushchev had browbeaten him at Vienna, Kennedy accepted Dean Acheson's argument that the Berlin issue was a "simple conflict of wills,"

---

[23] Smith, *What Happened in Cuba? A Documentary History*, p. 211.

and that no negotiations could be considered until the Soviets lifted their threat of turning over the access routes to East Germany. This argument refused to touch the Soviet Premier's real problem: the growing military power of West Germany, its strengthened ties with the West, its attractiveness to technicians and other experts living in East Germany, the very weak position of the East German Communist regime, the position of West Berlin as an espionage and propaganda center within the Communist bloc, the growing fear of the Soviet peoples over West Germany's power, and, finally, Khrushchev's realization that with his ICBM braggadocio punctured as only myth, he needed a major strategic victory. The Administration's reaction was, in the words of Secretary of State Dean Rusk, "to turn this thing over to my successor exactly as I inherited it." In a national broadcast on July 25, 1961, Kennedy asked that National Reserve troops be placed on active duty and announced a dramatic increase of nearly 25 percent in American military strength. His premise was simple. The Berlin "outpost is not an isolated problem. The threat is worldwide," endangering Southeast Asia, "our own hemisphere" and "wherever else the freedom of human beings is as stake," as well as Berlin. That city and Saigon were, in this crucial sense, alike. Kennedy, like Eisenhower, defined the Communist threat in global terms.[24]

On August 13, the Soviets built the Berlin Wall. The flow of young and skilled labor from East Germany to the West stopped, and Khrushchev partly sealed the bloc from Western influences. The United States protested, but the Wall stood, a final obstacle to hundreds of East Germans who were shot trying to escape to the West. It was mute and bloody testimony to the policy of both East and West which, since 1945, had preferred a divided rather than a neutralized and united Germany.

The Wall had solved one problem, at least temporarily, but Khrushchev's supposed strategic power continued to come under attack in the West. In mid-1961, the Defense Department revealed that only a "handful" of Russian ICBMs were operational. Administration officials wondered aloud about Soviet credibility in the military realm. This no doubt made Khrushchev's political situation in Moscow uneasy, a situation al-

---

[24] *Public Papers of the Presidents, Kennedy, 1961*, pp. 533–540.

ready under attack because of the Sino-Soviet split. The division within the Communist world had become irreparable by late 1960, and had led to the expelling of Sino-influenced Albania from the bloc. Two weeks after the Berlin Wall appeared, Khrushchev broke the three-year Russian-American moratorium on the testing of nuclear bombs by beginning a series of tests which climaxed with the explosion in November of a 58-megaton weapon, 3000 times more powerful than the bomb that had obliterated Hiroshima.

Kennedy responded with underground testing in September 1961, but, fully confident that the United States held a wide lead in nuclear-weapons capability, the President attempted to reconvene the Geneva Disarmament Conference which had been meeting intermittently since 1958. France refused to attend; having exploded his first nuclear device in September 1960, de Gaulle did not want to be bound by any restraints at this early stage of his career as a nuclear power. The Soviets again refused Western demands for inspection and international control. On April 25, 1962, Kennedy ordered the first of some thirty American tests which would occur during the following year.

The President viewed his first eleven months in office as a period of continual, international crisis, and it was in this context that he made two of his most fateful decisions. The first involved Laos. That former French colony was a key to Southeast Asia, for it rimmed China, both Vietnams, Cambodia, Thailand, and Burma. In 1958 a gimcrack agreement between center, right, and Communist forces collapsed when the center and right attempted to reconstitute the government and cut Communist influence. When Pathet Lao Communist forces began major guerilla action, the United States stepped up aid until by April 1961 over 300 American military advisors were in Laos and the country received over $32 million in economic assistance, three times the annual rate of 1955-1959. An Army *coup* and expanding Communist control in eastern Laos worsened the situation until the Eisenhower Administration supported a right-wing *coup* in December 1960. Receiving large amounts of aid from Russia, the Pathet Lao responded by launching a major offensive which, by the Vienna meetings in June, had conquered the eastern half of Laos.

As China began building roads to the Laotian border for its

own military power, the Soviets and Americans decided that the war must stop. With the support of Kennedy and Khrushchev, Great Britain and Russia reconvened the Geneva conference of 1954. The sessions agreed on neutralizing Laos, but the United States-supported government of Boun Oum refused to surrender any of its power. The Pathet Lao revived their attacks and Kennedy responded by channeling in American supplies, mobilizing United States troops in Thailand after signing a sudden military aid treaty with that country, and, most important, bringing about Boun Oum's downfall simply by stopping American economic aid. This opened the way for a coalition government to be formed under neutralist Souvanna Phouma in June 1962. Nineteen nations, including China, promised to respect Laos' territorial integrity and sovereignty, and the SEATO powers explicitly excluded Laos from their area of control. It was a tenuous agreement, but one in which a Soviet-American decision to enforce neutralization of a key area had moved Laos outside the torrid zones of the Cold War. "Thank God the Bay of Pigs happened when it did," Kennedy remarked privately. "Otherwise we'd be in Laos by now—and that would be a hundred times worse."[25]

The implications of that remark were not quite accurate, for meanwhile the President was making a pivotal commitment of American power to South Vietnam. The regime of Ngo Dinh Diem had become very unpopular by 1958, for it had stopped agrarian reforms begun by Ho in the countryside, cancelled elections, arrested political opponents, and concentrated power in the hands of Diem, his brother, and his brother's wife, Madame Ngo Dinh Nhu. Anti-Diem guerilla attacks were stepped up in 1958. Two years later Ho's government in Hanoi acknowledged and encouraged the southern pro-Communists by establishing the National Liberation Front (NLF). The American-trained South Vietnamese Army could not handle the guerillas, but it also disliked Diem and tried unsuccessfully in November 1960 to overthrow the President. The Vietcong guerillas meanwhile grew in number to nearly 10,000 in 1961, receiving support from the peasants and, for the first time, from Communist China.

With this civil war intensifying, President Kennedy sent Vice-

---

[25] Sorensen, *Kennedy*, p. 644.

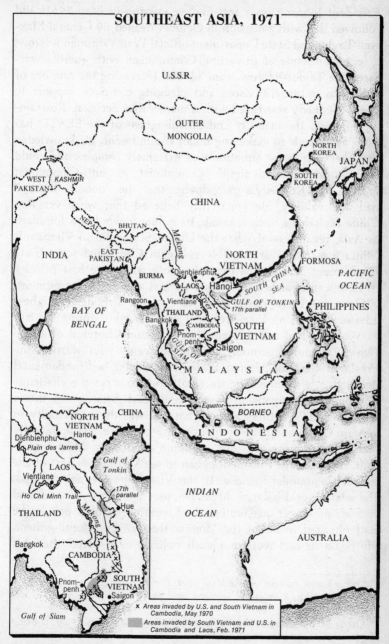

SOUTHEAST ASIA, 1971

U.S.S.R.

OUTER
MONGOLIA

WEST *KASHMIR*
PAKISTAN

CHINA

NORTH
KOREA

SOUTH
KOREA

JAPAN

INDIA

EAST
PAKISTAN

NEPAL

BHUTAN

BURMA

Mekong

Dienbienphu

NORTH
VIETNAM

Hanoi

LAOS

Rangoon

Vientiane

THAILAND

Bangkok

GULF OF TONKIN
17th parallel

*SOUTH CHINA
SEA*

FORMOSA

*PACIFIC
OCEAN*

PHILIPPINES

BAY OF
BENGAL

CAMBODIA

Pnom-
penh

SOUTH
VIETNAM

Saigon

*GULF OF
SIAM*

M A L A Y S I A

Equator

BORNEO

I N D O N E S I A

NORTH
VIETNAM

Dienbienphu

Hanoi

Plain des Jarres

CHINA

Gulf of
Tonkin

LAOS

Vientiane

Ho Chi Minh Trail

17th
parallel

Hue

*INDIAN
OCEAN*

THAILAND

Mekong R.

Bangkok

CAMBODIA

Pnom-
penh

SOUTH
VIETNAM

Saigon

AUSTRALIA

Gulf of Siam

X Areas invaded by U.S. and South Vietnam in
Cambodia, May 1970

Areas invaded by South Vietnam and U.S. in
Cambodia and Laos, Feb. 1971

President Johnson on a fact-finding mission in May 1961, and followed this with a mission in October headed by General Maxwell Taylor and State Department official Walt Whitman Rostow, a fervent disciple of thwarting Communism with guerilla warfare. The Taylor-Rostow team advised increasing the number of American military advisors and pledging complete support to Diem. Kennedy was faced with a momentous decision. Restraining him was the inability and unwillingness of the SEATO nations as a whole to make any major commitment, his knowledge that the Vietnamese situation was extremely complex and could not be divided into simple Communist vs. anti-Communist groups, and Kennedy's own doubts that the "domino theory" had any validity. He apparently believed that whenever Red China exploded a nuclear bomb, its influence would be dominant in Asia, regardless of what the United States did in Vietnam.[26] Military members of the "Never-Again Club" and some State Department officials, particularly those who gave first priority to European affairs, also warned against any large commitment.

Opposing these views were some of the President's highest advisors, including Vice-President Johnson who, during his trip to Vietnam, had called Diem the "Winston Churchill of Asia" (which Diem unfortunately believed), and who warned the President that the United States must make a "fundamental decision . . . whether we are to attempt to meet the challenge of Communist expansion now in Southeast Asia . . . or throw in the towel."[27] Others argued that this was the opportunity to contain China and that Vietnam's long coastline and apparently stable government provided optimum conditions. Most important, however, the President began to see Vietnam as part of the global Communist menace. If the Vietcong were not stopped, the whole world balance might be upset.[28] Kennedy soon found himself no longer questioning the Eisenhower-Dulles policies he had inherited, including the "domino theory," but adopting them. He could in fact work out such policies even better than his

---

[26] Arthur Krock column in *The New York Times*, February 14, 1965, p. E9.

[27] Philip Geyelin, *Lyndon B. Johnson and the World* (New York, 1966), pp. 34–40.

[28] Arthur M. Schlesinger, Jr., *A Thousand Days* . . . (Boston, 1965), p. 548.

predecessor because now the special conventional forces were being developed to do the job. Kennedy also had more motivation, since abroad (and also at home), he was determined to blot out the image given his Administration by the Bay of Pigs, the Vienna meetings, and the Berlin Wall. For an Administration which prided itself on its "realism," its political pragmatism, and its determination to save the newly emerging nations which were "the great battleground . . . of freedom,'' these arguments were irrefutable. The force was already present. The United States Pacific Command was a great military power with its 300,000 men, the largest mobile force on the globe (the Seventh Fleet), and logistics problems solved by bases in Okinowa, the Philippines, and Japan.

Within the fifteen months following the Taylor-Rostow report, Kennedy expanded the American commitment from 500 to 10,000 men, allowed these "advisors" to engage in combat, ordered United States Air Force units to strike Vietcong strongholds in South Vietnam, and promised full support to Diem. The Vietnamese President interpreted this promise to mean that he could intensify his authoritarian methods without worrying about any questions, or a possible pullout, from the American side.[29] The American-Diem forces attempted to secure the countryside with a Strategic Hamlet program which uprooted and then concentrated peasants in a fortified village.

This decision was signal and symbolic, for it, like many other policies adopted in 1961 to mid-1962, indicated that the Kennedy Administration could not lessen the Cold War tensions but only intensify them. These policies differed in no important essential from the Eisenhower policies after 1954. The new Administration was only more efficient and determined in carrying them out. When a reporter remarked in the autumn of 1961 that he wanted to write a book about the President's first year in office, Kennedy inquired, "Who would want to read a book about disasters?"[30]

---

[29] David Halberstam, *The Making of a Quagmire* (New York, 1965), pp. 67–69.

[30] Told by Elie Abel, quoted by I. F. Stone in *New York Review of Books*, April 14, 1966, p. 12.

CHAPTER X

Southeast Asia—and Elsewhere (1962-1966)

W HAT COULD HAVE BEEN the greatest of disasters nearly occurred one year later. The Cuban missile crisis, as President Kennedy remarked to Premier Khrushchev, at one moment
approached the point "where events could have become unmanageable." This confrontation rechanneled the policies of the
United States and the Soviet Union, affecting, indeed, many
facets of world affairs.

The roots of the crisis ran back to Khrushchev's ICBM-ori-
ented foreign policies after 1957 and his intense concern with
removing NATO power from West Berlin. By 1962 these policies
were related, for the Soviets needed credible strategic force if they
hoped to neutralize Western power in Germany. By the spring of
1962, however, high American officials had publicly expressed
their skepticism of Soviet missile credibility. President Kennedy
further observed in a widely publicized interview that under
some circumstances the United States would strike first. In June,
Defense Secretary McNamara indicated that American missiles
were so potent and precise that in a nuclear war they could
spare cities and hit only military installations.[1]

Khrushchev and Marshall Rodion Malinovsky angrily responded that contrary to McNamara's beliefs, cities would be the
first victims in any nuclear war. The Soviet Premier warned Kennedy against engaging "in sinister competition as to who will be
the first to start a war." For the first time in five years, however,

---

[1] Stewart Alsop, "Kennedy's Grand Strategy," *Saturday Evening Post*,
March 31, 1962, p. 14; *Documents on American Foreign Relations, 1962*,
edited by Richard P. Stebbins, (New York, 1963), pp. 232–233.

Khrushchev emphasized Soviet bomber strength instead of missiles. As for West Berlin, Kennedy's quick military buildup in 1961 had blunted Khrushchev's demands and, apparently, had wounded the Premier's power within the Kremlin.

In the summer of 1962 Khrushchev moved to regain the initiative in the strategic realm. In late August an American U-2 reconnaissance plane flying fourteen miles above Cuba reported the first Soviet surface-to-air missile site. Forty-two Russian medium bombers were next observed on Castro's airstrips. On October 14, high Administration officials expressed their disbelief that the Soviets and Cubans would try to install offensive, ground-to-ground missiles, particularly after President Kennedy had expressly warned against any such attempt in mid-September. This disbelief was also based on Khrushchev's repeated assurances that he would not jiggle East-West relations during the American congressional election campaign. On that same day of October 14, however, the first photographs were taken of a launch pad under construction which could fire ballistic missiles with a range of 1000 miles. Several days later a 2,000-mile missile site was observed under construction.

The President was in a delicate political situation. Some Senators, led by Republican Kenneth Keating of New York, for weeks had warned of threatening Soviet moves in Cuba. These reports, plus the frustrations which Castro was causing so many Americans, created in the early autumn what one acute observer called "a war party" which demanded military action against Cuba.[2] The elections were less than three weeks away. In this pressure tank, a special committee of top Administration officials began virtual round-the-clock meetings to consider the response to the Soviets. The alternatives narrowed down to a blockade or an air strike against the missile sites. Dean Acheson, supported by General Maxwell Taylor and the Joint Chiefs of Staff, argued vigorously for the air strike, even though such an attack would probably kill Soviet technicians working on the sites. Other officials changed their minds several times in the course of five days, but Under Secretary of State George Ball slowly won support for a

---

[2] Richard H. Rovere, "Letter From Washington," *New Yorker*, October 6, 1962, pp. 148–157.

blockade. McNamara supported Ball with the argument that if the blockade failed, the air strike option could still be used. Attorney-General Robert Kennedy, pointedly alluding to the attack on Pearl Harbor, endorsed Ball's position with the words, "My brother is not going to be the Tojo of the 1960's." Acheson so strongly opposed the final decision that he resigned from the committee.[3]

At 7:00 P.M. on October 22, the President broke the well-kept secret to the American people. Because the Soviets were building bases in Cuba "to provide a nuclear strike capability against the Western Hemisphere," Kennedy announced, the United States was imposing "a strict quarantine on all offensive military equipment" being shipped into Cuba. American military forces, he added, were on full alert, and the United States would "regard any nuclear missile launched from Cuba against any nation in the Western Hemisphere as an attack by the Soviet Union on the United States, requiring a full retaliatory response upon the Soviet Union." He appealed to Khrushchev to remove the offensive weapons under United Nations supervision.

The Premier replied four days later in a long, rambling letter which apparently offered removal of the missiles in return for an American pledge not to invade Cuba. A second letter the next day raised the price to the dismantling of the American Jupiter missiles in Turkey. The special committee, worn-down by ten days of the most intense pressures ("I saw first-hand," Theodore Sorensen later remarked, ". . . how brutally physical and mental fatigue can numb the good sense as well as the senses of normally articulate men"[4]), now made the crucial decision to bypass the second letter and accept the first. On Sunday morning, October 28, as American military officials prepared an air strike on the missile sites for Tuesday morning, Khrushchev endorsed the American offer.[5] Sixteen Soviet ships sailing toward Cuba turned around in midocean to return to Russian ports. The crisis was over.

The effects, however, will ripple on at least through the lifetime of the generation that lived through those October days.

[3] Elie Abel, *The Missile Crisis* (Philadelphia and New York, 1966), pp. 63–64, 70, 81, 88, 118–119.

[4] Sorensen, *Decision-Making in the White House*, p. 76.

[5] *Documents on American Foreign Relations, 1962*, pp. 392–404.

In a speech of February 27, 1963, Khrushchev explained that in removing the missiles he had saved the world from a possible nuclear disaster. This step back from the brink set the tone for a Soviet policy line, which was epitomized in a June 1964 press announcement that "in order to guarantee the final preponderance of the forces of socialism over the forces of capitalism, to win victory in peaceful competition, peace is essential." Even Soviet military support of "wars of liberation" became considerably more conditional.[6] In the summer of 1963, the United States and Russia negotiated and signed their first agreement to limit the arms race by prohibiting aboveground nuclear testing. These policies intensely angered the Chinese, widening the Sino-Russian split nearly to the point of a complete break. The Chinese called Khrushchev foolish for putting the missiles into Cuba and cowardly for removing them. They feared the growing Russian-American cooperation and deprecated the less militant Soviet policy.

The crisis did not enhance Khrushchev's personal power within the Soviet bloc. His decline, combined with the Sino-Soviet breach and the warmer East-West relations, opened new opportunities for the satellites in Eastern Europe to regain more autonomy. Some competent observers believed that the fear of Germany, as much as Russian control, kept the Warsaw Pact nations together. Certainly no generalization could fit the spectrum of intellectual freedom which stretched from Poland's liberalism to Albania's Stalinism, the agricultural collectivization which was almost total in Russia but declining in Poland and Yugoslavia, the use of terror which was greatest in Czechoslovakia but little evidenced in Poland, or the ideological framework which was rigidly dogmatic in Albania but quite loose in Yugoslavia and Poland.[7] By 1963, anyone who talked about a monolithic Communist threat was discussing a world that no longer existed.

---

[6] Garthoff, *Soviet Military Policy*, pp. 200–201, 213.
[7] H. Gordon Skilling, "National Communism in Eastern Europe Since the 22nd Congress," *Canadian Journal of Economics and Political Science*, XXX (August 1964), pp. 313–327.

In contrast to Khrushchev's decline, President Kennedy emerged from the missile crisis with new support and political charisma. His own conception of this power was exemplified when he abandoned the Cuban exile movement which had hoped to reclaim the island by force. At American University in Washington, D. C., on June 10, 1963, Kennedy spoke of peace "as the necessary rational end of rational men," and dramatically appealed to the Soviets to seek a relaxation of tensions. This speech sped the negotiations of the nuclear test ban treaty, a pact which Kennedy then drove through the Senate over the strong opposition of American military officials and a few scientists led by Edward Teller of the University of California. Teller argued that the ban would prevent the obtaining of requisite knowledge to develop an antiballistic-missile defense system to protect American cities, since the development of that system would require aboveground testing. He predicted that the arms race would be stimulated as a result and that, because the treaty discriminated against nascent nuclear powers who would want to test, would lead to the disintegration of NATO.[8]

NATO's deterioration was actually well underway. De Gaulle and Adenauer had been angered when Kennedy offered to negotiate bilaterally with the Soviets over Berlin in August 1961, and when the United States twice rejected (in August 1961 and January 1962) de Gaulle's pleas for establishing a joint directorate for military strategy. These rejections reaffirmed the French determination to build an independent nuclear power. De Gaulle viewed the British application for admission to the Common Market in 1961-1962 as the stalking-horse of American economic and political power. The French pondered Kennedy's July 4, 1962 speech which urged Europe to join in a "declaration of interdependence," but which pointedly omitted any mention of possible nuclear sharing. This speech, together with American trade legislation that allowed large reciprocal cuts in tariffs, indicated that the United States sought increased economic leverage in Europe. De Gaulle's mistrust intensified

[8] U.S. Congress, Senate, Committee on Foreign Relations, 88th Congress, 1st Session, *Nuclear Test Ban Treaty* (Washington, 1963), pp. 422–423, 427.

during the missile crisis when Acheson flew to Paris to "inform," not "consult," (the words were de Gaulle's) the French on the confrontation. The French President fully supported Kennedy, but the episode convinced Paris officials that the United States would involve them in a nuclear exchange without consulting them beforehand. Immediately after the crisis subsided, de Gaulle decided to veto the British application for membership in the Common Market.

His evaluation was apparently confirmed at the Macmillan-Kennedy conference at Nassau in December. The United States unilaterally cancelled its development of the Skybolt missile on which the British had hoped to base their nuclear striking force. Instead, Kennedy offered nuclear submarine and warhead information to Macmillan. The President pointedly did not make a similar offer to France. In January, de Gaulle dramatically announced that he would veto the British entry into the Common Market. He explained that Great Britain had nit-picked for sixteen months of negotiations in an effort to bend the Common Market to British interests, but had surrendered control of her own defense to the United States in a mere 48 hours at Nassau. De Gaulle, however, had made this decision for a more fundamental reason. He feared that if Great Britain entered the European Economic Community, "the end would be a colossal Atlantic Community dependent on America and directed by America, which would not take long to absorb this European Community." Shortly afterward, a Franco-German friendship treaty was signed, which de Gaulle hoped would be the axis for an independent European diplomacy. The French leader next began to prepare the withdrawal of French naval forces from the NATO command.

De Gaulle correctly believed that in the wake of the missile crisis East-West tensions would ease; in the long run, a united Europe led by France would be able to influence international diplomacy if that Europe was free of both Russian and American control and if France had its own nuclear power. He also feared unchecked American military and economic power, believing that because the United States would use the power unilaterally and irresponsibly, the French could suffer annihilation without representation. Finally, the French President's foreign policies enjoyed large support at home. Since 1919, at least, the French had distrusted Washington's policies in Europe. De Gaulle provided the rationale and was developing the power to check the Americans.

While the missile crisis did not advance Kennedy's "Grand Design" for Europe, it tragically accelerated the American rush into Vietnam. Key Washington policy-makers assumed that the results of the October confrontation signified a standoff between the two superpowers. Both had clearly indicated their reluctance to use nuclear power. The United States had won primarily because Khrushchev unwisely challenged Kennedy in the Caribbean where American conventional naval power was decisive. Within months, both sides were discussing the easing of Cold War tensions. If the assumption was correct that the two great powers mutually feared each other's nuclear power, then, the Kennedy Administration concluded, the leaders of the emerging nations might feel that they had considerable opportunity to play West versus East or, as in Southeast Asia and Africa, to undertake revolutionary changes without fear that either the United States or Russia would be able to shape these changes. If nationalist leaders acted on these beliefs, the newly-emerging world could become increasingly unmanageable, perhaps dangerously radical from Washington's point of view.[9] Such a view of course meshed perfectly with the other American fear that the Communist policy line of support for (but not direct involvement in) "wars of liberation" had been established in 1960-1961 precisely to exploit the emerging nationalisms. Despite the traditional American liberal rhetoric which professed a faith in self-determination, the Kennedy policy-makers determined to control these nationalisms. The New Frontiersmen particularly dedicated themselves to shattering "wars of liberation" within such nationalist movements. Vietnam would be used as the example.

The President also focused on Southeast Asia because he hoped to discipline what he believed to be the expansiveness of

---

[9] The best analysis is Walt Whitman Rostow, "Domestic Determinants of U.S. Foreign Policy; The Tocqueville Oscillation," *Armed Forces Journal*, June 27, 1970, 16D–16E; see also Rostow's *From the Seventh Floor* (New York, 1964).

Communist China. In 1949-1950 Kennedy, then a member of the House of Representatives, had joined Republicans in denouncing the Truman Administration for supposedly "losing" China. He softened these views during the 1950s, but in preparing to run for the presidency in 1960 he was reluctant to consider disavowing the use of nuclear weapons: "I wonder if we could expect to check the sweep south of the Chinese with their endless armies with conventional forces?"[10] In his first State of the Union Message the new President warned that "In Asia, the relentless pressures of the Chinese Communists menace the security of the entire area—from the borders of India and South Viet Nam to the jungles of Laos."[11] After the missile crisis, Kennedy summarized his position in a conversation with André Malraux, French Cultural Affairs Minister. Assistant Secretary of State for European Affairs William R. Tyler has described this talk:

[Kennedy] wanted to get a message to de Gaulle through Malraux . . . that really there was no reason why there should be differences between us and France in Europe, or between us and our European Allies, because there was no longer a likely Soviet military threat against Europe [since the Cuban missile crisis]. . . . But the area where we would have problems in the future . . . was China. He said it was so important that he and de Gaulle and other European leaders should think together about what they will do, what the situation will be when China becomes a nuclear power, what will happen then . . . this was the great menace in the future to humanity, the free world, and freedom on earth. Relations with the Soviet Union could be contained within the framework of mutual awareness of the impossibility of achieving any gains through war. But in the case of China, this restraint would not be effective because the Chinese would be perfectly prepared, because of the lower value they attach to human life, to sacrifice hundreds of millions of their own lives, if this were necessary in order to carry out their militant and aggressive policies.[12]

The missile crisis and the Berlin confrontation in 1961 also

[10] Kennedy to George Kennan, Jan. 21, 1960, Oral History Interview with Mr. Kennan, March 23, 1964, Kennedy Library. Used by permission.

[11] Quoted in Chester Cooper, *Lost Crusade* (New York, 1970), p. 171.

[12] Oral History Interview with William R. Tyler, March 7, 1964, Kennedy Library; and Mr. Tyler to author, December 10, 1971.

reinforced the Administration's belief that it knew how to threaten to apply or, if necessary, actually apply conventional military power to obtain maximum results. White House officials joked that poor John Foster Dulles had never been able to find a suitable war for his "massive retaliation"; these pragmatic Kennedyites, however, had apparently solved the great riddle by perfectly matching power to crisis. One false premise ultimately wrecked this self-satisfaction: in Berlin and Cuba the Russians had backed down (Castro, noticeably, had been willing to fight to keep the missiles); in Vietnam, the United States dealt with nationalist Vietnamese who like Castro had much to win by continuing to fight against apparently overwhelming American firepower.[13]

This fatal flaw did not clearly appear in 1962-1966. On the contrary, during the autumn of 1962 the President's policies seemed to be proved correct during the brief war between India and China. India provoked the war during a border dispute over territory more important to the Chinese than to the Indians. The Chinese attacked with devastating force, destroying both the myth of Indian power and the American hope that India could serve as a cornerstone in the containment of China. The Chinese carefully occupied only some of the disputed territory, voluntarily withdrawing from other conquered areas. On November 20, Prime Minister Pandit Nehru urgently asked Kennedy for aid. An American aircraft carrier moved across the southern Pacific towards India, but before it could become a factor the crisis ended.[14] Some Washington policy-makers nevertheless drew the false conclusion that the Chinese had backed down only after receiving warnings from the United States and, independently of the American move, from Russia.

Kennedy's advisers displayed similarly unwarranted confidence in their ability to control power in late 1962 when they decided to turn Laos into a pro-American bastion. They thereby helped destroy the Geneva Agreements which the United States

---

[13] David Halberstam, "The Programming of Robert McNamara," *Harper's*, February 1971, p. 68.
[14] Allen Whiting's review of Neville Maxwell's *India's China War* in *Washington Post*, May 25, 1971, p. B6.

had solemnly signed in midsummer, 1962. Under the Agreements, all foreign troops were to withdraw from Laos. The Communist Pathet Lao were to join neutralist Souvanna Phouma's coalition government. American military advisers, indeed, began to leave, but the Central Intelligence Agency stepped up the supplying of the Meo Tribesman, an effective guerilla army operating behind Pathet Lao lines. Through its aid programs and encouragement to right-wing factions in the capital of Vientiane, the United States pressured Souvanna Phouma to accept the CIA's activities and to squeeze the Pathet Lao out of the coalition government. Fighting erupted on the strategic Plain of Jarres in April, 1963. North Vietnam, which ostensibly refused to remove all its troops from Laos until the United States stopped supplying the Meo Tribesman, accelerated its aid to the Pathet Lao. The United States increased its own assistance from the CIA and through aid agreements purchased Thailand's Air Force to fly supporting missions and train Laotian pilots.

In April, 1964, however, a right-wing *coup* in Vientiane made Souvanna only a figurehead leader. The Pathet Lao retaliated with an offensive that threatened to conquer the entire Plain of Jarres. The United States then began initially small but systematic bombing raids on Laos which Washington carefully tried to keep secret. To save a supposedly pivotal domino, the Kennedy-Johnson advisers were confidently escalating their application of power. Roger Hilsman, who had served as Assistant Secretary of State for Far Eastern Affairs for both Presidents, admitted in 1965 that "We all understood perfectly well that [the Geneva Agreement of 1962] was just the starting gun. . . . If we had . . . used the negotiations as an excuse to withdraw from Laos . . . we in effect would have been turning it over to the Communists."[15] The actual result, however, was that at the very time the United States escalated its commitment to South Vietnam, the key area of Laos became uncontrollable and formed an open channel for aid to the National Liberation Front in South Vietnam.

In 1962-1963 the assumptions that would govern American

---

[15] D. Gareth Porter, "After Geneva: Subverting Laotian Neutrality," in Nina S. Adams and Alfred W. McCoy (eds.), *Laos: War and Revolution* (New York, 1970), pp. 179–212.

policies in Vietnam fell into place. First, Vietnam was vital to American interests because, in John F. Kennedy's words of 1956, "Vietnam represents the cornerstone of the Free World in Southeast Asia, the Keystone to the arch, the finger in the dike. . . . Her economy is essential to the economy of all of Southeast Asia; and her political liberty is an inspiration to those seeking to obtain or maintain their liberty in all parts of Asia—and indeed the world."[16] As Kennedy emphasized in his May 25, 1961 address to Congress, the battle of "freedom versus tyranny" was being waged in newly-emerging areas such as Vietnam. While belittling the foreign policies of the previous administration, the Kennedy advisors gulped down whole the Eisenhower "domino" theory. More precisely, Dulles' and Eisenhower's formulation of the 1950s remained valid because without an open Southeast Asia for her raw materials and markets Japan, essential to the entire American strategic policy in the western Pacific, would have to turn toward her traditional market of China.

The Kennedy Administration assumed, second, that China not only was to be isolated but, as some thought she had been in India, militarily disciplined. Both the Chinese and the Russians were to be taught that "wars of liberation" were not possible in areas the United States considered vital to its own interests. Third, the missile crisis, the India-Chinese conflict, and the emerging Laotan situation gave the Administration confidence in its ability to escalate military power while keeping it under control. Because of McNamara's work, moreover, the military power was available. For the first time in their history, Americans entered war with a great army at the ready, a force created by self-styled "realists" who, in the tradition of Forrestal and Acheson, believed that they could ultimately shape world affairs with American firepower.

These assumptions—the validity of the domino theory (particularly its economic implications for Japan), the century-old American fear of a "Yellow Peril," and the belief held by American liberal spokesmen that, as children of Niebuhr, they knew the secrets of using military force effectively—these governed the Kennedy Administration as it moved deeper into Vietnam.

---

[16] Quoted in Cooper, *Lost Crusade*, p. 168.

In 1962, Secretary of Defense McNamara had observed, "Every quantitative measurement we have shows we're winning this war."[17] Some factors in Southeast Asia, however, could not be computed. Twelve thousand American military personnel were involved in the conflict, yet the Vietcong continued to gain ground. The strategic hamlet program, geared to secure the countryside, was failing despite, or perhaps because of, the determination of the Diem regime. The peasants disliked being forced to leave their homes and to be resettled elsewhere, particularly by a government that had condemned any meaningful land reform program. "No wonder the Vietcong looked like Robin Hoods when they began to hit the hamlets," one civilian American official remarked.[18] Vietcong successes mounted despite their kidnapping and brutal murdering of village and hamlet officials.

Kennedy's hope of reversing the situation rested on the ability of Diem's government to wage a successful military campaign while stabilizing South Vietnam's political situation. Saigon's military capability was dramatically called into question on January 2, 1963 in the village of Ap Bac, approximately 50 miles from Saigon. A small Vietcong force was surrounded by a Vietnamese army that was ten times larger, but despite the urgings of American advisers to attack, the South Vietnamese refused. The Vietcong then methodically shot down five American helicopters, damaged nine more, killed three Americans, and disappeared. Apparently only United States soldiers had the will to fight in Vietnam, but Kennedy carefully pointed out after one fire-fight between Vietcong and American personnel that the United States forces in Vietnam were not "combat troops," and that if the situation changed, "I, of course, would go to Congress."[19] He was not prepared to do this in 1963. Nor was the White House even prepared to inform adequately the Congress and the public.

With an American presidential election little more than a year away, and his own belief that in 1964 his main challenge

---

[17] Schlesinger, *Thousand Days*, p. 549.
[18] Halberstam, *Making of a Quagmire*, pp. 186–187.
[19] Cooper, *Lost Crusade*, pp. 193–194; also in *Public Papers of the Presidents, 1962*, p. 228.

would come from the right-wing of American politics, Kennedy was careful to keep the best possible, even if misleading, light on Vietnamese affairs. American newspaper correspondents who candidly reported Diem's failures were rewarded either with Kennedy's unsuccessful attempt to give one critical correspondent a "vacation" from Vietnam, or with rejoinders to their questions like the one given by Admiral Harry Felt, Commander of American forces in the Pacific: "Why, don't you get on the team?"[20] The "credibility gap" did not begin with Lyndon Johnson's presidency.[21] In 1963 that gap measured the growing abyss between the actual situation in Vietnam and the self-assurance of the Kennedy Administration that it could manipulate military power to control nationalist revolutions.

By late summer, 1963, the abyss was so wide that it could no longer be covered. Throughout the early part of the year Diem, with the assistance of his brother Nhu Dinh Diem and Madame Nhu, ruthlessly suppressed domestic opposition. When Washington protested the Nhus' activities, Diem and his brother openly objected to this pressure. On May 22, Kennedy revealed the growing strain by commenting that if Diem wanted American personnel out of Vietnam they would leave "immediately." (At almost the same time, however, the Defense Department again announced that the "corner has definitely been turned" toward victory.) The beginning of the end for Diem and Nhu occurred on May 8 when Diem's troops shot into a crowd of Buddhists who were celebrating Buddha's birthday by waving religious flags, thereby violating the regime's rule that forbid the exhibit of any banner but the government's. The firing climaxed years of bitterness between the Roman Catholic regime of Diem and Buddhists who comprised more than 80 percent of the country's population. Many Buddhist leaders wanted no part of the war, no part of any foreign intervention in their nation, and no part of the Diem regime. They represented a new, potentially radical nationalism that neither the Diem regime nor the American officials in Vietnam could understand, let alone cope with. In June,

---

[20] Halberstam, *Making of a Quagmire*, p. 72.
[21] James Aronson, *The Press and the Cold War* (New York, 1970), pp. 182–183.

Buddhist-led antigovernment riots spread through Saigon. Diem retaliated by raiding Buddhist pagodas. Several Buddhists burned themselves to death in public protest, an act that Madame Nhu sarcastically welcomed as a "barbecue show." Students in normally quiet schools and universities joined the Buddhists. Diem confronted a full-scale rebellion.

The Kennedy Administration's confusion in dealing with the revolutionary situation became glaringly evident during the crisis.[22] While continuing to announce that the military program was going well, the White House attempted to push Diem into making necessary domestic reforms by cutting off relatively small amounts of military and economic aid. That move, however, was sufficient to encourage anti-Diem elements in the army. On November 1 and 2, with, at least, the knowledge and approval of the White House and the American Ambassador in Saigon, Henry Cabot Lodge, a military junta captured Diem and his brother.[23] Within hours the two men were shot and the junta assumed power. Three weeks later President Kennedy was assassinated in Dallas, Texas.

President Lyndon B. Johnson inherited a set of badly decomposed foreign policies. Although in the last weeks of his life Kennedy had said that the war was for the Vietnamese to win or lose, the American consent given for Diem's overthrow, and the Administration's full commitment to fighting what were intended to be limited wars with the conventional forces that Kennedy had so painstakingly developed, indicated that the United States would, if necessary, become further involved in Southeast Asia. Certainly Kennedy would have done nothing to change radically the American involvement until after the 1964 elections. By then

---

[22] *The Pentagon Papers*, as published by *The New York Times* (New York, 1971), pp. 163–177, 191–196. *The Pentagon Papers* is a condensed version of a massive study of Defense Department documents on the Vietnamese involvement. Commissioned by Secretary McNamara as a secret analysis, the larger study was written and compiled by three dozen experts and finally covered 3000 pages of analyses and 4000 pages of supporting documents. The shorter *Pentagon Papers* is crucial and revealing, but it should be used carefully because it contains little from either State Department or Presidential files.

[23] *Ibid.*, pp. 158–159, 215–232, especially Lodge to Bundy, October 30, 1963, No. 57, pp. 226–229.

he might have been unable to throw four years of policy suddenly into reverse. In Europe, the Administration's "Grand Design" was coming apart piece by piece, allowing de Gaulle to assume the leadership in the Western European community. The Alliance for Progress was crumbling, the victim of the false assumption that enough money and bureaucratic technicians could tinker with and adjust the dynamic nationalisms of an economically unbalanced Latin America to the policy objectives of a prosperous, satisfied, and expanding United States.

As these policies encountered the inevitable obstacles, bitter infighting appeared among Washington officials. The White House staff blamed the State Department for not having sufficient imagination and initiative to solve important diplomatic problems. Two talented biographers of Kennedy who were on the White House staff, Theodore Sorensen and Arthur Schlesinger, Jr., wrote their histories from this point of view. Their interpretation seemed naive, for it glossed over several points. Nothing on the record indicated that the White House and State Department ever argued much over whether the United States should become more involved in the newly-emerging nations; the argument was usually over how. If the State Department could not always discover the appropriate tactics, the fault lay perhaps in contradictions of the policy, not State Department incompetency.

There was no indication, moreover, that President Kennedy and Secretary of State Dean Rusk differed on fundamental points of policy. This is important, since Kennedy must have appointed and kept this key official in the full knowledge that Rusk, having served under Dean Acheson and Robert Lovett, accepted the military-oriented policies that those two officials had followed. Rusk had also been Assistant Secretary of State for Far Eastern Affairs during the Korean conflict. It did not require Kennedy's acute perception to conclude that Rusk, indeed, like the President himself, might have an uncommon commitment to building positions of military strength around the periphery of China. The Kennedy Administration bequeathed to Lyndon Johnson deteriorating foreign policies along with the test ban and, much to Johnson's discomfort, the overpowering image and somber rhetoric of the fallen President.

The new Chief Executive's first important diplomatic pronouncement explained that he would continue his predecessor's Vietnam policies.[24] The ensuing policy, as well as the style with which it would be carried out, could be understood in terms of the President's own history and resulting world view.

Lyndon Johnson's Administration was what happened in the United States when the historical legacies of Woodrow Wilson, Franklin D. Roosevelt, and the American frontier merged in the 1960s. The Wilsonian influence has permeated American foreign policy, even in the policies of those who in their writings have condemned Wilson's "moral diplomacy." Wilson believed that the American mission was to extend individual liberties throughout the world, but this was not out of altruism; it was rather out of the belief that American liberties could not long exist at home unless the world was made safe for democracy. The basis of liberty at home was found in the economic system, for as Wilson once observed, without "freedom of enterprise there can be no freedom whatsoever." Lyndon Johnson's own version was that "the very basis of a great nation is an educated mind, a healthy body, and a free enterprise system." With this established, the President could repeat time after time during the 1964 campaign that "Our cause has been the cause of all mankind." Whether the American system could work as well in the boiler-houses of newly emerging nations as it had during its 300-year growth, and several mutations, in the United States, was not discussed by the President. He simply moved to the conclusion: "Woodrow Wilson once said: 'I hope we shall never forget that we created this nation, not to serve ourselves, but to serve mankind.'"[25]

Emerging as a national political figure during the 1930s, and further developing the New Deal's domestic programs in the 1950s as the most powerful Senate leader in history, Johnson understood that even a well-functioning free enterprise system needed frequent governmental injections to provide balance and some economic justice. The New Deal, for example, had developed a poverty-stricken region of the United States through the

---

[24] Ibid., pp. 232–233.
[25] The Johnson quotes are cited from The New York Times, June 28, 1967, p. 24; and Public Papers of the Presidents, 1964, pp. 1242, 1103.

Tennessee Valley Authority's electrical-power system in the 1930s. "The over-riding rule which I want to affirm," the President remarked in Denver in 1966, "is that our foreign policy must always be an extension of our domestic policy. Our safest guide to what we do abroad is always what we do at home. . . ." This concern was easily translated to Vietnam: "I want to leave the footprints of America there. I want them to say, 'This is what the Americans left—schools and hospitals and dams. . . .' We can turn the Mekong [River area] into a Tennessee Valley."[26] The role of the government therefore, both in the United States and Vietnam, was first to clear away the obstacles (the unenlightened American businessman in the 1930s, the Vietnamese Communist in the 1960s), build the infrastructure (the Tennessee Valley and the Great Society at home, the Mekong Valley projects in Vietnam), and then let free enterprise develop the resources, and therefore the freedoms, of the areas.

Johnson had an equally simple view of how this was to be accomplished, a view formed when he grew up in the frontier of central Texas. His incredible ambition and energy exploited the opportunities of Texas and Washington, D.C., until he was privately wealthy and politically supreme. He had risen by making sharp distinctions between friends and enemies. "We are not a formal people," he observed in 1965. "We are not a people so much concerned with the way things are done as by the results that we achieve. Since the frontier really opened we have been this way." This remark, perilously close to an ends-justifies-the-means point of view, could serve as a rationalization for both Kennedy's and Johnson's conduct of the Vietnamese conflict. After all, as the President declared in 1965, "America wins the wars that she undertakes. Make no mistake about it." If the struggle became difficult, Johnson could again use the development of the American frontier as an example to reassure Americans that not they but a more inexorable power put them into Vietnam: "We had the good fortune to grow from a handful of isolated colonies to a position of great responsibility in the world. We did not deliberately seek this position; in a real sense the

---

[26] *The New York Times,* August 27, 1966, p. 10; Interview with Harry Graff in *The New York Times Magazine,* March 20, 1966, p. 133.

force of history shaped it for us."[27] History during the 1960s became a mere political tool to wield rather than a burden requiring understanding and humility.

Given this vision of American history, the President determined he must do nothing less than create a Great Society at home and wage the Cold War abroad. He demanded consensus for these objectives: "We cannot keep what we have and we cannot preserve the brightening flame of home for others unless we are all—repeat *all* committed; all—repeat *all* willing to sacrifice and to serve wherever we can, whether it be in Vietnam, whether it be at home." Recalling the venerated Franklin D. Roosevelt of 1938 to 1941, Johnson believed himself justified using the widest possible presidential powers in foreign policy in order to shape this consensus. For there was the other side of the coin if Americans did not "sacrifice": "There are 3 billion people in the world and we have only 200 million of them. We are outnumbered 15 to 1. If might did make right they would sweep over the United States and take what we have. We have what they want."[28] Given such a world view, if discontent appeared at home the dissenters too quickly could be labeled "appeasers" of the "Munich variety"; national press and television could justifiably be manipulated; and policies acquitted by the latest poll, pulled from a coat pocket, which demonstrated through apparently incontrovertible quantitative data that "body count" indicated the war was being won in Vietnam and consensus reigned at home.

Johnson's policies in Vietnam were not aberrations, but were the culmination of nearly three-quarters of a century of American foreign policy. He only presented those policies—and their consequences—more starkly than had his predecessors. In this sense his continuation of Kennedy's approach to Vietnam was natural, but like the New Frontier, the Great Society's hope for military-imposed stability in Southeast Asia soon vanished. Saigon politics was in chaos. Seven different governments rose to power in South Vietnam during 1964, three during the weeks of August

---

[27] *Public Papers of the Presidents, 1965*, pp. 770, 821; *Ibid., 1966*, p. 984.
[28] *Ibid., 1964*, p. 1640; *Ibid., 1966*, p. 1287.

16 to September 3 alone. This was the struggle within the civil war.

Nor was the civil war itself abating. The State Department Director of Intelligence, Thomas Hughes, remarked on June 8, 1964, that "by far the greater part of the Vietcong forces in South Vietnam are South Vietnamese, the preponderance of Vietcong weapons come not from Communist countries but from capture, purchase, and local manufacture."[29] In such a civil war, the United States could not find sufficient leverage to roll back the National Liberation Front. When Hanoi offered to negotiate in August 1964, the United States consequently rejected the proposal, arguing fifteen months later when the offer was finally revealed that Ho Chi Minh was not serious about making an equitable settlement, and that the military situation at the time gravely weakened the American negotiating position. The presidential campaign in the United States may also have been a factor. Johnson did not want to be open to the charge of appeasement, particularly when his Republican opponent, former Senator Barry Goldwater of Arizona, urged a "Let's Win" policy of total military victory.

The war entered a new phase on August 2, 1964 when North Vietnamese torpedo boats attacked an American destroyer *Maddox* in the Gulf of Tonkin. Bounded by North Vietnam and China, the Gulf was a sensitive strategic area. Despite American warnings and the reinforcement of the fleet, the attack was repeated on August 4. Hanoi claimed that the American ships had been participating in South Vietnamese attacks on two North Vietnamese shore areas. *The New York Times* also reported that the destroyers had collaborated with South Vietnamese commando raids.[30] President Johnson, however, interpreted the attack as "open aggression on the high seas," adding in an ironic historical prophecy, "We Americans know, although others appear to forget, the risk of spreading conflict." He insisted that "The attacks were unprovoked."[31] Without consulting NATO or SEATO allies or the United States Congress, the President or-

---

[29] Quoted in Geyelin, *Lyndon B. Johnson and the World*, p. 193.
[30] *The New York Times*, August 5, 1964, p. 4; *Ibid.*, August 4, 1964, p. 2.
[31] *Public Papers of the Presidents, 1964*, p. 928.

dered the first American air attack on North Vietnamese ports in retaliation.

Four years later in Congressional hearings, Secretary McNamara admitted that the American warships attacked in the Gulf had been cooperating with South Vietnamese forays against North Vietnam. Since February 1964, the United States had developed a program of clandestine attacks on North Vietnam. Termed 34A, these operations included parachuting sabotage teams, commando raids, and the bombardment of coastal installations. As the Saigon political situation deteriorated, these raids were stepped up, although the Administration concealed them from Congress. Before the attack of August 4, the American ships, the *Maddox* and *Turner Joy*, knew that the South Vietnamese were to conduct 34A raids in the area. McNamara later testified that the two ships were to attract North Vietnamese forces away from the 34A operations. He further admitted that the American vessels were authorized to move within four miles of the North Vietnam coastline, well within the area that Hanoi claimed to be its national waters. This evidence contradicted McNamara's statement of August 6, 1964: "Our Navy played absolutely no part in, was not associated with, was not aware of, any South Vietnamese actions, if there were any."[32]

The truth, however, appeared much too late to prevent Congress from making one of its worst foreign policy errors. The President requested a resolution supporting "all necessary measures" that the President may take to "repel any armed attack" against American forces. He demanded and received more, since Congress also gave advance consent that the President could "prevent further aggression" and take "all necessary steps" to protect any nation covered by SEATO which might request aid "in defense of its freedom." This "Gulf of Tonkin Resolution" sailed through the House of Representatives after forty minutes of debate with a vote of 416 to 0. In the Senate, however, Senator Gaylord Nelson, Democrat of Wisconsin, attempted to amend the

---

[32] U.S. Senate, 90th Cong., 2nd Sess., Committee on Foreign Relations, *The Gulf of Tonkin, The 1964 Incidents* (Washington, 1968). *The Pentagon Papers*, pp. 234–242, 258–279, also analyze the 34A operations and Gulf of Tonkin attack.

resolution so that it would not justify a widening of the conflict. He was stopped by J. William Fulbright, Democrat of Arkansas and Chairman of the Foreign Relations Committee, who argued that the President should be trusted, and that an amendment would require further consideration by the House at a time when speed and the appearance of national unity were essential. The Senate then voted 88 to 2 (Democratic Senators Wayne Morse of Oregon and Ernest Gruening of Alaska dissenting) to give the President virtually unlimited powers in the Vietnamese conflict. During the next four years Johnson waged war without an explicit declaration of war from Congress. He argued that the Gulf of Tonkin Resolution and the President's powers as Commander-in-Chief of the military gave him sufficient authority to send one-half million Americans into combat in Vietnam. The Senate would finally repeal the resolution in 1970. In the meantime, American constitutional processes, ironically used during these years by the Executive as a rationale to fight dissent at home, were gravely weakened.

To examine the Vietnam war in isolation would be a grave historical error. The conflict was not an exception to the world view of American foreign policy-makers during the 1960s. Vietnam was only one of a number of revolutions in the newly emerging world with which Johnson had to deal during his first eighteen months in office. Since 1960, Africa had been the most chaotic area. In all of Africa in 1945 only Egypt, Ethiopia, Nigeria, and South Africa could lay claim to independence. The remainder of the continent was under British, French, Spanish, or Portuguese control. The World War destroyed the power of European colonialism, afterward the Suez crisis and then the termination of British control of Ghana in 1957 (giving the first black African state its independence in the postwar era), set off a chain reaction. In 1960, sixteen new African states joined the United Nations. By 1970, fifty African nations were independent. Many of these states were national entities only in the sense that colonial authorities had formerly imposed central governments over the areas. Tribal ties often remained stronger, factionalizing the new nations, creating insoluble problems for nationalistic leaders, and thereby allowing army generals to use military force to consolidate their own as well as their nations' power. Nearly all new African nations, moreover, had been poorly prepared by the colonialists for independence. Necessary capital, technical skills, stable governmental institutions, and educated elites were in short supply. Both Washington and Moscow suffered serious reverses in attempting to come to terms with these changes.

The United States' position among black Africans was precarious because it refused to use sanctions to penalize the Republic of South Africa for its policy of *apartheid*, under which a small white minority of less than 20 percent of the population isolated and ruthlessly suppressed the black majority. That dilemma intensified in November 1965 when Southern Rhodesia, with a white population of 200 thousand and a black population of nearly four million, broke away from the British Empire to establish another *apartheid* system. The United States publicized its dislike for these *apartheid* policies, but refused to go further. Vast economic investments, strategic naval ports in South Africa, a reluctance to oppose military allies (such as Portugal) which still controlled colonial African territories, and a fear that such action would be a precedent for other nations passing judgment on the American domestic racial situation—all of these factors prevented the United States from effectively opposing *apartheid*.

Washington officials, however, did not hesitate to intervene in the Belgian Congo during the 1960s. This area, tragically unprepared by Belgium for independence, became a sovereign nation on June 30, 1960. Katanga Province, led by Moise Tshombe and bolstered by European and American copper and cobalt interests, attempted to secede from the Congo and become an independent state. In the ensuing two-year struggle the most popular nationalistic Congolese leader, Patrice Lumumba, was murdered by Katanga authorities. Order was restored only after the United Nations, with vast American support, helped the Congolese government capture Tshombe and reunite the country in January 1963. The United States had decided that removing Tshombe was less distasteful than allowing the continuation of a civil war that could become an open invitation to Soviet or Chinese intervention. The Soviets actually supported the UN intervention, but independently and outside UN channels.

Congolese stability proved short-lived. In the spring of 1964 three revolts began a left-wing nationalist attempt to overthrow the government. By this time the United States had replaced Belgium as the most powerful foreign element, having spent more than six million dollars attempting to bolster the central government. As rebellion spread, the Central Intelligence Agency formed a mercenary army and air force, many of whose planes were piloted by exiled Cubans. The multilived Tshombe returned to head this central government. He recruited white mercenaries from southern Africa, Europe, and the United States. The rebels opened contact with Communist China, although Communist influence in the movement was extremely small. The antigovernment forces tortured and executed perhaps 20,000 opponents. When they gathered 280 Belgians and 16 Americans as hostages, the United States organized a quick Belgian paratroop strike.[33] On November 24, 1964 the hostages were freed, and the rebels were dispersed. Shortly thereafter, Tshombe was driven from power by a military regime led by General Joseph D. Mobutu. The political structure remained unstable, and Tshombe's use of white mercenaries might have been a pivotal error, since it enraged African nationalists. American influence continued to grow until by 1967 Belgians had to make appointments through the United States Embassy to talk with Congolese governmental officials.[34] When rebellion again erupted in the summer of 1967, however, powerful Senators, led by Richard Russell, Democrat of Georgia, so strenuously objected to further aid for Mobutu that the State Department acquiesced. Racial tensions at home, as well as the rising combat fatalities in Vietnam, were beginning to limit American initiatives in other newly-emerging nations.

Africa ranked much lower on Washington's priority list than either Vietnam or Latin America. In the latter area, Johnson continued the downgrading of the Alliance for Progress, placing control of policy under a new Assistant Secretary of State, Thomas C. Mann. A fellow Texan, Mann's top priorities were the stabilization of Latin American politics, the protection of American private investments in the area, and a vigorous struggle against Communism. He willingly accepted military govern-

---

[33] Richard J. Barnet, *Intervention and Revolution; The United States in the Third World* (New York, 1968), pp. 248–251.
[34] *The New York Times*, August 3, 1967, p. 2.

ments in Latin America, particularly if these regimes replaced reform-liberal governments that threatened to pass destabilizing economic measures. The acceptance of such a military *coup d'etat* occurred first in Brazil in 1964. The new Brazilian military regime would become one of the most stable—and repressive—governments in the hemisphere.

When President Johnson did attempt to increase investment in social enterprises such as education or health, his policies were attacked by the Treasury Department and its new Secretary Henry Fowler. The Secretary's uppermost concern was not Latin American development but the correction of the worsening dollar deficit being incurred by the United States in international trade. Since the late 1950s, Americans had spent more overseas than they had sold. The deficit was made up by shipping gold abroad. By the mid-1960s the United States gold supply had shrunk 40 percent since 1945, and the situation threatened to get out of hand as Vietnam costs spiraled upward in 1965-1966. One of the first victims of America's inability to balance its international budget was the Alliance for Progress.

Fowler and the Treasury insisted that support for American exports (the most important suction for drawing money back into the United States) receive preference over all overseas social investments. The Treasury Department inserted an "additionality" clause in aid grants. Under this clause, Latin American recipients of American aid promised to spend all of that money on American goods, even though those goods were more expensive than, say, similar British or French goods. "Additionality" drastically drove up the cost of development for the Latin Americans. The President of Colombia observed sardonically in 1968, "Colombia has received two program loans under the Alliance. I don't know if we can survive a third."[35] This intensified attention to securing more exports also made the Johnson Administration very sensitive to any unsettling factor that might threaten markets in Latin America. By 1966 the Alliance had failed to achieve its objectives. Inflation was so rampant in Argentina,

---

[35]Jerome Levinson and Juan de Onís, *The Alliance that Lost Its Way: A Critical Report on the Alliance for Progress* (Chicago, 1970), is the best analysis; see especially pp. 120–123.

Brazil, and Chile that investors put their money in magazine subscriptions and airplane tickets—to anywhere—as fixed investments.[26] Worse, the Alliance had created rising expectations in Latin America, expectations that demanded more than American support for military regimes or the use of Latin America as a mere export market for United States goods. But worse was to come.

In the Dominican Republic on April 24, 1965, a civilian government headed by Donald Reid Cabral was attacked by liberal and radical followers of Juan Bosch. The nation's 3.3 million people were among the poorest in Latin America. Between 1916 and 1940 the government had been controlled by American Marines and customs officers, but the United States had withdrawn by 1940 in favor of Rafael Trujillo. The dictator, whom Franklin D. Roosevelt accurately characterized as "an s.o.b." but "our s.o.b.," brutally ruled and ruthlessly exploited his countrymen until he was gunned down by assassins in May 1961. When the dictator's relatives attempted to claim his power, President Kennedy deployed American naval units to safeguard the provisional government. In December 1962, the reform party led by Juan Bosch obtained 60 percent of the votes in a national election. Ten months later, Bosch was the victim of an army *coup d'etat* that was supported by conservative businessmen, landholders, and church leaders. Neither the White House, whose staff had become dissatisfied with Bosch and viewed him as a mere "literary figure," nor the State Department protected Bosch's popularly elected government. The Reid Cabral junta which assumed power was soon deserted by both conservative and radical forces; it was deserted by everyone, apparently, except the United States. When Reid Cabral insisted on running for president in the June 1965 elections, and when Washington then extended a $5-million loan to his regime, pro-Bosch forces overthrew what was only the shell of a government.

Two days of fighting between the rebels and army forces followed. On Monday, April 26, the rebels began arming thousands of civilians. By April 28, the military seemed to have the upper hand, but Washington officials, acting on conclusions too hastily

---

[36] *The New York Times*, January 31, 1965, F10.

CENTRAL AND SOUTH AMERICA
IN THE 1954-1970 ERA

UNITED STATES

CUBA
Batista overthrown 1959
Attempted anti-Castro invasion 1961
Soviet military aid, U.S. quarantine 1962

Miami

BAHAMAS
(Br.)

DOMINICAN REP.
U.S. broke diplomatic ties 1960
Trujillo assassinated 1961
Diplomatic ties restored 1962
U.S. and O.A.S. intervention 1965

MEXICO

Mexico
City

BR.
HONDURAS

Havana

JAMAICA

GUATEMALA
Arbenz
overthrown 1954
Castillo Armas
assassinated 1957
EL SALVADOR

HONDURAS
Diaz overthrown 1956

HAITI

PUERTO
RICO

CARIBBEAN SEA

Pérez Jiménez overthrown 1958
Anti-Nixon riots 1958

BARBADOS

NICARAGUA
Canal Zone

TRINIDAD AND TOBAGO

COSTA RICA

Caracas
VENEZUELA

GUYANA

PANAMA
Anti-U.S. riots 1959

Bogotá

SURINAM (Neth.)
FR. GUIANA

Rojas Pinilla forced out 1957

COLOMBIA

ECUADOR

Quito

PACIFIC OCEAN

PERU

BRAZIL

Anti-Nixon riots 1958
Military coup 1962
Military coup 1968

Lima

Brasília

BOLIVIA
La Paz

Average annual per capita income
late 1960's

Argentina	$800
Barbados	428
Bolivia	165
Brazil	350
Chile	465
Colombia	262
Costa Rica	380
Cuba	310
Dominican Rep.	212
Ecuador	183
El Salvador	245
Guatemala	264
Guyana	250
Haiti	75
Honduras	209
Jamaica	431
Mexico	600
Nicaragua	347
Panama	477
Paraguay	192
Peru	241
Trinidad & Tobago	515
Uruguay	537
Venezuela	902

PARAGUAY

Asunción

Rio de Janeiro

Salvador
Allende
elected 1970

CHILE

Buenos
Aires

URUGUAY

Santiago

Montevideo

ARGENTINA

Punta del Este Conferences
1961, 1962

ATLANTIC

OCEAN

Under $200

$200-399

$400-599

Over $600

256

formed by the American Embassy in Santo Domingo, concluded that Marines would have to land to prevent a Castro-type revolution. Johnson and Mann had taken a tough line on Castro. Despite approaches from the Cuban government in the autumn of 1963 which hinted at its desire to have normal relations with the United States, Washington had replied very cautiously. When Castro then suggested an agenda for the talks, Johnson was President. Although he saw the Cuban memorandum, Johnson had refused to make any conciliatory move.[37] By late 1964 the United States, working through the Organization of American States (OAS), had successfully encouraged every Latin American nation except Mexico to break off diplomatic relations with Cuba. Faced with the Santo Domingo revolt, the Administration adopted a view that American policy-makers had amplified from the Truman Doctrine to the Kennedy-Johnson interpretation of Vietnam: the revolt was part of a larger challenge, and a challenge in any area was thus a challenge to American security everywhere.

The initial public pretext for landing nearly 23,000 troops was the protection of Americans in strife-torn Santo Domingo. This rationale was probably publicized in part because the United States action violated Articles 15 and 17 of the OAS Charter which prohibited intervention "directly or indirectly, for any reason whatever, in the internal or external affairs of any other State." On April 30, however, Johnson gave a different reason: "people trained outside the Dominican Republic are seeking to gain control." When the American Embassy issued a poorly documented list of 58 (or 53) "identified and prominent Communist and Castroite leaders" in the rebel forces, American newspapermen on the scene considered the list propaganda, not fact, and agreed with Bosch's assessment that "This was a democratic revolution smashed by the leading democracy of the world."[38] In intervening unilaterally, the United States maneuvered a very reluctant vote of consent from the OAS, but Johnson's disdain for the organization's failure to be enthusiastic about the American

---

[37] Oral History Statement by William Attwood, November 8, 1965, Kennedy Library. Used by permission.
[38] *Newsweek*, May 17, 1965, p. 52.

Marines was unconcealed. "The OAS," the President remarked privately, "couldn't pour ——— out of a boot if the instructions were written on the heel."[39]

The President went further. On May 2, 1965, he announced that the "American nations cannot, must not, and will not permit the establishment of another Communist government in the Western Hemisphere." He warned that change "should come through peaceful process," and pledged that the United States would defend "every free country of this hemisphere." The importance of this "Johnson Doctrine," like that of the Truman and Eisenhower Doctrines, depended on how broadly the United States would define "Communism" and how easily force would be committed to defend "every free country." The contradictions inherent in the Administration's policies (in both Southeast Asia and Latin America) appeared on May 9 in an interview with Mann. Having just intervened with a large force, the Assistant Secretary of State said that the United States only wanted every nation to choose its "own government free of outside interference." Expressing the hope that "democratic" elements would triumph in future Dominican elections, Mann also observed that because the country had gone "through a long period of dictatorship," the people were only "just beginning" to understand the complexities of "democratic societies."[40]

In the spring of 1966 a conservative government led by Joaquin Balaguer assumed power through nationwide elections. Four years later Balaguer was reelected, but amidst increasing violence. Although the opposition pulled out of the campaign, more than 200 political murders occurred. During the first six months of 1971, political killings happened at the rate of one every forty-eight hours. Balaguer's police evidently committed most of the crimes. "Even under Trujillo we had nothing like this," said a veteran Dominican reporter.[41] The conclusion to the American interventions would not be written for years. The effect on Latin Americans was incalculable.

The Administration's policy came under severe attack at home,

---

[39] Geyelin, *Lyndon B. Johnson and the World*, p. 254.

[40] *The New York Times*, May 9, 1965, p. E3.

[41] *Washington Post*, July 15, 1971, p. F7.

but most critics were concerned with the evolving pattern of American intervention around the globe and the resulting justifications issued by official sources. In this sense, Santo Domingo was a microcosm of South Vietnam. During the 1964 presidential campaign, Johnson had answered Goldwater's demands for bombing North Vietnam with the remark on September 25, "We're not going north and drop bombs at this stage of the game" because "I want to think about the consequences of getting American boys into a war with 700 million Chinese." The same day, however, William P. Bundy, Assistant Secretary of State for Far Eastern Affairs, commented, "Expansion of the war outside South Vietnam . . . could be forced upon us by the increased pressures of the Communists." The difference between Goldwater and Johnson in 1964 could be found less by comparing party platforms (for both accepted the interventionist, anticommunistic policies of Truman through Kennedy), than by listening to the candidates' rhetoric. The "real foreign policy issue of this campaign," Johnson proclaimed on October 21, "is whether we will use our great power with judgment and restraint." Bundy, however, proved the more accurate prophet. At the time Johnson was campaigning, his closest advisers had decided that North Vietnam would have to be bombed. Target lists were drawn up, bombings were expected to begin at the outset of 1965, and only the President's permission, which his advisers now thought to be "inevitable," remained to be obtained. These counselors further understood that the bombing, once undertaken, would only be a stopgap measure to shore up the revolving South Vietnam regimes until American ground troops could be rushed into action.[42]

On February 8, 1965 the American bombing raids on North Vietnam began. The ostensible reason was a Vietcong attack on the American camp at Pleiku, killing seven Americans; this was one of a series of attacks against United States bases that had taken place since the autumn. In March, the President began "Rolling Thunder," a systematic, long-term bombing program against the North. Curtis LeMay, Air Force Chief of Staff, thought it time: "We are swatting flies when we should be going

---

[42] *Pentagon Papers*, pp. 307–342.

after the manure pile." By April, however, the bombing had only stiffened Hanoi's resistance. Johnson ordered more than 20,000 American troops into Vietnam, and now they were openly instructed to enter into combat. The inescapable logic of the commitment began to become apparent. Over 100,000 United States troops went to Vietnam in approximately four months. The escalation saved the tottering South Vietnamese government, but at an unimagined price.

"Rolling Thunder" was aimed at cutting off supplies being infiltrated from the North as well as helping to stabilize South Vietnam politically. It accomplished neither objective. Hanoi, with aid from Russia and China, matched the American escalation step by step, sending 60,000 men into the South in 1966 (three times the number of 1965), and increasing daily tonnage of supplies by 150 percent. Bombing had little effect on the primitive supply route that needed to provide only six tons of goods a day (an amount that could be carried by several hundred coolies) to keep the Vietcong refueled. Bombings North and South, moreover, probably killed a ratio of two civilians to one Vietcong, according to one estimate; American-Vietnamese search-and-destroy operations on the ground perhaps killed as many as six civilians for each Vietcong.[43] Ground fighting increased with Americans assuming the burden. In April 1966 for the first time more Americans were killed in action than South Vietnamese.

On the political side, prospects only slightly improved. In June 1965 strongman Air Vice-Marshal Nguyen Cao Ky came to power as Premier. A North Vietnamese who had fought with the French against Vietnamese independence forces and later made a widely publicized remark praising Adolf Hitler, Ky was nevertheless welcomed by American officials because he promised to provide the necessary political stability. But desertions continued to rise dramatically in the South Vietnam Army. Inflation and corruption, appearing almost in proportion to the intensified American effort, decimated the Vietnamese economy. By February 1966 McNamara admitted that even if bombing destroyed all of North Vietnam's power systems, oil, harbors, and dams,

---

[43] Roger Hilsman, *To Move a Nation* (New York, 1965), p. 530.

"they could still carry on the infiltration of the men and equipment necessary to support some level of operations in the South."[44]

These disasters were visible in 1966 for any American who cared to see them. Too often the scene was blurred by statistics that poured out of Washington, most of them misleading. "Ah, *les statistiques!*" a Vietnamese general explained to an American, "Your Secretary of Defense loves statistics. We Vietnamese can give him all he wants. If you want them to go up, they will go up. If you want them to go down, they will go down."[45] The view was also distorted by various peace initiatives. In an April 7, 1965 speech at Johns Hopkins University, President Johnson offered what he termed "unconditional discussions" and proposed an internationally financed Asian Development Bank for peacetime reconstruction. Hanoi responded with four points that would form the basis of its diplomacy for the next six years: (1) A withdrawal of American troops and bases from South Vietnam and a cessation of bombing. (2) Both Vietnams were to promise to have no foreign military bases or alliances. (3) South Vietnamese affairs were to be resolved according to the program of the National Liberation Front. (4) The reunification of Vietnam was to be carved out by the Vietnamese themselves. Point (3) was especially sticky, but actually peace discussions were impossible from the American view because of the deteriorating military situation. During his first months in office, moreover, President Johnson had ruled out any neutralization of South Vietnam. This undercut totally his professions for "unconditional discussions." "Your mission," he informed Henry Cabot Lodge in Saigon, "is precisely for the purpose of knocking down the idea of neutralization wherever it rears its ugly head."[46]

For their part, the North Vietnamese would settle for nothing less than a complete withdrawal of American power and the reunification of the country on their terms. They were not about to be betrayed as they felt they had been in the 1954 Geneva

[44] *The New York Times*, February 16, 1966, p. 1.

[45] Hilsman, *To Move a Nation*, p. 523.

[46] *Pentagon Papers*, pp. 285–286, especially cable from President to Lodge, March 20, 1964, Document No. 65.

Conference. By 1965 the Vietnamese civil war could no more be compromised than was the American Civil War a century earlier. These irreconcilable attitudes also doomed a dramatic American move in late December 1965, when the President began a bombing pause of thirty-seven days, sending senior diplomats throughout the world to explore possibilities for negotiations. During the truce North Vietnamese infiltration continued and the United States buildup increased even more rapidly.

The White House now aimed for military victory, for once a nation fell to "Communism," (an elastic term applied to revolutionaries whether in China or Iraq, Cuba or Santo Domingo) or became unsteadily "neutralized," American liberty in the world was decreased and Communism occupied a springboard for toppling other "dominoes." In this sense, the enemy of the 1960s was China. On the one hand, the Johnson Administration believed that because of internal difficulties the Chinese would not intervene in Vietnam as long as the fighting remained away from their borders. On the other hand, "Over this war—and all Asia— is another reality: the deepening shadow of Communist China," as the President told the nation in his Johns Hopkins speech. "The contest in Vietnam is part of a wider pattern of aggressive purposes." During the same month McNamara explained most fully in a private conversation why the United States was in Vietnam.

The alternative to fighting, he observed, was not to negotiate a neutral non-Communist South Vietnam since this was impossible. The real alternative was a Chinese-dominated Southeast Asia, which would mean a "Red Asia." If the United States withdrew, a complete shift would occur in the world balance of power. Asia would go Red, American allies would be shaken, and at home there would be a "bad effect on [the] economy and a disastrous political fight that could further freeze American political debate and even affect political freedom." Chinese attitudes might soften over the decades, but this would take longer than had the Russian change, for China "started from farther back than [the] Soviet Union in [the] industrializing process. The Soviet Union was contained by a military alliance in an expansionist period. So [it is] possible to contain China in her expansionist phase by similar alliances." To stop China, the United

States would not recognize "any sanctuary or any weapons restriction. But we would use nuclear weapons only after fully applying non-nuclear arsenal."[47]

The Secretary of Defense offered this explanation at a time when the Chinese were suffering a series of devastating foreign policy setbacks that helped to cause a severe internal upheaval within China between 1966 and 1968. During the 1960s Peking had tried to establish a third bloc by modifying Mao's revolutionary principles for the newly-emerging nations in order to cooperate with factions in such industrialized, bourgeois nations as Japan, France, and Canada which opposed both the United States and Russia. In Vietnam, Mao was even willing to accept a neutralist arrangement so long as the United States left the area. The Chinese sent no significant aid to the Vietcong until mid-1963, and large support arrived only after the American escalation in early 1965. In mid-1965, however, China suffered humiliating defeats. A domestically generated *coup* in Indonesia led by nationalist army elements, and having little to do with the American presence in Vietnam, destroyed pro-Peking Communists in a bloodbath. Castro's Cuba, revolutionary Algeria, Egypt's Nasser, and a number of African nations publicly attacked Chinese policies, restricting or severing diplomatic ties. Despite her explosion of an atomic bomb in 1964 and a thermonuclear device in May 1966, Chinese diplomatic leverage dissipated.

These failures influenced Mao to launch a "cultural revolution" within China, transforming foreign policy and enabling him to eliminate personal enemies within Peking who had advocated the third-bloc strategy. The turning point came in September 1965 when General Lin Piao, second in command to Mao, announced that China would encourage wars of liberation throughout the newly emerging nations because these countries, comprising the southern, agrarian areas of the world, were inextricably involved in various phases of conflict with the northern-urban nations. This was the signal that China would give up its attempt to create a third bloc by cooperating with capitalist nations, and would return, instead, to advocating third-world revolution. Lin

---

[47] "Memorandum" of Background Session with Robert McNamara, April 22, 1965, in Arthur Krock Papers, Princeton University Library.

Piao gave no hint that China would become directly involved in any of the revolutions. Peking would only encourage them, and from a distance. Lin Piao warned other revolutionaries to help themselves as the Chinese had done.

In Washington, however, policy-makers led by Secretary of State Dean Rusk immediately compared Lin Piao's statement to Hitler's *Mein Kampf*. The President announced that Lin Piao had confirmed that if the domino of Vietnam fell, others would follow[48] Chinese experts like Harvard's John Fairbank deplored this interpretation. Nearly 200 scholars of Asian affairs urged a re-evaluation of the policy towards China, but without success. They observed that regardless of how the rhetoric was interpreted, Chinese capabilities and power could not and might never be able to achieve Lin Piao's objectives. Developments in Indonesia, Cuba, and Africa confirmed this view.

As usual, the greatest irony could be found in Vietnam. Although the United States supposedly was fighting to contain China, American bombing of the North compelled Hanoi to move away from China and closer to the Soviet Union. Following the Lin Piao statement, China pleaded with Hanoi to fight a protracted struggle that would tie down and bleed American power. Ho Chi Minh disliked such advice. He saw no logic in an indefinite conflict that would benefit only China's objectives. He wanted to defeat the United States rapidly, since a long war would leave a weakened North Vietnam more open to Chinese pressure.[49] Meanwhile, much to the consternation of the Chinese, the Soviet Union replaced China as the most important source of aid and support for Ho's regime. Worse, in early 1966 clashes between Chinese and Russian troops occurred along their long common border. The Chinese were being squeezed from two directions by Russia; they were losing influence in Hanoi as well as other key third-world capitals; and they were undergoing a catastrophic revolution internally whose causes were quite di-

---

[48] *Public Papers of the Presidents, 1966*, p. 936; see also *The New York Times*, August 31, 1966, p. 9.

[49] David Mozingo, "China's Foreign Policy and the Cultural Revolution," Interim Report: Number 1, International Relations of East Asia Project, Cornell University, Ithaca, New York, 1970.

vorced from American actions in Southeast Asia. At this point in 1965-1966, the Johnson Administration decided to send 400,-000 American soldiers to save Vietnam from China.

The Soviet Union was the primary, perhaps sole nation that benefited from American intervention. With United States' attention and resources tied down in Southeast Asia, Russia made a dramatic recovery in world affairs between 1965 and 1971. After 1958 the Russian economy had grown at a considerably slower level than previously, discouraging hopes of challenging the American economic supremacy. The decline also weakened Khrushchev's power within the Kremlin. In the autumn of 1964 the Premier announced a new economic program that deemphasized heavy and defense industries. He apparently tied this with an approach for a *detente* with the West German government, a policy which, if it had worked, might have slid the army and defense industries down the economic priority list. Dissenting Party leaders and some military officials combined to oust Khrushchev in October 1964, dividing his posts between two former protegeés of Stalin, Alexei Kosygin, who became Premier, and Leonid Brezhnev, the new First Party Secretary. This change occurred as the United States stepped up its effort in Vietnam. Kosygin was actually visiting Hanoi at that moment in February 1965 when, for reasons best known to the State Department, the United States chose to begin the bombing.

The Russian response to American escalation was measured, partly because of the new regime's concern with domestic affairs. In contrast with Khrushchev's flamboyance, the new leaders emphasized steadiness, order, and efficiency. Brezhnev and Kosygin placed greater dependence on the internal police, particularly in a series of trials aimed at quieting younger intelligentsia and Jews who challenged the new repression. As Soviet influence in Hanoi increased in 1965-1966, Moscow would do nothing to mediate between the United States and North Vietnam, in part because the two sides were irreconcilable, but also because the war, as long as it remained limited, helped Russian policies. The Soviets began a rapid buildup of intercontinental ballistic missiles until by 1968 they approached parity with the United States. At the same time, Kosygin pushed for a nonproliferation agreement under which nations possessing nuclear weapons would not use these devices against other countries or aid nonnuclear nations in developing such weapons. An agreement of this kind would inhibit American use of nuclear devices in South Vietnam and would prevent West Germany and Japan from acquiring a nuclear arsenal. In 1968 the two superpowers negotiated such a pact.

As the Soviets doubtless intended, the nonproliferation treaty intensified strains on an Atlantic alliance already weakened by the American involvement in Vietnam. France refused to sign it, and West Germany moved toward approval most reluctantly. The United States immersion in Vietnam also heightened tensions. When McNamara privately warned the NATO defense ministers that China must be checked before she had missile capability to hit Europe or the United States, one European diplomat remarked, "McNamara wants us to start worrying now about China, but most of us have enough to worry about here in Europe."[50] France, harboring bitter memories of Dulles' actions in Southeast Asia a decade earlier, condemned the "foreign intervention" of the United States. These disagreements were symptoms of the disintegration within the Atlantic Alliance that had been underway since the mid-1950s. In the spring of 1966, American policies received a further blow when de Gaulle announced that France would formally withdraw from NATO military organizations within three years. At the same time that NATO was weakened, however, the French cooperated in strengthening the Common Market. Agreements were reached on the thorny issue of agricultural prices. Aided by new West German governments that were opening fresh chapters of diplomacy by initiating diplomatic relations with the Communist bloc nations, de Gaulle advanced his policies for a Europe independent of the United States in both the military and economic realms.

The Western Europeans refused outright to send men for the American buildup in South Vietnam. Of the forty nations linked to the United States through treaties, only four (Australia, New Zealand, South Korea, and Thailand) had committed combat troops by the end of 1966. Korea and Thailand did so only after the United States promised to pay handsomely for their troops.

---

[50] *The New York Times*, December 16, 1965, p. 1.

Japan, whom American officials had long considered the linchpin in their Asian defense plans, grew critical of the escalation in the war. Johnson was especially disappointed that neither West Germany nor India would help. If Indian Prime Minister Shastri got "off his can" and indicated, at least, some moral judgments in favor of the United States, the President commented, Shastri could better call on him if India "should happen to get in more trouble with Red China." Moreover, the Indians "can get some arms pretty cheap."[51]

No matter where he looked, Johnson had difficulty finding allies for his policies. Soviet military and diplomatic leverage meanwhile grew as unstable conditions spread in Africa and Latin America. The trouble with foreigners, the President observed, "is that they're not like folks you were reared with."[52] By mid-1966, however, the problems with the allies were rapidly becoming minor in comparison with the eruptions of the "folks" at home.

---

[51] "Confidential Memo on Turner Catledge's Conversation with President Johnson," December 15, 1964, Black Book No. 3, Krock Papers, Princeton.
[52] Quoted in Gayelin, *Lyndon Johnson and the World*, p. 15.

CHAPTER XI

The Fringes and the Center of the Cake (1966-1971)

S ince the early 1950s, American scholars and journalists had offered hosannahs to the idea of "consensus." The nation was supposedly united in pursuing common goals at home and abroad. The pressure of McCarthyism only partly explained this phenomenon. Equally important was the ideological transformation occurring among American liberal spokesmen. Since the time of Andrew Jackson they had traditionally praised social pluralism as the best guarantee of individual freedom. Encouraging many different socioeconomic interests to exist and compete against one another, the theory went, would prevent any one faction as, for example, big business, from becoming overly dominant in the society.[1] Between 1947 and 1960 that attitude changed. Americans denigrated pluralism to seek unanimity around anticommunism overseas and post-New Deal policies at home. In his famous Inaugural Address of 1961, John F. Kennedy issued the ultimate statement of American consensus rhetoric during the Cold War era. The United States would "support any friend," or "oppose any foe," warned the new President. Hence, he intoned, "Ask not what your country can do for you, ask what you can do for your country."

As Kennedy spoke, the consensus was shattering. New Left intellectuals attacked the assumptions on which consensus history and political science had been written during the 1950s. Black students staged sit-ins to win equal rights, thereby serving

---

[1] For good analyses of the rise and fall of American pluralism see two books by Theodore J. Lowi, *The End of Liberalism* (New York, 1969), and *The Politics of Disorder* (New York, 1971).

notice that they would no longer wait on doubtful long-term economic policies to create a just society for all races. Blacks joined with whites in reform-radical movements on both the university and national political levels. Reaction on the right soon appeared when Governor George Wallace of Alabama challenged the traditional two-party system by running for president on an independent ticket.

Lyndon Johnson, who placed the highest value on consensus support, inherited this breakdown, along with Vietnam, from the Kennedy Administration. Not understanding the problem until too late, Kennedy and Johnson took the United States into Vietnam on the assumption that as a single people Americans would "oppose any foe." As Johnson escalated the fighting in 1964–1965, the consensus further disintegrated. Teach-ins began at universities in 1965. The society thereby discovered how to carry on a debate that was lacking in both the White House and Congress. Draft resistance grew, defying Johnson's wielding of the tremendously increased presidential powers which liberal intellectuals had admired and sought to increase during the early 1960s. As many liberal New Dealers hastened to free themselves of the President's growing dilemma, his White House National Security Adviser, McGeorge Bundy, bitterly commented that "liberals" are "a prejudiced lot who don't distinguish between style and substance; they don't realize the President has his fist in the dike."[2]

The President meanwhile found it impossible to have both guns and butter: "Because of Vietnam," he observed on January 12, 1966, "we cannot do all that we should, or all that we would like to do." As he cut back on education, poverty, and health programs, terrible violence erupted in ghetto areas during 1966-1967. Following the assassination of Martin Luther King in April 1968, a riot in Washington was quelled only after United States Army troops and trucks moved into the city, using the Capitol Hill lawn as a bivouac area. Three major political assassinations (John F. Kennedy in 1963, Martin Luther King and Robert F. Kennedy in 1968) occurred within a national context in which an

---

[2] Interview with Henry Graff in *The New York Times Magazine*, March 20, 1966, p. 130.

important precedent and rationale for violence came from the federal government itself—not only in Vietnam, but in its refusal to pass adequate gun-control legislation at home.[3] The United States was experiencing a nightmare. The President, to use his phrase, "hunkered down" like a jackrabbit in a sandstorm.

United States power, however, was finally disciplined not by dissent at home but by defeats and the blunting of that power in Southeast Asia, Africa, Latin America, and Europe. As he failed to win the final military victory in Vietnam and as consensus collapsed at home, Johnson found his own private consensus by making major policy at a Tuesday luncheon group consisting of Rusk, McNamara, Bundy, and later Walt Whitman Rostow, who replaced Bundy. These men had involved the United States in Vietnam and little evidence appeared that they would be able to reexamine their own assumptions. Only McNamara was having second thoughts. More than most members of the Administration he was becoming aware of the dilemma of trying to do good while also wielding great power.[4] In mid-1967 he publicly testified that the bombing of North Vietnam was not working. As Johnson saw that McNamara had "gone dovish on me," the President sent the Defense Secretary off in February 1968 to become head of the World Bank.

Throughout late 1967 and early 1968, the Administration argued that the war was making noticeable progress. Such news was especially welcomed as the Democrats faced the upcoming presidential election. Then in January 1968, after announcing a seven-day truce to celebrate the Tet Lunar New Year holiday, the Vietcong launched a devastating attack in which they assaulted the American Embassy in Saigon, controlled part of the capital for a time, and held Hue several days. The onslaught provoked the United States to launch virtually indiscriminate bombing raids on Saigon and other major cities in order to drive out the attackers. The President asked Dean Acheson to undertake a reevaluation of the involvement. Acheson reported that Johnson

---

[3] Richard Hofstadter's Introduction, *American Violence; A Documentary History*, edited by Hofstadter and Michael Wallace (New York, 1970), p. 30.
[4] David Halberstam, "The Programming of Robert McNamara," *Harper's*, February 1971, p. 58.

was being "led down the garden path" by his advisers. And in the New Hampshire Presidential Primary, Senator Eugene Mc-Carthy of Minnesota, running as an anti-Johnson Democrat on the war issue, polled a surprising 42 percent of the votes.

On March 31 the President dramatically announced a restriction of the bombing of the North to obtain Hanoi's entry into negotiations at Paris. At the same time Johnson declared that he would not be a candidate in the November elections. How seriously the Administration wanted to deescalate the war is open to question. The State Department secretly told American Ambassadors in Asia that it expected Hanoi to reject the President's invitation to negotiate, and thus "give us a clear field for whatever actions" may be "required."[5] To maintain military pressure while negotiations were discussed, Johnson raised American troop levels in Vietnam from 486,600 to 535,500 during the summer. The North Vietnamese finally began the discussions, but otherwise the President's initiative was frustrated. Frustration continued at home as well. When the Democratic National Convention met at Chicago, riots pockmarked the streets and parks. Six thousand armed troops flew into the city. The President could not go to his party's convention without gravely endangering his life. Amidst the chaos, the party nominated Vice-President Hubert Humphrey, with Maine's Senator Edmund Muskie (who had led the opposition at the convention to a peace resolution) as his running mate.

Blacks rioted in Miami where the Republican convention was held, but despite the death of three blacks this was relatively overlooked by the media as the party nominated Richard Nixon for President. The former Vice-President had risen from the political grave between 1962 and 1966, attacking Johnson for not winning in Vietnam, supporting Goldwater in 1964, and in the process becoming the main Republican spokesman. He mysteriously promised a plan for settling the war, but indicated no major departure in foreign policy. This became apparent when he privately commented that Woodrow Wilson "was our greatest Pres-

---

[5] "Cable to Envoys in Asia," March 31, 1968, *The Pentagon Papers*, pp. 622–623.

ident of this century. . . . Wilson had the greatest vision of America's world role." Nixon's primary criticism of the World War One President was that "he wasn't practical enough."[6] The Republican nominee believed that the most important discontent was not among the left and radical young, but to the right of the political spectrum. To be "practical," therefore, he named as his Vice-Presidential nominee Spiro Agnew, governor of the border state of Maryland. Agnew made headlines by declaring that Humphrey was "squishy-soft" on Communism and law and order.

Nixon's analysis of American attitudes seemed correct. President Johnson desperately tried to take Vietnam out of the campaign by opening peace talks in Paris, but his South Vietnamese allies refused to sit down at the same table with the Communists, thus delaying the opening of the discussions. Saigon's refusal to do so on the Saturday before the elections evidently stopped a large migration of voters from Nixon to Humphrey, thereby possibly providing the Republican with his extremely narrow margin of victory (0.7 percent of total votes cast).[7]

Overall, however, the Vietnam issue was more complex. George Wallace, who represented hard-line foreign policies, received a surprising 13.5 percent of the vote. More significant, voter surveys indicated that a slight plurality of Democrats who supported antiwar Eugene McCarthy in the primaries preferred Wallace in the November election over either Nixon or Humphrey. Indeed, if Vietnam had been the single issue, Johnson had the best chance of winning, since polls showed that a large majority were willing to go along with his policies in 1968. Of those who were not, supporters of military escalation were nearly twice as numerous as those advocating unilateral withdrawal. And contrary to the images on the television screens, voting analyses showed that young people under thirty were more "hawkish" than the over-fifty generation. The young were also more likely to vote for Wallace than were older voters. The noncollege, conservative American in his twenties, not the radical student, determined

---

[6] Gary Wills, *Nixon Agonistes* (New York, 1970), pp. 20–21.
[7] Jules Witcover, *Resurrection of Richard Nixon* (New York, 1970), p. 460.

the results on election day.[8] Americans apparently voted less on Vietnam than on the so-called "social issues" of race, rioting, and crime in the streets. In regard to the war, the majority of Americans saw no better alternative than to follow President Johnson's course.

Nixon understood this on entering the White House. He realized that militarily Vietnam was a bottomless pit draining resources better applied at home or in more vital areas of the world. Henry Kissinger, the new President's National Security Adviser on foreign policy, had long considered Europe, not Asia, the fulcrum of world politics. Both men also realized that although the antiwar forces at home were not strong enough to embarrass them seriously,[9] the war would have to be terminated before these forces, and considerably more important, the voters on the right and center, turned their displeasure regarding an extended, expensive, unwinable war against the President in 1972. To accomplish these objectives, Nixon introduced with flourishes the concept of "Vietnamization": training South Vietnamese to defend themselves while withdrawing American combat troops. The concept was not new. Eisenhower, Kennedy, and Johnson had unsuccessfully tried it between 1955 and 1965. Between 1969 and mid-1971 American troops in Vietnam were reduced from 550,000 to approximately 200,000. The withdrawal, however, exposed the central problem of Vietnamization, for the South Vietnamese government grew weaker as it was stripped of essential American military protection. The Administration tried to find what Kissinger, before he became the President's adviser, once called a "decent interval," that is, a respectable amount of time between the point American troops withdrew and the South Vietnamese government fell with, perhaps, attendant repercussions on American politics.

The President attempted to obtain this decent interval during the spring of 1970 with an American-South Vietnamese invasion of Communist staging areas in neighboring Cambodia. Since vast amounts of supplies were captured and Vietcong activity de-

---

[8] *Washington Post*, October 1, 1969, p. A23; Richard M. Scammon and Ben J. Wattenberg, *The Real Majority* (New York, 1970), pp. 38–49, 92–93.
[9] *Washington Post*, February 28, 1971, p. B3.

creased in South Vietnam, the Administration termed the invasion a success. Other results, however, proved more enduring. At home demonstrations and riots against the operation were climaxed by the shooting of four young students at Kent State University. The nation once again went into a state of shock. In Cambodia, the Communists met the invasion by retreating from the staging areas and by concentrating on consolidating their hold over other areas of Cambodia. After the United States troops withdrew, a new pro-Western Cambodian government found itself in a state of seige. Approximately 45,000 Communist troops controlled one-third to one-half of the country. The Nixon Administration apparently nevertheless believed that because of the short-term military success of the operation and the supposedly successful pacification program in South Vietnam, the Saigon government could be preserved despite the American withdrawal. In February 1971, the President tried to repeat the Cambodian operation, but this time in Laos. (See map, page 227.)

South Vietnamese troops with overwhelming American air support moved into Laos in an attempt to cut off the main supply lines running from North Vietnam into the South. The operation, the Administration claimed, would be the acid test for the capabilities of the South Vietnamese Army and, therefore, for the President's "Vietnamization" program. The Laotian invasion turned quickly into disaster. Communist forces outflanked and destroyed South Vietnamese units, driving them back in headlong retreat. The Vietcong meanwhile challenged the supposedly successful pacification efforts in the South, shelling cities, raiding supposedly secure villages, and even attacking several American military bases that Washington had considered militarily invulnerable. The United States responded by stepping up the bombing of the Laotian supply trails, a policy that had continued secretly since 1964 and was drastically increased in 1968 when President Johnson restricted the bombing of North Vietnam. Laos, indeed, became the most heavily bombed area in world history. By 1969-1970 the bombing had become indiscriminate as jets dropped 500-pound bombs, delayed-action bombs, napalm, and antipersonnel bombs on villages, buffaloes, cows, rice fields, and schools as well as on Communist outposts. Some 150,-000 Laotians became refugees as their villages were obliterated.

But by mid-1971 the Communists were in a stronger position in Laos than at any time since 1962.[10]

The Laotian debacle evidently changed White House policies. Although the Central Intelligence Agency continued large-scale clandestine aid to a Laotian army of 30,000 men, and although Washington reaffirmed its commitment to the South Vietnamese government of Nguyen Van Thieu, talk was no longer heard of a possible military victory. At the Paris peace negotiations, neither the Laotian nor Cambodian invasions induced the Communists to moderate their demands for a definite, stated time for American withdrawal. On July 1, 1971, the National Liberation Front and North Vietnamese advanced new peace proposals in which they offered to release several thousand American prisoners if, in return, the United States would agree to state a definite time for complete American withdrawal of forces and would allow the Vietnamese to settle the destiny of Vietnam without outside interference. The President refused to give such a date until Hanoi released the prisoners and the South Vietnamese government gave some promise of being able to defend itself. The latter event seemed far off and was becoming the sticking point of the negotiations. With the failure of the Laotian invasion and the after-effects, the contradiction of "Vietnamization" became clear: as American forces withdrew and South Vietnamese soldiers appeared incapable of defeating Communist troops, American leverage to force the releasing of the prisoners and to defend the Saigon government dwindled.

North Vietnam, that "raggedy-ass little fourth-rate country," as Lyndon Johnson once called it,[11] also intensified President Nixon's problems at home. Although he solemnly announced that the Laotian invasion would shorten the war, Americans by a 2 to 1 margin refused to believe him, concluding instead that it would lengthen the conflict.[12] They tired of supporting a Vietnamese regime that seemed incurably corrupt and incapable of mustering nationwide support. Nor was this impatience pacified

---

[10] Ibid., May 23, 1971, p. B1; Fred Branfman, "Presidential War in Laos, 1964–1970," in Adams and McCoy, Laos: War and Revolution, pp. 213–280.

[11] Halberstam, "Programming of McNamara," p. 64.

[12] The New York Times, February 28, 1971, p. 10.

by comments such as Lyndon Johnson's: "Certainly they have corruption and we also have it in Boston, in New York, in Washington and in Johnson City. Somebody is stealing something in Beaumont right now."[13] Surprisingly, the view contrary to Johnson's came from South Vietnam's Vice-President, Nguyen Cao Ky in mid-1971. Ky had become bitterly hostile to President Thieu, especially after Thieu had rammed measures through the legislature making it impossible for Ky to run against the President in the October 1971 elections. The elections, essential to Nixon's "Vietnamization" policy, were a farce, and Ky explained why:

South Vietnam is like a sinking boat, with a deceptively good coat of paint outside, and a helmsman [Thieu] who is unfaithful, disloyal, and dishonest. A whirl of wind and that boat will sink to the bottom. It is clear that the people have lost faith in the Government. . . . Corruption is rampaging. . . . Corruption has become public, open, and as it were, an incurable disease.[14]

Disapproval increased within the United States when, after "Vietnamization" had supposedly deescalated the war, Americans learned that during 1969-1970 approximately 25,000 South Vietnamese civilians had been killed in the fighting and 100,000 wounded. Such slaughter was dramatized during the spring of 1971 when a military court martial convicted Lieutenant William Calley, Jr., of killing at least 21 South Vietnamese civilians in 1968 at the village of Mylai. American opinion apparently disapproved the indictment, but the response was divided between those who thought Calley was only doing his duty in a war which no longer distinguished between civilians and the enemy, and those who wanted the Lieutenant's superiors brought to trial. Calley's commander observed at his own trial, "Every unit of brigade size has its Mylai hidden some place."[15] The impersonal violence of Mylai became apparent as well in American universities, ghettoes, and cities. Not surprisingly, a presidential commission discovered that the age group most attracted to violence in

---

[13] *Ibid.*, March 3, 1968, p. 5.

[14] *Ibid.*, May 17, 1971, p. 33.

[15] *Ibid.*, May 25, 1971, p. 13.

the United States was under 25, that is, those who grew up among nuclear weapons and Southeast Asian wars. Meanwhile, American soldiers, unwilling to be, perhaps, the last to die in such a war, used drugs in increasing amounts to avoid combat. Some 15,000 troops in Vietnam were addicted to heroin, the American government warned, and would bring the addiction home with them.

Most Americans worried about such consequences from a so-called limited war. The invasions of Cambodia and Laos also created strong domestic opposition to unchecked presidential use of violence overseas. A large student movement arose out of the Cambodian crisis in 1970 to support the passage of the Hatfield-McGovern Amendment providing that all American troops be removed from South Vietnam by the end of 1971. The students displayed neither the staying power nor the political organization to win such a battle. The amendment was defeated 55 to 39 in the Senate during early September, long after most students had deserted Washington. Congress, particularly the House of Representatives, proved singularly incapable of translating the rising domestic opposition to the war into legislation that could check presidential power in foreign affairs. This congressional impotency continued despite public warnings by several leading Senators that Henry Kissinger was more powerful in shaping policy than was Secretary of State William Rogers. Unlike the Secretary of State, however, Kissinger could not be summoned before Congressional committees to consult or to defend his policies, for as a personal adviser to the President, Kissinger could, and did, invoke executive immunity. Leaving the critical constitutional issues aside, Kissinger's power was significant in other respects, since he took a tougher line on policies in Southeast Asia, Central Europe, strategic arms negotiations, Latin American revolutions, and the Middle East crisis than did Secretary of State Rogers.

During the early 1970s, an overextended and overbearing United States power was challenged in the first instance not by an aware and politically effective American citizenry, but by inexorable economic problems at home and uprisings in Asia, the Middle East, Africa, and Latin America. The significance of Vietnam was that it was only the most dramatic and bloody of a series of global confrontations that successfully chopped away at

American power. The United States continued to be one of the two superpowers, but its empire began to resemble the British Empire of the 1770s which Benjamin Franklin described as like an overlarge cake which first disintegrated along its edges.

By the mid-1960s a highly unlikely point of vulnerability in the empire was the American economy, that undergirding of the postwar reconstruction and trade expansion in most areas of the world. The economy, however, had become less competitive in selling its own goods in foreign markets especially since 1966-1967, the years when spending in Vietnam ignited an uncontrollable inflation in the United States. Inflation drove up costs, thereby increasing and so making less competitive the prices of American goods. Unemployment rose. The Nixon Administration did little until mid-summer 1971 when governmental figures showed that for the first time since 1893 the country would buy more from abroad than it sold. The deficit balance would have to be paid by the United States either in gold (from a gold supply that had already dropped 50 percent in ten years), or in dollars. But the more dollars moved overseas to cover the deficit, the cheaper and less welcome they became, particularly as their value depended on a stumbling economy. The American financial structure, the greatest in all history, was in grave trouble.

On August 15, 1971 President Nixon suddenly announced a 90-day wage-price freeze to control inflation; established a 10 percent surcharge on foreign imports, thereby hoping to correct the deficit trade balance and make some key American products, such as automobiles, more competitive with cheaper foreign products at home; and, most dramatically, declared that for a period of time the dollar would no longer be redeemable in gold. This last announcement allowed an overvalued dollar to "float" in world money exchanges, finding its worth at a lower level than had been the case during the previous twenty-five years, when the American government had guaranteed its worth in a certain amount of gold. As the dollar became devalued, or cheaper, so too did American products whose value was based on the dollar. Hence this "floating" also helped the nation's export trade.

Once again, as for example in 1807, 1893, and 1914, not a neat theory of abstract power politics but simply an inability to make their economy function properly forced Americans to change drastically their foreign policies. By cutting the dollar from a guaranteed support in gold, the President ended a quarter century during which the Bretton Woods arrangement of 1944 had governed most of the world's exchanges. That arrangement had made dollars as good as gold, guaranteed by the world's greatest economic power, and had provided a lighthouse for postwar expansion. (It had also given the Americans who printed and used those dollars an edge in international commerce, much to the chagrin of Western Europeans such as the French.) Now with the domestic economy in trouble just a year before a presidential election, Nixon brought an era to a close. Another conference, similar to Bretton Woods, would probably be required to put the pieces back together again, since if currencies were allowed to "float" too freely to make them cheaper, currency wars resembling those of the 1930s could erupt, with similar economic, political, and diplomatic chaos following. As a second result, the United States would pay diplomatically for treating the system in this way. For the President took his step without consulting either Western European or Japanese leaders. These allies were shocked, particularly the Japanese who sold more than one-third of their exports to the United States. The Tokyo stock exchange took its worst beating in history the day after the President's announcement. Nixon treated his primary Asian ally in this fashion, moreover, at the same moment that he was making an equally dramatic turnabout in dealing with Japan's and the United States' central problem in the Pacific, the Peoples Republic of China.

On the Asian fringe of the cake, American, Japanese, and Russian policies had long aimed at the containment of 700 million Communist Chinese. By 1969 Mao Tse-tung completed his consolidation of the Cultural Revolution and began restoring normal diplomatic relations. The Chinese continued their policy line of the 1965 Lin Piao statement by announcing continued support for third-world revolutionary movements. Peking's primary thrust, however, attempted to crack the intensified Soviet-American policy to isolate China. During the spring of 1971 the Chinese dramatically invited a table-tennis team to become the first group of Americans to visit China since 1949. The timing indicated why Peking acted, since the invitation was issued at the same moment that the Russians were convening a Communist party congress to line up support internationally against the Chinese. Mao was playing the United States off against the Soviets, for as President Nixon withdrew troops from Vietnam and during 1969-1970 slowly opened some trade relations with China, Mao viewed Russia, not the United States, as the number one enemy. During the late 1960s the Soviets had built a force of nearly one million men along the Sino-Russian border, and stories circulated that they might destroy nascent Chinese nuclear weapons plants before Peking could develop an efficient strike force.

In mid-July 1971, President Nixon responded to the Chinese initiative by announcing that he would soon become the first American President to visit Peking. The surprise move astonished domestic and foreign opinion. In August, the State Department declared it would cease opposing China's entry into the United Nations; but Washington fought unsuccessfully to prevent the expulsion of Taiwan from the world body. Such a compromise was acceptable neither to China, which continued to claim Taiwan as part of its mainland empire, nor to Taiwan where Chaing Kai-shek's aged regime refused to surrender its hope of someday recapturing the mainland.

The President's Peking junket revealed his diplomatic priorities. Most important he wanted the major powers to reach a settlement in Southeast Asia that would, at least, temporarily stabilize the area, would allow further withdrawal of American troops, and thereby would remove one of the thorniest obstacles threatening the President's reelection in 1972. Although China in reality could exert little pressure on the North Vietnamese, an overall settlement was possible only if China participated. The Nixon policy also temporarily silenced critics of the Administration's failure to respond constructively to the July 1 proposals of the National Liberation Front and North Vietnamese at Paris. At home stunned Democratic Presidential hopefuls could only congratulate the President on his apparent *coup*. Immersed in inflation, rising unemployment, and a chronic international trade deficit that threatened to choke the economy, some Americans hoped that the vast, fabled China market would help provide relief once political relations were established. They were only dreaming the dreams of their ancestors who had created the China market myth during the crisis decades of the 1780s, 1840s, 1890s, and 1930s. Even if some trade could be obtained, a price would be paid, since American relations with Russia, Southeast Asian allies, and especially Japan suffered as a consequence of the new Chinese-American *detente*. For two decades the United States had pressured Thailand, Japan, South Korea, and Taiwan to pay high costs in order to contain China. Few Americans had been more outspoken in demanding these sacrifices during the 1950s and early 1960s than had Richard Nixon. He now began suddenly and radically realigning the Pacific power structure without consulting his closest allies.

Of most importance was Japan. During the summer of 1969, President Nixon defined a so-called "Asian Doctrine" in which he said that the United States expected Asians to defend themselves against Communism while American troops slowly withdrew from the western Pacific. The United States would provide material aid and a nuclear umbrella as the Asians supposedly helped themselves. The pivot of Nixon's Asian Doctrine was Japan, the leading industrial power in Asia, the third greatest industrial nation in the world, and the only Asian nation with the military-economic potential to offset China. To American eyes the Japanese seemed a natural ally against the Chinese, for as the West lived with the horrible memories of Munich in 1938, so the Chinese remembered the horrors of the Japanese invasions of the 1930s. These memories sharpened in the 1960s as Japanese capital penetrated countries around China, converted Taiwan into a virtual economic protectorate of Tokyo, developed the world's greatest ship-building industry, carried out military maneuvers with South Korea, and opened negotiations for a joint Japanese-Russian exploration of the tremendous mineral reserves in Siberia. Japan was on the move. The show of Chinese friendship toward the United States in 1971 was partially caused by Peking's hope that it could drive a wedge between this burgeoning Japanese power and the Americans.

The Japanese, however, had long held doubts about policies such as Nixon's Asian Doctrine. "It seems," one of Japan's Defense Agency's officials observed, "that the Pentagon wants us to play the infield while you play the outfield against the

Chinese."[16] Tokyo increased trade with China during the late 1960s, although diplomatic relations were not formally restored. The stumbling block was the virtual economic domination by Japan over Taiwan, the island that China claimed to be part of its main. By mid-1971 the realignment of Sino-American relations created a crisis between Washington and Tokyo. One Japanese official feared that the announcement of Nixon's visit to Peking "set back Japanese-American relations by ten years."[17] The crisis was compounded in August when the President issued his new international economic policies. Meanwhile Congress threatened a trade war against the Japanese because Tokyo continued to undermine American textile and steel industries with cheap exports to the United States, but refused to allow American capital to enter freely for investments in Japan. The events seemed reminiscent of the 1920s and early 1930s, another era when the United States had depended on Japan to help contain the Chinese and Russian revolutions. During the early 1970s, Japan continued to depend on American nuclear power, but the Defense Agency in Tokyo announced a plan that more than doubled the expenditure on armed forces between 1971 and 1976. Japan had the capability to become a nuclear power almost overnight.

Japan, not China, was becoming the third superpower, and it demonstrated increasing reluctance to be dependent either on the United States or on American power in the two areas where the United States had not been able to create order: Southeast Asia, a historic sphere of Japanese economic interest, and the Middle East, the region where Japan obtained more than 90 percent of her oil. For the cake's fringes were also dissolving in the world's greatest oil-producing area. The Arab-Israeli confrontation was the eye of the conflict. After the Suez crisis of 1956, the Soviet Union funneled over $1 billion in arms to build the armies of Egypt's Gamel Abdel Nasser. The United States and Western Europeans maintained the military balance by sending equally large amounts to Israel, but Washington also

---

[16] Quoted by George R. Packard III, in *Foreign Affairs*, XLVI, October 1967, p. 195.
[17] *The New York Times*, August 4, 1971, p. 2.

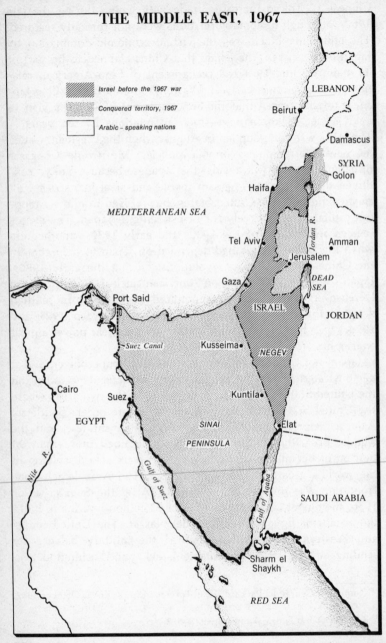

THE MIDDLE EAST, 1967

Israel before the 1967 war

Conquered territory, 1967

Arabic – speaking nations

LEBANON

Beirut

Damascus

SYRIA

Golon

Haifa

MEDITERRANEAN SEA

Jordan R.

Tel Aviv

Amman

Jerusalem

Gaza

DEAD SEA

ISRAEL

JORDAN

Port Said

Suez Canal

Kusseima

NEGEV

Cairo

Suez

Kuntila

SINAI PENINSULA

Elat

Nile R.

EGYPT

Gulf of Suez

Gulf of Aqaba

SAUDI ARABIA

Sharm el Shaykh

RED SEA

attempted to undercut Soviet influence and to protect western oil companies by sending arms to some Arab nations as well. The rebuilding of the Egyptian armies coincided with crises that Nasser faced inside Egypt and from anti-Egyptian factions within the Arab bloc. When skirmishes broke out in the spring of 1967 between Israeli and Syrian-Egyptian troops in disputed border areas, Nasser ordered a United Nations peace-keeping team that was stationed along the disputed Gaza Strip to leave. This left Egypt in control of the Gulf of Aqaba, the entranceway to Israel's key southern port of Elat. Despite Israeli pleas for help, the United States did little. Washington was totally immersed in Vietnamese affairs. On June 5, 1967, Israel suddenly struck. In a six-day war, the Israelis drove the Egyptians back across the Suez, humiliated the Egyptian and Syrian armies, and seized all of the prized city of Jerusalem.

The United States and the Soviet Union refused to intervene, but for the first time used the "hot line," a direct line installed between Washington and Moscow after the Cuban missile crisis, to reassure one another that each would stand aside. Within months, however, the Soviets moved to rebuild Nasser's army. The United States maintained the balance by providing sophisticated weapons to Israel. A confrontation between the two superpowers loomed, especially after Soviet ships and naval bases began appearing in the Mediterranean and Indian Ocean areas in 1969-1970. Since the 1946 Iranian crisis, these waterways had been dominated by the United States.

In late 1970 tensions decreased somewhat. Secretary of State Rogers initiated a plan by which Israel would withdraw from the Suez, Egypt would recognize Israel's existence and fair boundaries, and the two superpowers would guarantee the settlement. Then Nasser suddenly died in the autumn of 1970. Anwar el-Sadat became president. He agreed to enter into negotiations with the Israelis, but only after they retreated from the Suez. Israel rejected American pressure and refused to withdraw without further guarantees. Fourteen thousand Russians worked in the Egyptian industrial-military complex, and the American military no longer enjoyed its former preeminence in the area.

Nor did United States economic power enjoy its former status. American oil companies confronted numerous attempts by Middle Eastern and African governments to make their power more responsive to the revolutionary nationalisms erupting in the area. Perhaps the most significant internal revolt occurred in Libya where a group of young army officers overthrew a corrupt monarchy, ordered the closing of a large American air base, nationalized numerous foreign enterprises, and successfully demanded increased oil royalties from international companies. The Libyan action set off a chain of similar demands, until even the Shah of Iran, whom the United States had reinstalled in power in 1953, threatened punitive action unless the oil companies returned more proceeds to Iran. The great international companies, accustomed to dealing with weak and divided governments, suddenly faced a unified bloc of oil exporting countries. As a result, the companies were forced to pay almost $15 billion more in taxes over a five-year period. After a half-century, the oil-producing nations finally began to believe that "We are the Masters."[18]

The most significant "revolution," however, occurred in Latin America. The Nixon Administration had no alternative to the moribund Alliance for Progress. Terrorism and guerrilla activities increased in Venezuela, Colombia, Guatemala, and Bolivia. The President's only major policy response was to propose the doubling of the amount of military arms sold by the United States to Latin America.[19] The Andean nations of Bolivia, Peru, and Chile began taking separate paths. The Bolivian revolution nationalized some American oil holdings. In 1968, Peru came under the control of nationalistic army officers who suspended the electoral process, nationalized the powerful Standard Oil affiliate, placed rigid controls on foreign investment in basic industry, and instituted a program for distributing increased profits to workers. Most important were the events that took place in Chile.

That nation, unlike most Latin American countries, had a long history of successful parliamentary government and one of the highest rates of per capita income ($465). For several decades the Socialist party had been both more radical and popular than

[18] Gurney Breckenfeld, "How the Arabs Changed the Oil Business," *Fortune*, LXXXIV, August, 1971, pp. 113–117.
[19] *The New York Times*, May 19, 1971, p. 2.

the Communist party. In 1970 the head of the Socialist party, Salvador Allende, won the presidency as a coalition candidate of the left-wing parties. As the first avowed Marxist to rise to power in the hemisphere through free elections, Allende posed an unusual problem to the United States. The dilemma intensified when he began nationalizing the nearly billion dollars of American investment, particularly the copper industry. Chile opened diplomatic relations with Castro's Cuba and sent a delegation to Russia to sign a trade agreement. In local elections during the spring of 1971, voters approved Allende's policy by giving his coalition much greater support than it had the year before.

President Nixon publicly assumed a hands-off policy, announcing (perhaps with the Cuban missile crisis in mind) that as long as Chile did not threaten American national interests he did not want to be involved in Chile's internal politics. Allende responded by declaring that no foreign power would be allowed to have a base on Chilean territory. But on the economic level the United States government retaliated by refusing to help Chile with trade or developmental programs. American banks and governmental lending institutions such as the Export-Import Bank cut credit.[20] President Nixon then termed Chile's recognition of Castro a "challenge to the Inter-American system." Within Chile, Allende was attacked by conservative and ultra-leftists in his coalition. The extreme left, disavowed by Allende, forcefully seized large plantations, claiming that the president's socialization program was moving too slowly. Quite clearly, with the passing of the Alliance, Allende's experiment had offered one hope in the hemisphere for the working out of Latin American nationalistic needs and aspirations within a context of free elections and parliamentary decision-making. For this reason the importance of the American response to Chilean policies during the 1970s could not be overestimated.

The perimeters of the American empire were not only under attack in the newly emerging world. For Washington policymakers the most important long-term thrust came from the NATO countries of the North Atlantic community. Charles de Gaulle

---

[20] *Ibid.*, February 28, 1971, p. 3.

passed from power in 1969, but his policy of blunting American initiatives to foster greater independence for Europe continued to be practiced. An unexpected practitioner was Canadian Prime Minister Pierre Trudeau. Canada's industry, periodicals, banks, and even television had been increasingly dominated by the United States since 1945. During the late 1960s, Canada opened major trade avenues with China. In 1971, Trudeau became the first Canadian Prime Minister to travel in the Soviet Union, signing a pact with the Russians that provided for regular consultations. Although he made it clear that he was not imperiling Canada's participation in NATO or the North American Air Defense System (NORAD), Trudeau nevertheless added that the trip was partially motivated by a concern that the "overpowering presence" of the United States endangered "our national identity from a cultural, economic and perhaps even military point of view."[21]

European leaders similarly attempted to move toward more friendly policies with the Soviets. Chancellor Willy Brandt of West Germany undertook a historic mission when, in 1970, he attempted to settle the quarter century old boundary disputes between his nation and Poland. Brandt announced that the agreement would be ratified only after the Soviet Union agreed to recognize Allied rights in Berlin. Because the Soviets moved toward a Berlin settlement very slowly, Brandt's policy foundered. The chancellor nevertheless had gone too far for such Americans as Dean Acheson. The former Secretary of State, joined by other elderly architects who had formulated the Cold War policy in the late 1940s, conjured up visions of another Nazi-Soviet pact. Acheson urged that German ties to the West be strengthened, not loosened. President Nixon joined Acheson in a bipartisan utterance of these warnings.

This concern seemed misplaced in the early 1970s. West Germany was securely tied to the West through both NATO and, of greater importance, the Common Market. The worry of Acheson and Nixon, therefore, had to be understood on another level. They were less concerned that Brandt was leading his nation away from Western Europe than that Western Europe, led by Brandt's

---

[21] *Washington Post*, May 21, 1971, p. 1.

and France's initiatives, was moving away from the United States points of view. This concern had substance. When the Common Market abolished all internal tariffs in 1968, it was becoming an economic power potentially equal to the United States. During 1970-1971, the member countries further announced that within a decade they hoped to have a common currency relieving them of their overwhelming dependency on the dollar as the medium for international trade. Europeans correctly believed that they depended on a dollar that was constantly weakening because the United States could control neither its inflation nor its constant deficit in international trade. By 1971 nearly 60 billion dollars had become "Eurodollars" (that is, they were being used almost solely in Europe) because, in part, world investors and traders believed that the European economy overall was sounder and more profitable than the American. Common Market countries could do little in the early 1970s but suffer the failure of the United States to solve its economic crisis generated by the Vietnam War, plan their own common currency, which within a decade might drive out the cheapened dollars, and complain—as did France's President Georges Pompidou when he remarked, "We cannot keep forever as our basic monetary yardstick a national currency [the dollar] that constantly loses value as a result of purely internal [American] policies. The rest of the world cannot be expected to regulate its life by a clock which is always slow."

Pompidou moved to integrate Great Britain into the Common Market. With this enlarged membership, and if Brandt's policies opened a new era of increased economic opportunities inside the Soviet bloc, the Western European nations would be able to rival American economic power. In its determination to be free of this United States leverage, moreover, the Common Market could well develop into a separate, even competing bloc. Already in 1971 vast American farm exports, which for centuries had found natural markets in Europe, were threatened by tariffs raised to protect Common Market farmers. At this point, Acheson's and Nixon's qualms could be understood, since once major economic blocs appeared (especially in Western Europe and Japan, as well as in the long-developed Comecon economic community of the Soviet bloc), the United States would again confront the dilemmas of 1945. At that time, Acheson and others had used the British loan and Marshall Plan arrangements, among other tools, to extinguish such blocs. This extinction was fundamental to the success of postwar American foreign policies. Now the feared blocs seemed to be mushrooming in key areas of the globe.

During the early 1970s the United States had two effective means of halting the growth of these blocs. The first was the political manipulation of American military power, particularly the 310 thousand troops stationed in Europe to provide security against possible Communist attack. In 1970-1971, United States senators, led by Democratic majority leader Mike Mansfield of Montana, tried to pass legislation forcing the President to reduce by half the number of these troops. If passed, the "Mansfield Amendment" would have dramatically increased congressional control of the President's foreign policy powers and also would have reduced the drain of dollars going abroad to pay for these troops. The Senate met stonewall opposition from Western Europeans and the White House. West Germany especially opposed the move, since the troops provided psychological assurance and gave Brandt a card to play in negotiations with the Soviets. By removing the need for increased investment in military goods, the American troops also allowed the Western European economies to develop competitive consumer-goods industries. President Nixon, aided by Acheson and other Democratic foreign policy formulators of the 1940s and early 1960s, successfully fought the Mansfield Amendment because he also realized that the troops provided admirable cards in playing for European stakes.

The second instrument available to the United States for controlling European affairs was the emergence of the multinational corporation. The maturation and expansion of this type of organization is perhaps the single most important development in international affairs during the late 1950s and 1960s. Although the United States sells more than 200-billion dollars worth of products in overseas markets, only one-fourth of this comes from the traditional source of exports. The remainder is produced and sold by American plants in foreign countries. Although existing since the mid-19th century, the multinational corporation has become dominant only since 1945, particularly since the formation of the Iron and Steel Community in 1950; and then the Common Market in 1958 opened the promise of a vast, tariff-free and secure trading area. Table 11.1 shows the development and thrust of private long-term direct investment abroad by Americans since 1960 (in billions of dollars)[22]:

TABLE 11.1

	1960	1965	1968 Prelim- inary	1968 Oil Only	1968 Manufac- turing Only
All	31.9	49.5	64.7	18.8	26.4
Canada	11.1	15.3	19.5	4.0	8.5
Latin America	7.5	9.4	11.0	3.0	3.7
Europe (all)	6.7	14.0	19.4	4.6	10.8
Common Market nations	2.6	6.3	9.0	2.1	5.4
Africa (all)	.9	1.9	2.6	1.6	.4
South Africa	.3	.5	.7	.1	.3
Middle East	1.1	1.6	1.8	1.7	.1
Far East	1.2	2.0	2.9	1.1	1.1
Oceania	1.0	1.8	2.8	.6	1.5

If American portfolio investment in overseas securities is added to the above, the total United States private investment abroad amounted to $19 billion in 1950, $49 billion a decade later, $81 billion in 1965, and $101 billion estimated in 1968.

This record of American economic expansion since 1950 is doubtless the most incredible economic phenomenon in the history of any nation. If it is true that where your treasure is there will your heart be also, the table vividly illustrates the vital interests of the United States and how those interests have expanded, especially in the Common Market and Canada. The implications are clear. Although suffering economically at home between 1966 and 1971, American corporations dominated world production. The United States multinational corporation formed the third greatest economic power in the world, behind only the American

---

[22] U.S. Department of Commerce, *Statistical Abstract of the United States, 1970* (Washington, 1970), pp. 765–766.

domestic economy and economy of the Soviet Union, ranking ahead of the economies of Japan, West Germany, France, or any other nation. The top twenty multinational organizations produced goods equal to the entire gross national product of Great Britain. The top four could finance Belgium's governmental budget from their profits alone. Europe was being gripped by what one French author called, "The American Challenge." When asked whether Belgium was in danger of becoming an American colony, a Belgian economic affairs minister replied, "We already are."[23] During the late 1960s, however, European multinational corporations become prominent, increasing their rate of growth more rapidly than American firms and buying out corporations within the United States itself.

The political effects proved to be enormous. Nation-states were incapable of controlling the multinational corporation, and few scholars or governments were devoting adequate attention to the phenomenon. The United States, for example, might try to isolate economically certain Communist nations, but American corporations simply set up production plants in countries not having these restrictions and proceeded to carry on trade with China or Russia. When Washington officials attempted to increase private investment in Latin America and other newly-emerging nations, American corporations increased their interests but, as Table 11.1 indicates, they increased even more rapidly their investments in more secure areas like the Common Market and Canada. This diversion of funds in particular sucked capital out of Peru, Bolivia, and Chile after 1965. Investments of this kind made sense in terms of profits, but they only widened the already unbridgeable abyss between the rich and the poor nations. During the late 19th century the national American corporation sought to bring order, efficiency, and profits out of the politico-economic chaos left behind by the Jacksonians and the Civil War. The multinational corporation has begun to do the same thing on a global scale.

---

[23] Richard J. Barber, *The American Corporation* (New York, 1970), pp. 257–260; *The New York Times*, January 15, 1968, p. C51; George W. Ball, "Multinational Corporations and Nation States," *Atlantic Quarterly*, V (Summer, 1967), pp. 247–253.

Although this economic phenomenon created new ties between East and West, it did little to moderate the diplomatic tensions between the United States and Russia. A treaty banning the use of nuclear weapons in outer space, signed after rapid negotiations on January 27, 1967, was followed by an agreement not to proliferate nuclear weapons to nonnuclear powers. Since 1964, however, and even before President Johnson escalated the fighting in Vietnam, the Soviets rejected numerous American overtures for better East-West understanding.[24] The rejections were motivated by internal problems, a reluctance to be too closely associated with the United States while Americans were fighting in Vietnam, and by developing tensions within the East European sphere.

Bloc questions became most pressing in 1968 when Czechoslovakia's leaders attempted to liberalize their economic and political system while they remained within a one-party Communist structure. By midsummer, the reforms were moving so rapidly that the Soviet leadership concluded that they endangered party rule throughout the bloc and opened avenues for increasing West German influence in Eastern Europe. In August, Soviet troops moved into Prague to overthrow the liberal faction led by Alexander Dubcek. Soviet party leader Leonid Brezhnev proclaimed the "Brezhnev Doctrine" under which Soviet intervention was justified because socialist nations had the right to save other socialists from "world imperialism" and the "counterrevolution" to preserve the "indivisible" socialist system. Before the intervention, the United States was so careful not to interfere in these Eastern European problems that Washington was charged with following another "Munich policy" of 1938. The Johnson Administration did little, not only because of military realities but also because the Brezhnev Doctrine on Eastern Europe was not unlike the Johnson Doctrine of 1965 in regard to Latin America. Separate spheres of interest were well established. Neither superpower cared for the development of blocs within its own sphere.

Although the Soviets followed a hostile policy toward the United States in Vietnam, and the two powers confronted one another in a tense Middle East, they moved in 1968 to open gen-

---

[24] Thomas W. Wolfe, *Soviet Power and Europe, 1945–1970* (Baltimore, 1970), pp. 266–269.

eral talks on the limitation of nuclear arms. The United States had enlarged its missile capability during the early 1960s, in part, as Robert McNamara admitted too late, because of false American intelligence estimates regarding the Soviet missile buildup.[25] After 1965 the Soviets determined to match the United States. In 1965 the latter had 934 Intercontinental Ballistic Missiles (ICBMs), in 1971, in accordance with deliberate policy, it had 1,054. The Soviets possessed 224 ICBMs in 1965, but had 1,510 in 1971. At the end of 1970, the United States maintained a sizeable lead in submarine-launched ICBMs, 656 to 350, but this gap was also rapidly closing. A nuclear parity was being reached, and it seemed to be in both powers' interest to freeze this balance and thus avert a needless spiraling upward of the arms race. Agreement became more imperative after 1966 when new monster weapons appeared. These included the Russian SS-9 and the American MIRV (Multiple-Independently-targeted-Reentry-Vehicle), which contained within a single missile multiple warheads capable of being targeted on widely separated areas. The Strategic Arms Limitation Talks (SALT) were stalled because of the Czech invasion, but finally began in 1969. During the next two years some progress was made, particularly on a possible freeze of defensive antiballistic-missile systems (ABMs). The Soviets had begun a small ABM system, and the United States initiated its own in 1967. By 1971 both nations appeared ready to stop building ABMs as part of a general arms control agreement.

The SALT negotiation was one of several events that promised a thaw in Russian-American relations during the early 1970s. Perhaps of most significance, Brezhnev offered discussions on a general military *detente* in Central Europe under which both the NATO and Warsaw Pact armies would reduce their forces. President Nixon responded positively, although clearly the negotiations would take years and would be extremely complex. A European *detente*, moreover, could not occur until the quarter-century old Berlin dilemma was solved. In August, 1971 a major breakthrough occurred. The Soviets promised new guarantees to

---

[25] Robert S. McNamara, *The Essence of Security* (New York, 1968), pp. 57–58.

keep access routes open into Berlin from the West. In return, the Allies agreed to downgrade Berlin's political significance for the West and to allow a Russian consulate in the city. This most explosive of East-West political issues began to be defused. American-Russian relations improved after six years of near-paralysis. Moscow officials had good reasons to welcome the change. The Soviets needed to take initiatives to offset the improved relationship between the United States and China. They also confronted immense domestic economic problems at home and within the Communist bloc, particularly from Rumania.

As the Russians sought a European settlement in order to be free to deal with the growing Chinese threat to the east, so the United States sought the settlement in order to care for its festering sores in Southeast Asia and at home. Americans would be hard put to survive another five years like those of 1966-1971. They had suffered a great deal, including the loss of more than 45,000 men in Vietnam, since President Johnson announced in August 1966, "The overriding rule which I want to affirm is that our foreign policy must always be an extension of our domestic policy. Our safest guide to what we do abroad is always what we do at home."

That statement carried interesting implications. Historically it indicated the one theme that had continually shaped American policies as a world power since the 1890s, that is, before Communism emerged as a challenge to United States objectives overseas. Johnson's "overriding rule" explained how the Vietnamese tragedy and the problems within the Atlantic alliance were not the results of unconscious assumptions and isolated decisions, however easy historians find such explanations to be; those events were firmly anchored in the history of the Cold War and the half century of American domestic and foreign policies before 1945.

During the mid-1960s two groups of dissenters had especially challenged the continuation of this historic policy. A university student-oriented "New Left" movement protested the Vietnamese involvement and the domestic social costs that this involvement demanded. Carl Oglesby, President of the Students for Democratic Society, thought something fundamentally wrong when "This country, with its thirty-some years of liberalism, can send two hundred thousand young men to Vietnam to kill and die in the most dubious of wars, but it cannot get a hundred voter registrars to go into Mississippi."[26] A second group of dissenters rallied around J. William Fulbright, Democrat of Arkansas and Chairman of the Senate Foreign Relations Committee. After concluding that President Johnson had misled him on the Administration's intentions in Vietnam, Fulbright became an outspoken critic of the Johnson and Nixon governments. His natural conservatism rebelled against the rapidly growing power of the presidency. He counseled restraint in the use of American military and political force, and emphasized that the dynamic element in international affairs was increasingly "the power of nationalism in Southeast Asia and, indeed, in all the world's emerging nations." By 1971 the "New Left" and Fulbright had been joined by many Americans in their opposition to the Vietnam conflict and the escalation of presidential power in foreign affairs.

President Nixon proved sensitive to these pressures, but only after his military "Vietnamization" policies were destroyed with the failure of the Laotian invasion in early 1971. He thereby differed from Lyndon Johnson. The Texan was a consummate politician who maintained a domestic consensus even while pursuing foreign policies that derived more from the corruption of Wilsonian liberalism (which held that Communism was monolithic and, hence, believed world power acted as a row of dominoes), than from the special interests of the American socioeconomy. Nixon, however, had little opportunity to perform such wonders. He enjoyed neither the nation's trust nor the political abilities of a Johnson. Nixon had to be politically responsive, not to the most needy and impoverished groups in the society, but to socioeconomic interests that, amidst inflation and domestic repression, had decided that Vietnam was no longer worth the price. The President's first term in office would therefore leave paradoxical legacies: the withdrawal from Southeast Asia and the readjustment of depleted American power to world realities, but also the wasting of years in which the terrible divisions at home should have been ameliorated racially, economically, and politically.

---

[26] Paul Jacobs and Saul Landau, *The New Radicals, A Report With Documents* (New York, 1966), pp. 65–69, 74–82, 261.

And although the President withdrew troops from Asia, he opposed a too rapid disengagement, fearing it would tempt Americans "to turn inward—to withdraw from the world, to back away from our commitments. That deceptively smooth road of the new isolationism is surely the road to war."[27] Such fears of "isolationism" seemed to be misplaced during the early 1970s. The United States had more than a half million troops stationed overseas in more than two dozen major military bases. Over $100 billion of private American capital was invested abroad. The United States was increasingly attached militarily to foreign powers. Since 1945, it had given away or sold nearly $50 billion in military equipment and services. The selling of military arms accelerated during the 1960s, as President Kennedy and, then, Presidents Johnson and Nixon attempted to use these sales to aid the nation's deficit balance of international payments.

Military spending was out of control. The government's General Accounting Office concluded after a survey of 146 completed military contracts worth $4.2 billion that the average rate of return on contractors' capital, before taxes, was 56.9 percent, nearly three times more than the pretax profits for all American manufacturers.[28] A study by the highly respected Brookings Institution predicted that even if the United States left Vietnam, given President Nixon's foreign policies, the American defense budget would rise from $76 billion in the 1972 fiscal year to $82 billion in 1974 and $88 billion in 1976.[29] There was little hope that increased funds could be found for necessary domestic measures. "I get no comfort out of the fact," Dean Rusk once observed, "that the defense budget of the United States [in 1968] is roughly equal to the gross national product of all of Latin America."[30] Little danger seemed to exist that the United States would, as President Nixon feared, become "underinvolved."

The question would be the more difficult problem of the nature of the involvement. A quarter century after the Truman Doctrine, which had neatly divided the world between the enslaved and the

---

[27] Radio Address accompanying "U.S. Role in the World, 1971," text in *The New York Times*, February 26, 1971, p. 13.

[28] *Washington Post*, March 2, 1971, p. 1.

[29] *The New York Times*, May 2, 1971, p. 28.

[30] *State Department Bulletin*, February 19, 1968, p. 230.

free, Americans confronted not a monolithic Communism but the incredibly more complex dilemma of how to help maintain order and stability amidst the revolution of autonomy that was erupting in the newly-emerging nations. This problem had become central to policy-makers in the mid-1950s, resulting a decade later in the determination to fight "limited war" in areas where these revolutions occurred. "Limited war," however, was a misnomer. From mid-1965 until the end of 1967 only, the United States dropped more bomb tonnage on Vietnam than was dropped by the Allies on Europe during all of World War II. At home this type of conflict resulted in increasingly unlimited commitments which depleted educational resources, enlarged an already rigid government bureaucracy, sliced domestic welfare programs, and increased already awesome presidential powers. Scholars and politicians who had lauded the widest use of presidential power since 1933 began to have second thoughts.

Sometime during the last half of the 19th century, at the point when American foreign policy switched from focusing on conquering a continent to expanding global economic and strategic interests, the nature of foreign policy decision-making changed radically. Critical decisions were increasingly made in isolation and away from public or congressional supervision by a few men who were influenced by a relatively small number of socioeconomic interests. Harry Truman guaranteed the continuation of this process when he developed the consensus on anti-Communism in the late 1940s. After that, and until the late 1960s, anyone questioning the sacrosanct decisions of global policy could be accused of being "unrealistic" or an "appeaser" who undermined the necessary consensus at home. Part of the increased presidential power was the natural product of the complexity of foreign policy which, as the Founding Fathers knew, made necessary the granting of many foreign policy decisions to the Chief Executive. But this increased power was also caused by the failure of Congress and the concerned public to care enough to become educated and sufficiently active politically to make the President accountable and responsible. Civilian policy-makers, not a mysterious "military-industrial" complex, committed the United States to "support any friend" and "fight any foe." That these civilians were not saved from their own "realist" view of power was not only their personal fault but the fault of Congress and the public who might have held them accountable before 45,000 American lives and many times that number of Vietnamese were tragically lost.

The question was not whether the United States had sufficient power or whether American officials were courageous enough to apply enough power. The crux of the problem was whether the American system could delineate the ends for which that power could most properly and profitably be used, and whether the system as it evolved in the 20th century made the decision-makers properly accountable to those who would pay the terrible price of error. The few academics, politicians, or businessmen who had tried to do what was needed, that is, to make a radically new appraisal of policy by questioning the basic objectives, were too often dismissed as not being "realists," that is, they were not realistic and sufficiently tough-minded about the importance and capability of military power in the postwar world. Yet never during the first two decades of the Cold War era was the overall supremacy of American power in doubt. The results of such dominance were, among others, the weakening of the Atlantic Community, a tragic involvement in Vietnam, revolutionary anti-American movements in Latin America and Africa, and accelerating economic problems at home. More ominous, this dominance of power had led American officials and public opinion to believe in a military solution for primary, unsolvable problems. Supposedly the most politically sophisticated and certainly the most prosperous people in the world, Americans answered the political and economic challenges in the newly-emerging nations with responses in the Bay of Pigs, Santo Domingo, and Southeast Asia which, by relying on "realistic" military solutions, were confessions of political and economic failure. Even more fundamentally, Americans had, in John F. Kennedy's word, "welcomed" the responsibility of answering these challenges at least as early as the Truman Doctrine.

The "realists" who dealt in military power believed that the United States could reshape the world while producing both guns and butter. Americans, they hoped, might be saved from the fate of other great empires which, like Ben Franklin's cake, began to fall apart as they became overextended. The ultimate irony occurred when Richard Nixon, the man many "realists" most detested during the 1952-1969 era, began papering over the policy disasters of the New Frontier and Great Society, retrenched in an economy that proved incapable of producing both guns and butter without disastrous side effects, moved toward conciliation with China, and—most poignant of all—gave sermonettes during the summer of 1971 warning that the United States would emulate the decline of the Greek and Roman empires unless Americans disciplined themselves. Nixon thereby proved to be the most valid Niebuhrian of the Cold War era, for his personal insecurity, slippery political basis, and the nation's deteriorating economic position made him more aware of human and national limitations than either of the two preceding presidents.

These human and national limitations can be understood, and with the least pain, by comprehending how American history since the 1890s, and particularly since 1945, had climaxed in the dilemmas of the early 1970s. Certainly a misunderstanding of history, or perhaps a failure to read it adequately, condemned the policy-makers of 1945 to 1970 to measure opponents by the figure of Adolf Hitler, to equate any hesitancy to use power with the tragic isolationism of the 1930s, and to call too many international crises another "Munich" or "Manchuria of 1931." "Realists" tended to justify commitments of military power with false historical analogies (perhaps the worst of all forms of argument) and were condemned to make fatal foreign-policy blunders. By the early 1970s that power which Niebuhr very much feared had been partially checked not so much by Americans, but by Western Europeans, Africans, Latin Americans, and Southeast Asians who had begun to melt away the edges of the American empire. A larger question remained: Could Americans adjust to this challenge to their empire without yielding to the temptations of panic and witch-hunts at home and counterrevolutionary activities abroad?

Niebuhr died in June 1971, at a time when the United States withdrawal from Vietnam, the publication of *The Pentagon Papers*, and economic recession forced many Americans to painful introspection. In one of his last essays, Niebuhr dealt with the question of how he had changed his mind during the late 1950s and 1960s. "Perhaps there is not much to choose between communist and anticommunist fanaticism," he observed, "particularly when the latter, combined with our wealth, has caused us to stumble into the most pointless, costly and bloody war in our history." Niebuhr recalled that during the late 1940s he had advocated a "realism" without realizing that it

. . . like all realism [was] excessively consistent. It is one of the mysteries of human nature that while most of us are unconscious of an inevitable mixture in our motives, we try to atone for this error by too constant emphasis on 'the law in our members which wars against the law that is in our minds.'[31]

As the evacuation of Vietnam hopefully ended a quarter century of Cold War foreign policies in the United States, Russia, and China, so also Niebuhr's final words hopefully terminated an era of supposed "realism" in American foreign policy.

---

[31] Reinhold Niebuhr, "Toward New Intra-Christian Endeavors," *Christian Century*, LXXXVI, December 31, 1969, pp. 1662–1667.

Bibliography for Additional Reading

BIBLIOGRAPHIC TOOLS:

Bulletin of the Public Affairs Information Service (New York) has been a standard reference for important works since its initial publication in 1915. *The Universal Reference System. Political Science, Government and Public Policy Series, Vol. I. International Affairs*, prepared under the direction of Alfred de Grazia (New York, 1965) is a staggering achievement of annotating and intensively indexing important books, pamphlets, and articles in the field. For Soviet policy the indispensable work is Thomas Taylor Hammond, *Soviet Foreign Relations and World Communism; A Selected Annotated Bibliography of 7000 Books in 30 Languages* (Princeton, 1965). Considerably more modest but helpful is Henry L. Roberts, *Foreign Affairs Bibliography . . . 1942-1952* (New York, 1955). For U.S. Government documents, see Laurence F. Schmeckebier and Roy B. Eastin (eds.), *Government Publications and Their Use* (Washington, 1961). For the Kennedy years, James Tracy Crown has published a fine annotated work, *The Kennedy Literature* (New York, 1968).

JOURNALS:

The most important and influential is *Foreign Affairs*, a quarterly published by the Council on Foreign Relations in New York City; *Foreign Policy*, a new journal with more diverse views, is very useful. Good sources of contemporary documents and statistics are *State Department Bulletin*, the U.S. Department of Commerce's *Commerce Today*, and *Vital Speeches*. For the Soviet side, *Current Digest of the Soviet Press* is the basic source, while *International Affairs* (Moscow) includes important articles. *Soviet Law and Government* has important essays translated from various Russian periodicals. The historical background can be found in *Slavic Review*. Excellent analyses of the Soviet and West European scenes are in *Survey, Encounter*, and the Royal Institute's *International Affairs* as well as in the *Annals of the American Academy of Political and Social Science*. Several journals combine first-rate articles on the contemporary scene with essays on recent history: *World Politics, American Political Science Review, The Journal of Conflict Resolution, Review of Politics, International Organization, World Affairs, Military Affairs, Canadian Journal of Economics and Political Science*, and *Current History*. For dissenting views, see *I. F. Stone's Weekly* and the *Bulletin of the Committee of Concerned Asian Scholars. Journal of Inter-American Studies* and *Inter-American Economic Affairs* are helpful on the hemisphere's problems. Along with Department of Commerce publications, the Chase Manhattan Bank's *International Finance* is an important biweekly publication on the world's financial affairs.

GENERAL WORKS, UNITED STATES, 1945–1971:

Indispensable are the Council on Foreign Relations' *The United States in World Affairs*, an annual, well-researched, and incisively written survey; and the Council's yearly *Documents on American Foreign Relations* which, along with the London Royal Institute's annual *Documents on International Affairs*, are the best documentary sources for the Cold War era. Geoffrey Barraclough, *An Introduction to Contemporary History* (New York, 1964), puts the Cold War in historical perspective. John Lukacs, *History of the Cold War* (Garden City, N.Y., 1961, 1966) stresses Central and Western European affairs. Interesting analyses from the perspective of international relations experts are Roger D. Fisher, *International Conflict for Beginners* (New York, 1969), very lightly written; and Ernst B. Haas, *Tangle of Hopes; American Commitments and World Order* (Englewood Cliffs, N.J., 1969). A fine study is Anatol Rapoport's *The Big Two: Soviet-American Perceptions of Foreign Policy* (Indianapolis, 1971).

Overall views that emphasize American policy include Seyom Brown's excellent summary, *The Faces of Power; Constancy and Change in United States Foreign Policy From Truman to Johnson* (New York, 1968); Robert E. Osgood, Robert W. Tucker *et al.*, *America and the World: From the Truman Doctrine to Vietnam* (Baltimore, 1969); Edgar E. Robinson *et al.*, *Powers of the President in Foreign Affairs* (San Francisco, 1966) with studies of Truman, Eisenhower, and Kennedy; the Secretaries of State are helpfully analyzed in Norman Graebner (ed.), *An Uncertain Tradition* (New York, 1961). "New Left" overviews include Denna Frank Fleming, *The Cold War and Its Origins, 1917-1960,* 2 vols. (Garden City, N.Y., 1961); David Horowitz, *From Yalta to Vietnam* (a revised edition of 1967 formerly published as *Free World Colossus*); Horowitz's editing of a series of essays, *Containment and Revolution* (Boston, 1967) of which the Bagguley essay is especially helpful; Thomas G. Paterson's editing of *Cold War Critics* (Chicago, 1971); Richard J. Barnet, *Intervention and Revolution; The United States in the Third World* (New York, 1968); and William Appleman Williams, *The Tragedy of American Diplomacy* (New York, 1962), the most stimulating interpretive work on the Cold War and its origins.

Voluminous documentation can be found in the U.S. Department of State's *American Foreign Policy, 1950-1955* (2 vols.) and the single annual volumes that have been published on the 1956 though mid-1960s events; the latter are entitled *American Foreign Policy; Current Documents*. Equally important is *Public Papers of the Presidents of the United States*; these annual volumes cover the public announcements, speeches, and news conferences of each President since Harry Truman.

SPECIFIC TOPICS IN UNITED STATES POLICY SINCE 1945:

Relations with world organizations can be examined in Ruth B. Russell's mammoth work, *A History of the United Nations Charter; The Role of the United States, 1940-1945* (Washington, D.C., 1961); Lincoln P. Bloomfield, *The United Nations and U.S. Foreign Policy*, revised edition (Boston, 1967); James M. Boyd, *United Nations Peace-Keeping Operations: A Military and Political Appraisal* (New York, 1971); and Richard N. Gardner, *In*

Pursuit of World Order; U.S. Foreign Policy and International Organizations, revised edition (New York, 1966). On American defense policies, the historical background is provided in Raymond G. O'Connor (ed.), *American Defense Policy in Perspective* (New York, 1965); Urs Schwarz, *American Strategy: A New Perspective* (New York, 1966), an excellent short study. Robert A. Levine, *The Arms Debate* (Harvard, 1963) attempts to categorize schools of military thought; Ernest R. May (ed.), *The Ultimate Decision: The President as Commander in Chief* (New York, 1960), provides a good historical background for its subject; and Harold Stein (ed.), *American Civil-Military Decisions; A Book of Case Studies* (Birmingham, Ala., 1963) is indispensable for anyone interested in the Cold War. Senator Henry M. Jackson (ed.), *The National Security Council* (New York, 1964) stresses the 1960s in the development of the NSC. Conflicting views on the subject may be found in Samuel P. Huntington, *The Soldier and the State* (Cambridge, Mass., 1957), and Allen Guttman, "Political Ideals and the Military Ethic," *The American Scholar*, XXXIV (Spring, 1965), 221-237. Good surveys on arms control and disarmament efforts are in Bernhard G. Bechhoeffer, *Postwar Negotiations for Arms Control* (Washington, 1961) which takes the story down to the Kennedy years; the moral aspects are emphasized in Robert C. Batchelder, *The Irreversible Decision, 1939-1950* (Boston, 1961). Two monumental volumes on the beginnings of the nuclear age are Richard G. Hewlett and Oscar E. Anderson, Jr., *The New World, 1939-1946*; Volume I of A History of the United States Atomic Energy Commission (University Park, Penn., 1962); and Richard G. Hewlett and Francis Duncan, *Atomic Shield, 1947-1952* (University Park, Penn., 1970), Volume II of the AEC study focusing on the Oppenheimer affair and the decision to develop nuclear weapons. William B. Bader's *The United States and Spread of Nuclear Weapons* (New York, 1968) is informed and frightening. This book should have had more attention focused on the American scientist; good accounts are Eugene B. Skolnikoff, *Science, Technology and American Foreign Policy* (Cambridge, Mass., 1967); Don K. Price, *The Scientific Estate* (Cambridge, Mass., 1965); and a classic study by Alice Kimball Smith, *A Peril and A Hope: The Scientists' Movement in America, 1945-1947* (Chicago, 1965).

The influence of domestic politics on American foreign policy —or the lack of such influence—can be found in Neal R. Peirce (ed.), *Politics in America, 1945-1966*, published by the Congressional Quarterly Service, 2nd edition (Washington, 1967); James N. Rosenau (ed.), *Domestic Sources of Foreign Policy* (New York, 1967); a series of studies by Angus Campbell, especially *The Voter Decides* (Evanston, Ill., 1954); Richard M. Scammon's and Ben J. Wattenberg's extremely provocative analysis of the 1968 election, *The Real Majority* (New York, 1970); and for specific topics, two books by Alfred Hero, *The Southerner and World Affairs* (Baton Rouge, 1945), and *The U.A.W. and World Affairs*, an analysis of United Automobile Workers' views (New York, 1965). Most valuable is Ronald Radosh, *American Labor and United States Foreign Policy* (N.Y., 1969). On Congressional influences, Malcolm E. Jewell, *Senatorial Politics and Foreign Policy* (Lexington, Ky., 1962); David N. Farnsworth, *The Senate Committee on Foreign Relations, 1947–1956* (Urbana, Ill., 1961); H. B. Westerfield, *Foreign Policies and Party Politics: Pearl Harbor to Korea* (New Haven, Conn., 1955); and for its special topic, Edward A. Kolodziej, *The Uncommon Defense and Congress, 1945-1963* (Columbus, Ohio, 1966). An analysis and approbation of Executive power is in Richard E. Neustadt's *Presidential Power*, which contains case studies from the late Truman and Eisenhower years. Bernard C. Cohen's *The Press and Foreign Policy* (Princeton, N.J., 1965), is a good place to start; James Aronson has written a muckraking account in *The Press and the Cold War* (Indianapolis, 1970). The American Assembly's *Cultural Affairs and Foreign Relations* (Washington, D.C., 1968) is an interesting collection of essays on arts, humanities, education, and science. What the voter does not know is analyzed in several works by Harry H. Ransom, especially his *Central Intelligence Agency and National Security* (Cambridge, Mass., 1958). The best comprehensive studies of American liberalism and its dilemmas in the early 1970s are Theodore Lowi's two books, *The End of Liberalism* (New York, 1969), and *The Politics of Disorder* (New York, 1971); see also Clifton Brock's *Americans for Democratic Action* (Washington, D.C., 1962). Niebuhr's thought may be traced through *The Irony of American History* (New York, 1952), *Christian Realism and Political Problems* (New York,

1953), *The World Crisis and American Responsibility* (New York, 1958); Gordon Harland, *The Thought of Reinhold Niebuhr* (New York, 1960); and Charles W. Kegley, editor, *Reinhold Niebuhr* (New York, 1956), especially the Bennett, Schlesinger, Jr., and Burtt articles. Kennan's changing views are seen in *American Diplomacy, 1900-1950* (Chicago, 1951); *Russia, the Atom and the West* (New York, 1958); and *On Dealing with the Communist World* (New York, 1964); but most particularly in his *Memoirs, 1925-1950* (Boston, 1967).

The economic developments of the Cold War era are described in Andrew Shonfield, *Modern Capitalism* (New York, 1966); and Emma Woytinsky, *Profile of the U.S. Economy: A Survey of Growth and Change* (New York, 1967); and particularly *The Economic Impact of the Cold War, Sources and Readings*, compiled and edited by James L. Clayton (New York, 1970), which stresses the military-industrial complex as a "social fact" changing the basic nature of the economy. Seymour Melman, *Pentagon Capitalism; the Political Economy of War* (New York, 1970) emphasizes the concept of "State-Management." Raymond F. Mikesell's several works are important, especially *U.S. Private and Government Investment Abroad* (Corvallis, 1962). Gerald D. Nash, *United States Oil Policy, 1890-1964: Business and Government in Twentieth Century America* (Pittsburgh, 1968), and Robert Engler, *The Politics of Oil* (New York, 1961) differ in emphases while they provide good introductions to their subject. Gordon L. Weil and Ian Davidson, *The Gold War; The Story of the World's Monetary Crisis* (New York, 1970) is superb and easy to understand. David Baldwin, *Economic Development and American Foreign Policy* (Chicago, 1966) is excellent on a broad subject; William Paddock and Paul Paddock, *Hungry Nations* (Boston, 1964) are good on the newly-emerging nations themselves; Herbert Feis, *Foreign Aid and Foreign Policy* is a helpful essay by a former State Department official (New York, 1964); and Raymond A. Bauer *et al.*, *American Business and Public Policy; The Politics of Foreign Trade* (New York, 1963) is most useful. On the multinational corporations the bibliography has expanded tremendously since 1968, but a huge, detailed introduction is Sidney E. Rolfe and Walter Damm, *The Multinational Corporation in the World Economy: Direct Investment in Per-*

spective (New York, 1970); and Charles P. Kindleberger's many books, particularly *American Business Abroad* (New Haven, Conn., 1969), are excellent shorter studies. Jack N. Behrman, long-time government administrator, has written *Some Patterns in the Rise of the Multinational Enterprise* (Chapel Hill, 1969); Rainer Hellmann presents the new trend in *The Challenge to U.S. Dominance of the International Corporation* (New York, 1970); and Jean Jacques Servan-Schreiber's popular *The American Challenge* (New York, 1968) urges Europeans to emulate or be swept over by American business methods.

On the outbreak of the Cold War, Gaddis Smith, *American Diplomacy During the Second World War, 1941-1945* (New York, 1965) is the best short study for background; William H. McNeill, *America, Britain, and Russia* (London, 1953) still a landmark in historiography although now replaced by Gabriel Kolko's *Politics of War* (New York, 1968), a long, detailed, stimulating and superb account of 1943-1945 diplomacy. Equally important, particularly since it extends American policies into the 1947-1950 era through brilliant biographical studies, is Lloyd C. Gardner, *Architects of Illusion; Men and Ideas in American Foreign Policy, 1941-1949* (Chicago, 1970), and Gardner has provided the best and most provocative study of the foreign policy of the entire 1933-1945 era in *Economic Aspects of New Deal Diplomacy* (Madison, Wisc., 1964). Robert Divine, *Second Chance: The Triumph of Internationalism in America During World War II* (New York, 1967) is important in understanding the bipartisanship fashioned during 1944-1945. Three different and stimulating interpretations of the causes can be found in Lloyd C. Gardner, Arthur Schlesinger, Jr., and Hans J. Morgenthau, *The Origins of the Cold War* (Waltham, Mass., 1970). Athan G. Theoharis, *The Yalta Myths: An Issue in U.S. Politics, 1945-1955* (Columbia, Mo., 1970), and Diane Clemens' study of *Yalta* (New York, 1970) are important contributions on the pivotal conference and its after-effects. European problems are detailed in U.S. Department of State, *The Conference of Berlin* (The Potsdam Conference), 2 vols. (Washington, 1960); Herbert Feis, *Between War and Peace* (Princeton, 1960); John L. Snell, *Wartime Origins of the East-West Dilemma over Germany* (New Orleans, 1959); Allen Dulles, *The Secret Surrender* (New York,

1966) which reveals how the Italian surrender injured Soviet-American relations; and especially John Gimbel's excellent study, *The American Occupation of Germany; Politics and the Military, 1945-1949* (Stanford, 1968). Richard N. Gardner, *Sterling-Dollar Diplomacy* (Oxford, 1956) is a classic on Anglo-American relations; and E. P. Penrose, *Economic Planning for the Peace* (Princeton, 1953) is the best detailed study. Asian policies are noted brilliantly in Gardner and Kolko, mentioned above, and are described by Herbert Feis, *The Atomic Bomb and the End of World War II* (Princeton, 1966) which seeks to rebut Gar Alperovitz, *Atomic Diplomacy* (New York, 1965).

On the Truman years, the following are essential: Barton J. Bernstein and Allen J. Matusow, *The Truman Administration: A Documentary History* (New York, 1966); Truman's *Memoirs*, 2 vols. (Garden City, N.Y., 1955, 1956), which should be used carefully and supplemented with *Public Papers of the Presidents*; Cabel Phillips' good short account, *The Truman Presidency* (New York, 1966); Arthur H. Vandenberg, *Private Papers* (Boston, 1952) which must be used with great care; James F. Forrestal, *The Forrestal Diaries*, edited by Walter Millis (New York, 1951), still an indispensable source; Robert Murphy, *Diplomat Among Warriors*, written by a career diplomat who somehow became involved in most Cold War crises from the 1940s into the 1960s; and finally Dean G. Acheson's detailed, condescending, but personal and therefore useful autobiography modestly entitled, *Present at the Creation* (New York, 1969) detailing his view of events between 1941 and 1952. The Secretaries of State are studied in George Curry's *James F. Byrnes* and Robert H. Ferrell's *George C. Marshall*, volumes XIV and XV, respectively, in *The American Secretaries of State and Their Diplomacy* (New York, 1965), while Byrnes' *Speaking Frankly* (New York, 1947) remains a good contemporary source; Gaddis Smith is writing the volume in the series on Acheson as Secretary of State. Joseph M. Jones, *The Fifteen Weeks* (New York, 1955) is a detailed study of policies leading to the Truman Doctrine and Marshall Plan; Harry B. Price, *The Marshall Plan and Its Meaning* (Ithaca, 1955) is the best volume on the Plan itself. Coral Bell's *Negotiation from Strength* (London, 1962) provides a critical view of Acheson's and Dulles' diplomacy. The atomic and then nuclear energy fight can be traced in Bernard M. Baruch, *Baruch, The Public Years* (New York, 1960); David E. Lilienthal's *Journals,* 2 vols. (New York, 1964), especially Volume II; a brilliant dissenting contemporary view, P. M. S. Blackett, *Fear, War, and the Bomb* (New York, 1948); and the two volumes on the history of the Atomic Energy Commission mentioned above. Two controversial, if very dissimilar men can be studied in E. L. and F. H. Schapsmeier, *Prophet in Politics; Henry A. Wallace and the War Years, 1940-1945* (Ames, Iowa, 1971); Ronald Radosh's unpublished Master's Thesis at the State University of Iowa (1960), "The Economic and Political Thought of Henry A. Wallace," the best of the Wallace studies; Karl M. Schmidt, *Henry A. Wallace: Quixotic Crusade, 1948* (Syracuse, 1960) which picks up where Radosh leaves off; and Wallace's own *Toward World Peace* (New York, 1948); Joseph McCarthy's 1950-1951 career is in his *Major Speeches and Debates* (Washington, 1953); Richard Rovere's *Senator Joe McCarthy* (New York, 1959, 1960) a standard and critical biography; William Buckley, *McCarthy and His Enemies* (Chicago, 1954, 1961) a defense; and Robert Griffith, *The Politics of Fear; Joseph R. McCarthy and the Senate* (Lexington, Ky., 1970), a prize-winning analysis.

The best single volume on the Korean conflict is David Rees, *Korea: The Limited War* (New York, 1964). Glenn D. Paige, *The Korean Decision* (New York, 1968) is an invaluable and almost minute-by-minute account of decision-making between June 24 and June 30, 1950 with an especially arresting thesis about how decision-makers use historical reference points as justification for policy; Roy E. Appleman, *South to the Naktong, North to the Yalu* (Washington, 1960), a good Army History with important documents used; L. M. Goodrich, *Korea; A Study of U.S. Policy in the United Nations* (New York, 1956) is standard; Allen Whiting, *China Crosses the Yalu* (New York, 1960) is a minor classic and indispensable in understanding the conflict. Acheson's account in his *Present at the Creation* should be measured against several of David S. McLellan's studies, especially "Dean Acheson on the Korean War," *Political Science Quarterly,* LXXXIII (March, 1968); Gaddis Smith, "A History Teacher's Reflections on the Korean War," *Ventures,* VIII (Spring, 1968), 57-65; and I. F. Stone's *The Hidden History of the Korean War*

(New York, 1952). The Truman-MacArthur conflict can be seen from different sides in John W. Spanier, *The Truman-MacArthur Controversy and the Korean War* (Cambridge, Mass., 1959) emphasizing the concept of "limited war"; Trumbull Higgins, *Korea and the Fall of MacArthur* (New York, 1960); MacArthur's *Reminiscences* (New York, 1964), which provides insight into why the United States became involved in Asia after 1900; and Ronald J. Caridi, *The Korean War and American Politics* (University Park, Penn., 1969) which focuses on the Republicans.

The events during the Eisenhower Presidency are detailed in Dwight D. Eisenhower, *The White House Years: Mandate for Change, 1953-1956* (Garden City, N.Y., 1963), and *The White House Years: Waging Peace, 1956-1961* (Garden City, N.Y., 1965), but should, like Truman's *Memoirs*, be used carefully. Emmet John Hughes, *The Ordeal of Power* (New York, 1963) is a highly critical work, especially on Dulles, while Louis Gerson's biography of Dulles in *The American Secretaries of State* series is considerably more favorable and detailed; Robert J. Donovan, *Eisenhower: The Inside Story* (New York, 1956) is a good contemporary account of the first term; while Norman Graebner's *New Isolationism* (New York, 1956) is more critical while relating Republican politics to foreign policy. Dulles' views can be found in his *War Or Peace* (New York, 1950); and Richard Goold-Adams, *John F. Dulles* (London, 1962) is an excellent short biography of Dulles. Adlai E. Stevenson, *The New America* (New York, 1957) shows in Stevenson's own words the inherent problems of running against Eisenhower in 1956. Lewis L. Strauss, *Men and Decisions* (Garden City, New York, 1962) is the autobiography of an important public servant which includes a flagrant attack on Oppenheimer and the scientist's supporters; Cushing Strout (ed.), gives the documents and useful introduction to the Oppenheimer case in *Conscience, Science and Security* (Chicago, 1963). On the pivotal Suez affair, Herman Finer, *Dulles Over Suez* (Chicago, 1964) is detailed and extremely critical of Dulles in general as well as during the crisis itself; Hugh Thomas, *The Suez Affair* (London, 1966), a more balanced, readable account, is partly based on oral history interviews and includes important documents; and Richard E. Neustadt's *Alliance Politics* (New York, 1970) emphasizes the bureaucratic malfunctioning during the crisis. Perhaps Garry Wills, *Nixon Agonistes*, with its several chapters on the 1950s, is the best short analysis of Eisenhower, Dulles, Nixon, and the 1950s.

The Kennedy material is well presented in James Tracy Crown's bibliographical study, *The Kennedy Literature* mentioned above. Kennedy's own views can be found in *Strategy of Peace* (New York, 1960); *To Turn the Tide* (New York, 1962); and *Public Papers of the Presidents*. A still revealing biography is James MacGregor Burns, *John Kennedy, A Political Profile* (New York, 1959); Arthur M. Schlesinger, Jr., *A Thousand Days* (Boston, 1965) is the most detailed, historical, and well-written of the favorable biographies; Theodore Sorensen, *Kennedy* (New York, 1965) is a sometimes revealing account written by the President's closest White House associate, which might be supplemented with Sorensen's *Decision-Making in the White House* (New York, 1963). Henry Pachter, "JFK as an Equestrian Statue: On Myth and Mythmakers," *Salmagundi*, I (Spring, 1966), 3-26 is the best critique of Schlesinger and Sorensen; while Wills' *Nixon Agonistes* provides rich, critical insights into the Kennedy years. Perhaps the best single contemporary insight into the Kennedy policies may be obtained by reading the Rockefeller Brothers Fund, *Prospects for Peace; The Rockefeller Panel Reports* (Garden City, New York, 1961), which was written, in part, by some of the top Cabinet members and counselors before they entered the Kennedy Administration. The mind of a key adviser can be examined in a series of works by Walt Whitman Rostow (also extremely influential during the Johnson Administration), *An American Policy in Asia* (New York, 1955); "Countering Guerilla Warfare," *New Leader*, July 31, 1960; *The United States in the World Arena; An Essay in Recent History* (New York, 1960); and *View From the Seventh Floor* (New York, 1964). Roger Hilsman, *To Move a Nation* (New York, 1967) is an insider's analysis of policies in the newly emerging areas, particularly Southeast Asia, and is sometimes unintentionally revealing. The Administration's military strategy and its background is given in Maxwell D. Taylor, *The Uncertain Trumpet* (New York, 1959); the Rockefeller Panel report listed above; Henry A. Kissinger, *The Necessity for Choice* (New York, 1961); Herman Kahn, *On Thermonuclear War* (Princeton, 1960, 1961);

the critique of Kahn by Erich Fromm, *May Man Prevail* (Garden City, N.Y., 1961); William W. Kaufmann, *The McNamara Strategy* (New York, 1964); Henry L. Trewhitt's biography, emphasizing Vietnam, *McNamara* (New York, 1971); and the revealing *The Pentagon Papers*, published by *The New York Times* (New York, 1971). Richard E. Neustadt's *Alliance Politics* (New York, 1970) discusses the Skybolt fiasco in 1962; while Elie Abel has done a model job on *The Missile Crisis* (Philadelphia, 1966); as has Henry Pachter, *Collision Course* (New York, 1963), although both may now be supplemented with Robert F. Kennedy's *Thirteen Days; A Memoir of the Cuban Missile Crisis* (New York, 1969); and Graham Allison, *Essence of Decision* (Boston, 1971).

The Kennedy and Johnson policies are compared in two fascinating books, Hobart Rowen, *The Free Enterprisers: Kennedy, Johnson and the Business Establishment* (New York, 1964); and Tom Wicker, *JFK and LBJ; The Influence of Personality Upon Politics* (New York, 1968). The best account of the early Johnsonian foreign policies remains Philip Geyelin, *Lyndon B. Johnson and the World* (New York, 1966), now to be supplemented with *The Pentagon Papers* mentioned above. (See also the Vietnam section below.) Louis Heren, *No Hail, No Farewell* is an interesting bittersweet account of the Johnson years by a knowledgeable British journalist stationed in Washington (New York, 1970); Eric F. Goldman, *The Tragedy of Lyndon Johnson* (New York, 1968) is a critical and rather sad account by a former White House Staff member. Johnson presents his own rebuttal in his memoirs, *Vantage Point* (N.Y., 1971), to be used with extreme care. The views of advisers can be found in the works listed above by Walt W. Rostow plus his *Politics and the Stages of Growth* (London, 1971), an attempt at a *magnum opus*; Maxwell D. Taylor, *Responsibility and Response* (New York, 1967), emphasizing how the United States must be "tough-minded" in the "poker game," but with an interesting thesis on the new multipower world; the McNamara works listed above; a semi-dissenter within the Administration, George W. Ball, *The Discipline of Power; Essentials of a Modern World Structure* (Boston, 1968); and a more radical dissent is found in Senator Fulbright's *Old Myths and New Realities* (New York, 1964); *The Arrogance of Power* (New York, 1966); and Tristram Coffin's biography,

Senator Fulbright (New York, 1966); while the "New Left" of the mid-1960s can be found in Paul Jacobs and Saul Landau, *The New Radicals* (New York, 1966).

A brilliant introduction to the Nixon Administration is Gary Wills' *Nixon Agonistes* listed above, and Jules Witcover, *The Resurrection of Richard Nixon* (New York, 1970) is a good political history which emphasizes the post-1964 years. The standard biography is Earl Mazo, *Nixon; A Political Portrait* (New York, 1968), while Nixon gives his own account of the 1948-1960 traumas in *Six Crises* (New York, 1961). His major policy statements of 1969-1970 can be found in *Setting the Course* (New York, 1970) and the President's key adviser's thoughts can be found in general form in Henry Kissinger, *American Foreign Policy; Three Essays* (New York, 1969), as well as in *The Necessity for Choice* mentioned above. Secretary of State William Rogers has given the Department's view in *United States Foreign Policy 1969-1970; A Report of the Secretary of State* (Washington, 1971), the first such State Department overview published since 1896, and an attempt, in part, to counter the annual foreign policy summaries instituted by President Nixon and coming out of the White House under Kissinger's direction. Two accounts are useful for understanding American foreign policy in the new world of the 1970s, Philip W. Quigg, *America the Dutiful* (New York, 1971), written by a pessimistic member of the "Establishment"; and particularly Zbigniew K. Brzezinski, *Between Two Ages; America's Role in the Technetronic Era* (New York, 1970), a brilliant work that cuts across Russian, Asian, and European as well as American policies in the coming "technetronic" age.

THE SOVIET UNION SINCE 1945:

Michael T. Florinsky (ed.), *McGraw-Hill Encyclopedia of Russia and the Soviet Union* (New York, 1961) is a useful reference. Adam Ulam's *Containment and Co-Existence* (New York, 1967) is an excellent analysis of Soviet foreign policy from 1917-1967; while Jan Librach, *The Rise of the Soviet Empire* (New York, 1964) also begins in 1917. John M. McKintosh, *Strategy and Tactics of Soviet Foreign Policy* (New York, 1963) deals with post-1945, but the best on that era is Thomas W. Wolfe, *Soviet*

Power and Europe, 1945-1970 (Baltimore, 1970), with more than one-half the account devoted to post-1954. Valuable documents are in Robert V. Daniels, *A Documentary History of Communism*, 2 vols. (New York, 1960); and especially for foreign policy, Myron Rush, *The International Situation and Soviet Foreign Policy; Key Reports by Soviet Leaders from the Revolution to the Present* (Columbus, Ohio, 1970), which has valuable editorial comments. For provocative interpretations, see George Frost Kennan, *Russia and the West Under Lenin and Stalin* (Boston, 1960); Philip E. Mosely, *The Kremlin and World Politics* (New York, 1960); Isaac Deutscher, *The Great Contest: Russia and the West* (Oxford, 1960); and three important books by Zbigniew Brzezinski, *The Soviet Bloc* (Cambridge, Mass., 1960, 1967); *Ideology and Power in Soviet Politics* (New York, 1961); and an interesting if uneven volume written with Samuel K. Huntington, *Political Power: U.S.A./U.S.S.R.* (New York, 1964). Essential for understanding Soviet politics are Robert C. Tucker, *The Soviet Political Mind* (New York, 1963), a brilliant account; Myron Rush, *Political Succession in the U.S.S.R.* (New York, 1965); Richard Lowenthal, *World Communism, The Disintegration of a Secular Faith*; and for an excellent case study, Michel Tatu, *Power in the Kremlin, from Khrushchev to Kosygin* (New York, 1967, 1968). Raymond L. Garthoff, *Soviet Military Policy* (New York, 1966), and H. S. Dinerstein, *War and the Soviet Union* (New York, 1962) are models of this type of study, as is Wolfe's volume mentioned above. Harry Schwartz has written several readable works on the economy, particularly *The Soviet Economy Since Stalin* (Philadelphia, 1965). There is no good biography of Stalin, but the most useful is Isaac Deutscher, *Stalin* (New York, 1960); Milovan Djilas, *Conversations with Stalin* (New York, 1962) is essential; and Marshall D. Shulman, *Stalin's Foreign Policy Reappraised* (Cambridge, Mass., 1963) is stimulating and controversial on the 1949-1953 years. Khrushchev has his say in *The Crimes of the Stalin Era*, annotated for the *New Leader* by Boris I. Nicolaevsky (New York, 1956, 1962), the best edition of the 20th-Congress "de-Stalinization" speech; and also in Khrushchev's probable memoirs, *Khrushchev Remembers* (Boston, 1970), which has interesting comments on American policies, especially those of John F. Kennedy. Good biographies are Edward Crankshaw, *Khrushchev, a Career* (New York, 1966), and Myron Rush, *The Rise of Khrushchev* (Washington, 1958). Essential for understanding Soviet foreign policies during the Khrushchev years is Arnold L. Horelick and Myron Rush, *Strategic Power and Soviet Foreign Policy* (Chicago, 1966).

On Eastern Europe and the Soviet bloc, a starting point is Robert F. Byrnes, *The United States and Eastern Europe* (Englewood Cliffs, N.J., 1967); while Soviet relations are emphasized in Margaret Dewar, *Soviet Trade with Eastern Europe, 1945-1949* (London, 1951), updated by Robert Owen Freedman, *Economic Warfare in the Communist Bloc* (New York, 1970), which stresses Soviet political control; and the Brzezinski books listed above. The most tragic story is in Tad Szulc's detailed study, *Czechoslovakia Since World War II* (New York, 1970); and J. Korbel, *The Communist Subversion of Czechoslovakia, 1938-1949* (Princeton, 1959). Soviet relations with other areas are analyzed in Walter Z. Laqueur's two valuable works, *The Soviet Union and the Middle East* (New York, 1959), and *Russia and Germany* (London, 1965). The Middle East relationship is continued in Aaron S. Ikleman, *Soviet Russia and the Middle East* (Baltimore, 1970). Max Beloff, *Soviet Policy in the Far East, 1944-1951* (London, 1953) continues to be useful, as is Beloff's and William Mandel's *Soviet Source Materials on USSR Relations with the Far East, 1945-1950* (New York, 1950), although both are better on China than on Korea. The relations with the newly emerging nations can also be studied in Thomas Thornton (ed.), *The Third World in Soviet Perspective* (Princeton, 1963). The historical background on the arms control problem is in Alexander Dallin *et al.*, *The Soviet Union and Disarmament* (New York, 1965); and Lincoln P. Bloomfield *et al.*, *Khrushchev and the Arms Race* (Cambridge, Mass., 1966).

WESTERN EUROPE, CHINA AND THE NEWLY EMERGING NATIONS

A good survey is Walter Laqueur, *The Rebirth of Europe: A History of the Years Since the Fall of Hitler* (New York, 1971). On American policy, Max Beloff, *The United States and the Unity of Europe* (New York, 1963) is useful, but the two most provocative accounts continue to be Richard J. Barnet and Marcus G. Raskin, *After 20 Years* (New York, 1965); and David P. Calleo, *Europe's Future* (New York, 1965), which is one of several good works on the subject by Calleo. Richard N. Cooper, *The Economics of Interdependence: Economic Policy in the Atlantic Community* (New York, 1968) is helpful on this key topic. On the historical background of the military arrangements consult, in addition to Barnet and Raskin and Calleo, Robert Osgood, *NATO: Entangling Alliance* (Chicago, 1962); and Lord Ismay, *NATO: The First Five Years* (Utrecht, 1956), by the former NATO Secretary General. German relations are studied, in addition to John Gimbel's book on 1945-1949 listed above, in Harold Zink, *United States in Germany, 1944-1955* (New York, 1957); Lucius D. Clay, *Decision in Germany* (Garden City, New York, 1950); Edgar McInnis *et al.*, *The Shaping of Postwar Germany* (New York, 1960), a good collection of essays; Manuel Gottlieb's valuable *The German Peace Settlement and the Berlin Crisis*; Wolfram F. Hanrieder, *West German Foreign Policy, 1949-1963* (Stanford, 1967); Richard Hiscocks, *The Adenauer Era* (Philadelphia, 1966), much preferable to Adenauer's own disappointing *Memoirs* (Chicago, 1966); and for the East-West issue, Charles R. Planck, *The Changing Status of German Reunification in Western Diplomacy, 1955-1966* (Baltimore, 1967). For French policies, the best analysis is Guy de Carmoy, *The Foreign Policies of France 1944-1968* (Chicago, 1967); while de Gaulle's three volumes of *War Memoirs* (New York, 1955-1960), now updated by two more volumes on the postwar world, are invaluable. *Full Circle: The Memoirs of Anthony Eden* (Boston, 1960) is indispensable for the 1950s and particularly for Suez. Arthur Whitaker's *Spain and the Defense of the West* (New York, 1961) is excellent; and William B. Bader, *Austria Between East and West, 1945-1955* (Stanford, 1966) provides the important context for the East-West withdrawal between 1953 and 1955.

For the Middle East, very useful books have been written by J. C. Hurewitz, especially his editing of the essays in *Soviet-American Rivalry in the Middle East* (New York, 1969); and Nadav Safran's several works are also useful, including his volume on *The United States and Israel* (Cambridge, Mass., 1963) and more recently his detailed *From War to War, The Arab-*

Israeli Confrontation, 1948-1967 (New York, 1969). Frank E. Manuel, *The Realities of American-Palestine Relations* (Washington, 1949) is still the standard on the era before 1949. George Lenczowski, *The Middle East in World Affairs,* 3rd edition (Ithaca, N.Y., 1962), gives a good overview of the area. On African affairs south of the Sahara, see Rupert Emerson, *Africa and United States Policy* (Englewood Cliffs, N.J., 1967); Alan P. Merriam, *Congo: Background of Conflict* (Evanston, Ill., 1961); and William Attwood, *The Reds and the Blacks* (New York, 1967), by an American Ambassador who served the Kennedy Administration in Guinea and Kenya. For the South African problem, consult William A. Hance (ed.), *Southern Africa and the United States* (New York, 1968), especially the Hance and Vernon McKay essays; and Waldemar A. Nielsen's earlier, *African Battleline: American Policy Choices in Southern Africa* (New York, 1965).

A good approach to understanding Latin America is Kalman H. Silvert, *The Conflict Society* (New Orleans, 1961). David Green's *The Containment of Latin America* (Chicago, 1971), is the best work on Latin America and the outbreak of Cold War during the 1940s; while important historical background is provided in Dexter Perkins' well-known *History of the Monroe Doctrine* (Cambridge, Mass., 1963), and J. Fred Rippy's *Globe and Hemisphere* (Chicago, 1958), which is valuable on the economic side. A major contribution is Jerome Levinson and Juan de Onís, *The Alliance that Lost Its Way; A Critical Report on the Alliance for Progress* (Chicago, 1970); and the OAS is analyzed in Jerome Slater, *The OAS and United States Foreign Policy* (Columbus, Ohio, 1967). A helpful but too often disappointing account of the Latin American view is Raymond Vernon (ed.), *How Latin America Views the U.S. Investor* (New York, 1966). The influence of Communism is superbly analyzed in Rollie E. Poppino, *International Communism in Latin America: A History of the Movement, 1917-1963* (New York, 1964); and more particularly in Stephen Clissold (ed.), *Soviet Relations with Latin America 1918-1968, A Documentary Survey* (London, 1970); and Cecil Earle Johnson, *Communist China and Latin America, 1959-1967* (New York, 1970). The Guatemalan intervention of 1954 is well analyzed in Ronald M. Schneider, *Communism in*

Guatemala, 1944-1954 (New York, 1958). On Cuba and Castro, Hugh Thomas' huge work, *Cuba; The Pursuit of Freedom* (New York, 1971) devotes its last 800 pages, or half the book, to post-World War II, with valuable sections on the United States reaction to Castro. The historical background is especially valuable in two books by Robert F. Smith, *The United States and Cuba* (New York, 1961), and his documentary history, *What Happened in Cuba?* (New York, 1963); while a useful short overview and bibliography is in Lester Langley, *The Cuban Policy of the United States* (New York, 1968). For contrasting interpretations of United States-Castro relations, see Theodore Draper's two books, *Castro's Revolution* (New York, 1962), and *Castroism, Theory and Practice* (New York, 1965); the American Ambassador's account in Earl E. T. Smith, *The Fourth Floor* (New York, 1962); and, on the other side, William A. Williams, *The United States, Cuba and Castro* (New York, 1962). For Santo Domingo in 1965, Dan Kurzman's *Santo Domingo: Revolt of the Damned* (New York, 1965) is by a first-rate correspondent, as is Ted Szulc's *Dominican Diary* (New York, 1965); the principal American negotiator tells his story in John Bartlow Martin, *Overtaken by Events: The Dominican Crisis from the Fall of Trujillo to the Civil War* (New York, 1966).

For Sino-American affairs, John K. Fairbank, *The United States and China, revised ed.* (Cambridge, Mass., 1971), is fine on China, weak on relations with the United States; Fred Greene, *U.S. Policy and the Security of Asia* (New York, 1968), emphasizes a greater Asian context and military affairs; Alexander Eckstein, *Communist China's Economic Growth and Foreign Trade: Implications for U.S. Policy* (New York, 1966), is very critical of American policies; A. T. Steele, *The American People and China* (New York, 1966), is interesting but too weak on pre-1949. Ross Y. Koen, *The China Lobby in American Politics* (New York, 1960) deals with internal American politics, is the best book on the subject, but evidently was taken off the market shortly after publication. A superb interpretation is David Mozingo, *China's Foreign Policy and the Cultural Revolution*, IREA Project, Interim Report, Number 1 (March, 1970, Ithaca, New York); and most helpful is a series of books by a A. Doak Barnett beginning with *China on the Eve of Communist Takeover* (New

York, 1962). Tang Tsou, *America's Failure in China, 1941-1950* (Chicago, 1963) has become the standard work on the period. On the Sino-Soviet split, see works by Donald S. Zagoria, William Griffiths, and especially O. Edmund Clubb, *China and Russia, the "Great Game"* (New York, 1971). The India-China relationship and its 1962 culmination is analyzed by Neville Maxwell, *India's China War* (New York, 1971). All too little has been published on the trends in Japanese-American relations. One place to begin is Edwin O. Reischauer, *The United States and Japan*, revised ed. (Cambridge, Mass., 1965); James Cary, *Japan Today: Reluctant Ally* (New York, 1962), seems increasingly prescient; and consult the excellent study of the 1951 treaty by B. C. Cohen, *The Political Process and Foreign Policy* (Princeton, 1957).

The literature on Vietnam has become so vast it is possible to list only several of the basic works. Joseph Buttinger, *Vietnam: A Political History* (New York, 1970) is the most comprehensive history and a condensation of a three-volume work. The best critical and historical account, complete with key documents, is George Kahin and John W. Lewis, *The United States in Vietnam* (New York, 1967), and can be supplemented by the excellent account of an "insider" turned critic, Chester L. Cooper, *The Lost Crusade; America in Vietnam* (New York, 1970). Another inside account by a Johnson Administration official is Townsend Hoopes, *The Limits of Intervention* (New York, 1969). Important background can be found in Franklin B. Weinstein, *Vietnam's Unheld Elections* (of 1956), published as Data Paper: No. 60, Southeast Asia Program, Cornell University, July 1966; and Franz Schurmann *et al.*, *The Politics of Escalation in Vietnam* (Greenwich, Conn., 1966). Key documents can be found in Marvin and Susan Gettleman and Lawrence and Carol Kaplan, (eds.), *Conflict in Indochina* (New York, 1970), which has nearly one-quarter of its space devoted to Cambodia; and Marcus G. Raskin and Bernard Fall (eds.), *The Vietnam Reader* (New York, 1965). The late Bernard Fall wrote several small classics on the coming of the war; see, for example, the collection of his articles, *Vietnam Witness, 1953-1966* (New York, 1966). The widely publicized massacres are recounted in Seymour M. Hersh, *My Lai 4* (New York, 1970), based on extensive interviews with American soldiers; and Richard Hammer, *One Morning in the War: The Tragedy at Son My* (New York, 1971), which tends to emphasize more the Vietnamese side. For crucial areas in Indochina, consult Nina S. Adams and Alfred W. McCoy (eds.), *Laos: War and Revolution* (New York, 1970); and Roger M. Smith, *Cambodia's Foreign Policy* (Ithaca, New York, 1965). A new and frightening dimension of newly emerging nations' affairs is superbly introduced in Lester R. Brown, *Seeds of Change; The Green Revolution and Development in the 1970's* (New York, 1970) which discusses a phenomenon that will especially influence Southeast Asian development or, as in the case of Pakistan in 1971, help bring about civil war.

References to Congressional documents, Congressional hearings, newspapers, and other secondary sources may be found in the footnotes of each chapter. Additional bibliography can often be found in the general surveys mentioned at the beginning of each topic listed above.

Acknowledgments

ROBERT DIVINE OF THE UNIVERSITY OF TEXAS, the editor of this series, Gaddis Smith of Yale, Myron Rush of Cornell, and Lloyd Gardner of Rutgers have immeasurably helped this manuscript by reading it in its entirety and making many constructive criticisms. To Lloyd Gardner and to Thomas McCormick of the University of Pittsburgh, William Appleman Williams of the University of Wisconsin, Fred Harvey Harrington, President of the University of Wisconsin, and Robert Bowers of Hanover College, I owe considerably more than mere thanks for professional advice. Knight Biggerstaff of Cornell read many of the sections on Asia and improved them greatly. William Gum of Wiley has been the most helpful and long-suffering editor that an author could wish for. Nancy Unger, also of Wiley, made this a better volume by taking care of the editorial work on the maps.

Tom Rogers, Coordinator of Research at Cornell, Frank Long, Vice-President of Research at Cornell, Stuart Brown, Dean of Cornell's College of Arts and Sciences, and Sandy Cheney, Associate Dean of that College, have literally made this book possible by providing the research funds that enabled me to investigate materials in various libraries and to have the manuscript typed. I particularly thank Mrs. Nancy Bressler of the Princeton University Library staff for making the Dulles and Baruch papers so easy to use and also for expediting the clearance of my notes through the Dulles Committee. Phillip Brooks and Phillip Lagerquist were very helpful at the Truman Library. I am, of course, primarily obligated to the fine library staff at Cornell, particularly to Giles Shepherd and Evelyn Greenberg. Herman

Phleger, General Nathan Twining, and Sherman Adams graciously consented to allow the use of the quotations from their oral history interviews in the Dulles manuscripts at Princeton. Mrs. Robert Ludgate and Mrs. John Quincy Adams of Ithaca typed most of the manuscript with great care under pressure from immediate deadlines.

I thank these persons who either supplied me with research materials or somewhat narrowed the boundaries of my ignorance by talking with me about the Cold War: David Brion Davis, Walter Pintner, Michael Kammen, and Richard Polenberg, all professors at Cornell in the Department of History; Andrew Hacker, Clinton Rossiter, John Lewis, and George Kahin in the Cornell Government Department; Paul Marantz, a graduate student in Government at Harvard; David Maisel, an undergraduate at Cornell; Raymond G. O'Connor, Professor and Chairman of the History Department at Temple University; Professor Barton Bernstein of Stanford; Professor Athan Theoharis of Wayne State University; John Windmuller, Professor in the Industrial and Labor Relations School of Cornell; and George Kennan of the Institute for Advanced Study at Princeton. I am particularly indebted to Professor Carl Parrini and the History Department at the University of Northern Illinois for allowing me to try out some of my ideas about the Cold War at their N.D.E.A. Institute in the summer of 1966. The dedication is to a person who has yet to lose a war—either hot or cold—and this has been fortunate for me.

WALTER LaFEBER

Index